Reshaping
Reason

Reshaping Reason

Toward a

New

Philosophy

John McCumber

Indiana University Press

BLOOMINGTON & INDIANAPOLIS

This book is a publication of

Indiana University Press
601 North Morton Street
Bloomington, IN 47404-3797 USA

http://iupress.indiana.edu

Telephone orders   800-842-6796
Fax orders   812-855-7931
Orders by e-mail   iuporder@indiana.edu

The paper used in this publication meets the minimum requirements of
American National Standard for Information Sciences—Permanence of Paper
for Printed Library Materials, ANSI Z39.48-1984.

Manufactured in the United States of America

Library of Congress Cataloging-in-Publication Data

McCumber, John.
    Reshaping reason : toward a new philosophy / John McCumber.
        p.   cm.
    Includes bibliographical references and index.
    ISBN 0-253-34503-0 (hardcover : alk. paper)
        1. Philosophy. I. Title.
    B72.M385 2004
    191—dc22

                                                            2004007895

1 2 3 4 5   10 09 08 07 06 05

In memory of Géza von Molnár
Mentor and Friend

Zu wissen wenig, aber der Freude viel
Ist Sterblichen gegeben . . .
  —Friedrich Hölderlin

Contents

viii   Contents

Preface

Toward the end of the eighteenth century, Immanuel Kant found philosophy blocked by an undigested quarrel between two groups he called "dogmatists" and "skeptics." Kant realized that old ways of thinking were inadequate to resolve this dispute and that a new "tribunal" would have to be instituted for that purpose. If it was to adjudicate philosophical disputes, this tribunal would itself have to be philosophical, a "tribunal of reason" founded on the "eternal and unchanging" laws of thought (*KRV* A xi). Knowledge of our thought is knowledge of ourselves, and obtaining it is for Kant the "most arduous of rational tasks." That task now fell to a new discipline, the "critique of pure reason" (*KRV* A xii), which would therefore furnish the needed tribunal.

At the beginning of the twenty-first century, philosophy's situation was even more dire than in Kant's time. The events of September 11 had abruptly moved philosophy from the peripheries of the cultural landscape to its exact center, for the suicide attack on a technological symbol of America was ultimately an attack on critical thought itself. It had to be answered, and answered well, by philosophers; otherwise the conflict would degenerate into a parochial "clash of civilizations" or even into a religious war.

But this sudden challenge found American philosophers unready. Their behavior and allegiances, for example, were stamped, to the tiniest detail and without exception, by whether they were "analytic" or "continental" philosophers. After fifty years, the quarrel between these two approaches was not merely undigested but had grown so confused, stale, and hopeless that each side rarely even mentioned the other. Indifference to philosophy, long rampant in the larger culture, thus overtook even philosophers themselves. Unable to settle their intellectual disputes, philosophers lost credibility within the academy; jobs, offices, and even whole departments followed (cf. *TD* 96f). The "death of philosophy" seemed imminent and was fondly proclaimed.

A Kantian call to self-knowledge, summoning all to the tribunal of reason, was obviously needed. None came, for in the centuries since Kant, the tribunal of reason itself had been undermined. Its original legitimacy had been founded on a view undoubted even by skeptics like Hume: that we can at least know our own minds. As Kant put it:

> Here nothing can escape us, because what Reason brings forth entirely from itself cannot remain hidden, but is brought to light through Reason itself, as soon as one has uncovered its common principle. (*KRV* A xx)

Kant's confidence in Reason was as naïve as it sounds. Today, after Freud, Marx, Heidegger, and the Postmodernists, the "eternal and unchanging" laws of thought themselves are in question. Can we then turn, for our tribunal, to what is transient and changing? Then philosophy would adjudicate itself with reference to the ways in which philosophers articulate and comprehend historical givens, the way mid-twentieth-century analytical philosophy articulated and explained the rise of science.

But philosophy, in America at least, is not doing as well with historical givens as it once did. Its failure to respond to September 11 is one example;[1] my own investigations of the history of the American philosophical community, published as *Time in the Ditch*, furnish another. They show that American philosophy may have suffered traumatic political pressures half a century ago—and, more damningly, that the very possibility that that had happened has never been acknowledged, much less confronted.

To be sure, philosophers can hardly be blamed for not acknowledging something of which they have no knowledge. Once the repugnant facts are known to them, and only then, can they decide whether to learn the hard lessons of those facts and be seekers of truth, or to remain what so many of their teachers had silently hoped they would be: seekers of convenient truth. In the meantime, American philosophers stand on the brink of philosophy, unknowing whether they are followers of Socrates, on the one hand, or of Anytus and Meletus on the other. Their behavior furnishes no indication of what philosophy can or should be.

Facts, which come and go in time, thus cannot furnish the needed tribunal—even when they are facts about philosophers themselves. Nor, clearly, can the now suspect "eternal and unchanging" laws of thought. But I believe there is a middle way between the temporal and the atemporal. What if reason can be seen to accord not with the passing contents of time, but with what we encounter as the structure of time itself? Might it not be that our experience of time, which as Kant argued is the universal form of all knowable particularities, gives the key for determining the "source, scope, and limits" (*KRV* A xii) of our rational powers?

The claim of this book is that it can. The traditional Kantian mind, with its unchangeable rational laws, can be replaced by a temporalized mind—one whose every single component and function has come to be and will pass away, and which has evolved rational tools to cope with that fact. The principles by which those tools operate constitute what I call "temporal reason."

No full account of such reason has ever been given. The need of it was not even broached until Heidegger's *Being and Time*—and Heidegger himself, unable to follow through on the task, quickly fell into what was widely seen as crude irrationalism.[2] Yet once we have broken through some crippling prejudices, the first part of such an account is surprisingly easy to give. The crux of the argument is that traditional philosophical thinking—i.e., the philosophical use of various forms of inference—is conducted in the present tense. Its goal and medium is the true assertion (sentence, belief, or proposition). True assertions, however, require the simultaneous availability—the "copresence"—of the assertions themselves and whatever it is that makes them true. Otherwise they cannot be verified, however true they are, and are philosophically useless.

The account of temporal reason offered here enriches such traditional philosophy by introducing methods which relate philosophical thinking to the past and future in ways which do not reduce to stating truths about them, but have definable goals and techniques of their own. I call these ways of relating philosophically to past and future "narrative" and "demarcation" respectively, and I give an account of them in chapter 2 (chapter 1 is introductory). Narrative and demarcation correspond loosely to our ordinary activities of telling stories and formulating questions, but when undertaken philosophically they have special constraints on them. When they are added to traditional patterns of inference, the result is a comprehensive view of reason which sees it as fully temporal— as relating equally to past, present, and future.

Quine is my standing archetype for the philosophical practice of inference; Hegel for that of narrative; and Heidegger for that of demarcation. That these three figures could cooperate on anything whatever may seem strange. When we look at things this way, however, we can see that in fact a whole posse of contemporary American philosophers, so to speak, is now riding to philosophy's rescue, converging from these three long-separated corners of the philosophical landscape.

First, analytical philosophers in the wake of Quine have had unparalleled success exploring reason in the present tense, without reifying its objects into atemporal fantasies; a new generation is situating itself with respect to the history of philosophy. A few of the names associated with this trend are Robert Brandom, Michael Friedman, Christine Korsgaard, John McDowell, and Michael Williams. Second, philosophers in the Hegelian tradition, such as David Kolb, Terry Pinkard, Robert Pippin, Pirmin Stekeler-Weithofer, Robert Williams, and Richard Dien Winfield are showing us that

Hegel is not making silly claims about some present entity (such as the *Zeitgeist* or the Absolute). They open the way to seeing Hegel as teaching us how to validate the present by reconstructing a certain sort of past. Finally, Heideggereans in the wake of Jacques Derrida, such as Robert Bernasconi, Stephen Erickson, David Krell, John Sallis, Reiner Schürmann, and Gary Shapiro, as well as Daniel Dahlstrom, provide rich resources for any philosophy which aims to open up futures.[3] While adequate discussion of these contemporary thinkers (and their fellows) is beyond the scope of the present book, I hope to undertake it in the future.

&

In chapter 3 I explore what sort of "reality" such temporal reason enables us to know. It seems frivolous just to say, "knowable reality," but the phrase has a point. In order to be "known" by us (as well as "experienced," "encountered," and "inferred," etc., by us), a thing must have certain characteristics. The specification of those characteristics counts as "ontology," for whatever existed but did not exhibit them could not be known by us and so would be, at best, an "ontos" without a "logy." In fact, temporal reason sees ontology itself in new ways—not as a universal "theory of being" but as a generalized recommendation as to how things should be understood, responded to, and acted upon.

Ontology so viewed is anything but a recondite and abstract discipline of importance only to philosophers. Indeed, various ontologies have played crucial roles in the history of the West.[4] In chapter 3, I will discuss seven of these historically significant ontologies. Once we understand what they are and how they function, we can see how they are grounded in yet another ontology, one still more basic than they, and I will discuss this as well.

The real business of temporal reason, however, is not "knowing" at all, for as chapter 2 has it, knowledge is an affair of the present tense only. What temporal reason undertakes is the rational construction of situations. It goes about this by reflectively placing things—components of situations—into a temporal flow, thus endowing them with, or allowing them to have, certain types of past and future.

The ultimate job of philosophy, as a situating activity in this sense, is to help us see how it is necessary to live. In chapter 4, I embark on this in a "marginal" way. The daunting central issues of traditional ethics are based on the concept of the free and fully aware moral agent, a concept which I (along with many others) find highly problematic. After discussing some of its problems, I will head for the "edge" of ethics, to the areas where our moral agency peters out or runs against the channels that history and custom have dug for it. From this angle, ethics is as much about the way relationships channel our actions as it is about those actions themselves.

There are ways to make sense of the overwhelming diversity of human relationships, for like everything human they are structured by the ways we experience time. I will give an elementary account of some of those basic relational structures and show how they apply, not merely to private affairs, but to one type of government itself. My claim, then, is that we can understand moral action and responsibility better when we see them from these edges as well as from the center.

That can hardly count as a complete ethics; indeed, nothing in this book is even remotely finished. Taking it for a finished work is like taking a collection of stem cells for a human being. But I do think that the book's second chapter codifies some aspects of a "new philosophy," different from current versions—and better, because more fully temporal. And I believe that the two following chapters present some promising first results.

&

Some of these results will matter, I think, to philosophers. Temporal reason views knowledge and reality as dynamically producing one another, in ways which can sometimes be disentangled—thus saving some versions of realism, if only on a case-by-case basis.

Ontologies, on this approach, do not subsist as argument chains in logical space, but arrive and depart in history and have their own sorts of validity in doing so. There is serious empirical evidence that conscious decision is not the beginning of action, but follows it in time. All these issues have bearing on traditional philosophical disciplines, such as epistemology, ontology, and ethics, which are rethought in this book.

Beyond philosophy, the array of philosophical methods presented in chapter 2 aims to help us humanists see how to do what science cannot: how to situate ourselves among scientific and other truths. Aristotle was right about science (at *Metaph* I.1 981a15–20); it can give us general information, such as what level of cholesterol is best in general or what type of bridge can be built over a river. But applying those findings requires inserting them into the ongoing life of a person or community, which in turn means seeing how the application would carry that life forward and what kinds of futures it would foreclose or open up: the kind of temporalized, "humanistic" situating activity to be explored in this book.

Group identity is arguably an affair of ongoing narrative, so the accounts of narrative in chapter 2 and of its ontological consequences in chapter 3 may prove useful to critical theorists, feminists, queer theorists, and race theorists. The account of the double nature of elementary human relationships explored in chapter 4 may be useful to therapists and educators of all sorts. The fact that the "double" in question is freedom/oppression has implications for political and economic theory.

I will allude to these consequences in the book, but I do not try to draw them in detail. This would have been a much longer book had I done that—but not, in my cramped and tired hands, a better one. What I present here is all that I, alone at this moment, can hope to do.

᠍᠍᠍᠍᠍᠍

Though this book is my effort, and all its many defects my fault, the "new philosophy" it presents is not emerging from a single head. In addition to the contemporary thinkers I mentioned above, almost everything in it can be found, attributed to some historical figure, in one or more of my previous books. To avoid self-referentiality I will not document this in detail; in general terms, the enlargement of the "philosophical toolbox" in chapter 2 was adumbrated in *Time in the Ditch*, which in turn drew on the extended analyses of Hegel and Heidegger in *The Company of Words* and *Metaphysics and Oppression* respectively. The view of ontology as a force in history was prepared by *Metaphysics and Oppression*, as was the critique of traditional concepts of agency in chapter 4. The classification of basic types of relationship in that chapter builds on foundations laid in *Poetic Interaction*.

The influence of philosophers past and present thus extends throughout the book; if I were to footnote them, the notes would be on every page. It would be insulting to those from whom I have learned so much to subject them to scholarly reportage and dissection; what is needed is an ongoing, and to some degree informal, discussion. In the rest of the book, these "discussions," though part and parcel of the argument, will be indented and italicized. Traditional scholarly references will remain in the notes. It is my hope that following these discussions will not only clarify the historical and contemporary affiliations of the new philosophy, but will provide illumination of philosophy's history and present state—if only, to be sure, from an unconventional perspective.

Finally, the contemporary figures I have mentioned are only a few examples of the threefold convergence I have in mind. Other thinkers—some analytical, some continental, some who do not consider themselves "philosophers" at all—are already beginning to philosophize along these lines. Still others are feeling it as a need, increasingly sharp.[5] The "new philosophy" is thus emerging from a variety of investigations underway today.

What if those investigators care to make common cause, with me and with each other? Then philosophy, far from having died, will, once again, have just begun.

Acknowledgments

I would first like to thank those who freed up for me the time to write this book. My UCLA Dean, Pauline Yu, and my Dean at Northwestern and again at UCLA, Eric Sundquist, were open to crucially creative arrangements concerning leaves. My colleagues in the Northwestern University German Department, in particular Peter Fenves, Franziska Lys, and Eva Stonebraker, tolerated my absence during those leaves; and did so with unwarranted good cheer. Prof. James A. Schulz, philosophus extraordinarius, gave a perceptive and helpful reading to the entire manuscript. Dee Mortensen of Indiana University Press has once again provided wise guidance. The humane intelligence of Françoise Lionnet has, as always, saved me from numerous disasters.

None of these people are responsible for the many defects in this book. At a time when the lurches of history and the hobgoblins of all-pervading power have in the view of many reduced responsible agency to a mere fantasy, it is with some relief that I can safely say that those defects are mine alone.

Abbreviations

AA	Kant, *Akademie-Ausgabe (Academy Edition)*
AT	Descartes, *Oeuvres,* Adam & Tannery Edition *(Works)*
CW	McCumber, *The Company of Words*
Emp.	Hardt & Negri, *Empire*
EN	Dewey, *Experience and Nature*
Enz.	Hegel, *Enzyklopädie der philosophischen Wissenschaften (Encyclopedia of the Philosophical Sciences)*
KPV	Kant, *Kritik der Praktischen Vernunft (Critique of Practical Reason)*
KRV	Kant, *Kritik der reinen Vernunft (Critique of Pure Reason)*
KSA	Nietzsche, *Kritisch-Studienausgabe (Critical Edition)*
KU	Kant, *Kritik der Urteilskraft (Critique of Judgment)*
Metaph	Aristotle, *Metaphysics*
MO	McCumber, *Metaphysics and Oppression*
NE	Aristotle, *Nicomachean Ethics*
PF	McCumber, *Philosophy and Freedom*
Phil Inv	Wittgenstein, *Philosophical Investigations*
PhS	Hegel, *Phänomenologie des Geistes (Phenomenology of Spirit)*
PI	McCumber, *Poetic Interaction*
SZ	Heidegger, *Sein und Zeit (Being and Time)*
TD	McCumber, *Time in the Ditch*
WdL	Hegel, *Wissenschaft der Logik (Science of Logic)*
Werke	Hegel, *Werke* (Moldenhauer & Michel Edition) *(Works)*

Reshaping
Reason

which we cause, of our own acts—is very rarely achieved. But attempting to understand what we are responding to when we act (omit, utter) is necessary to living a human life; to what degree can you *be* yourself if you do not *understand* yourself?

This all holds, in particular, for philosophy. The present work of philosophy, like all philosophy, is a congeries of acts, omissions, and utterances. It is produced by a human in such a way as to claim intelligence, and so is a set of responses. It is responsive not just to the various facts and phenomena it seeks to understand and which are contemporaneous with it, but to larger historical trends as well. Some of these trends are philosophical in nature—various developments in the history of philosophy which it tries to carry forward, evade, or stymie.

But the "history of philosophy" is never just philosophical. It is inextricable from the history of philosophers, and so from the stories of the communities which these philosophers form and in which they work. I have traced some aspects of the institutional history of recent American philosophy in *Time in the Ditch*. Here, I want to focus on the *philosophical* level of the overall situation, the state of the *logos* just before the intervention of this book—the state of philosophy to which it responds, its *pro-logos*.

The tale told in *Time in the Ditch* is, essentially, a story of decline: fewer departments, fewer tenure lines within departments, fewer journals, fewer publishers, an aging professoriat. That such institutional and social problems correspond to an intellectual crisis, indeed that philosophy's institutional and intellectual problems are two levels of a single crisis, may seem tendentious. Many philosophers, after all, have been trained to think that philosophy begins only when we negate all institutional considerations. Institutions, after all, are English, American, French, or

German, while philosophy (we learn) is on a different level. To put the matter linguistically, philosophy deals not with "snow is white" or "Der Schnee ist weiß" or "La neige est blanche," but with what is common to all these. Hegel called such scurrying to the universal shooting the Absolute "as if from a pistol" (*PhS* 26/16), but it is really we philosophers who are shot, into some unchanging and so abstract realm where even our shadows are lost. The trajectory is as old as the Presocratics—Thales' abstract realm was water, and Anaximander's was "the indefinite."

Though such unchanging realms have historically been important for philosophy, they are hardly necessary for it. Restricting philosophy to them was for millennia regarded as unphilosophical. It was Socrates who, as he declares in the *Apology*, turned from the investigation of nature to examining himself instead, and thereby turned philosophy, at least in part, into an investigation of self. In so doing, he placed philosophers under an obligation that no one, philosopher or not, could ignore—the demand that, even while trying to scurry to the universal, they pause and explain themselves. Poor Euthyphro, who was assuredly no philosopher, had to explain to Socrates why he was prosecuting his own father for murder—and why should anyone, especially a philosopher, think herself better than Euthyphro?

We (philosophers) must therefore explain ourselves, and we must do so in English, French, German, etc.—for we obviously cannot do it in "what is common to all these." We must do it, moreover, to people who are not philosophers. To refuse this task is to take the stance that philosophy is either a special taste whose merits cannot be explained to outsiders—or not worth doing at all.

Both stances are philosophical, because they make important statements about the nature of philosophy itself. But both are untenable. The latter leads obviously to a *tu quoque,* to refutation by "you do it too"; if philosophy is worthless, why are you doing it? The former stance is as self-contradictory as advocating universal lying. If, tonight at midnight, everyone on earth stopped telling the truth and started lying, there would be no way for new members of our species to learn to talk, and language itself would eventually die out. If I advocate that something like that should happen, I am using language to push for the destruction of language, which as Kant pointed out is a practical contradiction—another *tu quoque.*[1] Similarly for philosophy. If it is to survive, philosophers, even those who populate its most abstract realms, must explain themselves at least to those who will, perhaps, one day become philosophers. And since no one can tell just who those people are, philosophers must be ready to explain themselves not just to each other but to non-philosophers in general. If they do not do that, no one will become a philosopher, and philosophy will eventually die out. To do philosophy without explaining to non-philosophers *why* you do it is thus to do philosophy in a way which guarantees its extinction—another sort of practical contradiction.

Any philosopher must therefore hold that philosophy is an activity which is worthwhile and whose merits can and must be explained to outsiders. Such explanation is a Socratic task, for it means explaining *ourselves* as philosophers. Perhaps it is the philosophical task *par excellence.* Yet the apparent institutional decline of philosophy within the university suggests that it is not going well. If philosophers were making the case for philosophy, if they were explaining to others why they do it and why it should be done, more resources—if not, perhaps, many more— would be allocated to it.

That philosophers cannot explain themselves to non-philosophers may be a philosophical failing, then; but it is a philosophical failing with institutional consequences. To ask why it is occurring is to reach the point of intersection between the institutional and intellectual levels of philosophy's crisis. That crisis, I suggest, is *aporetic* in nature.

Philosophy's Aporia I: A General Account

An "aporia," as I will use the term, is a situation in which two sides disagree but cannot resolve their dispute because it presupposes a hidden, but mistaken, agreement. In the present case, the two sides would be philosophy which claims to study the various changeless and abstract realms into which philosophers have traditionally *escaped,* and philosophy which seeks instead to explain the lives they and others *lead.*

> This aporia, which opposes philosophy's atemporal intellectual orientation on the one hand to its changing institutional circumstances on the other, is nothing new. Plato was caught, there too, unable to explain the relation of the eternal Forms to the world we actually live in with anything more than a word—and, as Aristotle points out, a metaphor at that (methexis: Metaph I.9 991a20–23). As Plotinus pointed out in turn, the problem hardly goes away when the relation between unchangeable essences and the beings of which they are the essences is restated in terms of Aristotelian forms-in-matter (Enneads VI.3.4ff).

To dissolve the aporia, we need a more specific account of just what the disagreement is between the two sides, and of the common mistake they have made. Helpful in this will be an outline of the basic structure of the aporia as it arises today, and I will approach this from two directions. First, I will give a basic, general sketch of the *kind* of aporia that I think philosophy currently exhibits. Then I will give a broad-brush historical account of how an aporia of that type could actually have arisen within philosophy. Each approach should have some plausibility on its own. The general sketch should match with what philosophers see with their own eyes as they practice their discipline, and the historical account should resonate with what they learned, early on, about the history of the field. The convergence of the sketch with the account will increase the plausibility still further. Though the aporia I am about to state is a product of interpretation, then, there are reasons to believe that the interpretation is a plausible one.

It is this aporia to which this book offers a conscious response. As will become evident, however (I hope), the kind of philosophy I am proposing has other merits as well, and can be accepted or rejected independently of its success in resolving the aporia at hand.

We can begin the general account by considering philosophy loosely, as a way of doing certain things, *a* way, and several or many things (just which way, and which things, will be explained when I move to the historical level). When a way of doing things no longer works, we must either find a new way or stop doing those things. But what happens when those things are great and important and have to be done, and no new way turns up? What happens when that bind persists for a couple of generations? We might expect two sides to develop:

One side still adheres to the old way, even though it no longer works. Since the original goals of the "old way" can no longer be achieved in that way, those goals must be redefined; otherwise the old way itself must be abandoned. Those who refuse to abandon it therefore cut back their goals to match the old methods, but that still leaves them with the uncomfortable memory of the great goals they once had. One way to suppress that memory is by sealing themselves off from everyone who could call it up. If the goals were great and the memory widespread, this may eventually require excluding everyone but themselves. Cut off from its original tasks and goals, what was once only a way of doing things now becomes an island unto itself, peopled with things that were originally the mere artifacts and tools of a greater project but which now have been left with the status of brute, and so primary, realities. Those so-called realities are, however, really only fantasies, i.e., beings originally thought up by people for specific tasks that have now vanished. The unchangeable, universal realm has now become a sort of Fantasy Island, and I will call this wing of the general aporia the "Fantasy Island" approach.

The other side abandons the old way—but since no new way shows up, it merely struggles. After some time, its practitioners accept that no new way is going to come along and that their confusion is permanent. At that point, this approach ceases to be a mere phase leading toward something else and becomes—like Fantasy Island—a goal in itself. This struggling is both honest and worthy of pursuit, i.e., good. But all that can make it good is its distance from Fantasy Island, for there is nothing else by which it can measure itself. So it holds its confusion to be not only honest and good, but (because it increases the distance) liberating as well. It is a liberation which departs from the old ways without settling into any new ways, and so is a form of subversion. I will call this second wing of the aporia the "Subversive Struggle."

It is tempting to apply this to contemporary philosophy

by seeing Fantasy Island as the domain of analytical philosophy, with its timeless *ficta* of absolute truth, purity of reference, and validity of argument. It is also tempting to see the Subversive Struggle as postmodernism, priding itself on liberating us from the binary oppressions of metaphysics (e.g., True and False, Valid and Invalid, Right and Wrong) without installing any new fantasies in their places. Tempting—but wrong; Fantasy Island and the Subversive Struggle are not merely two different schools of philosophy, to one or the other of which every would-be philosopher must declare allegiance early on. They are, first and foremost, two tendencies that wrestle within each of us and produce, in contemporary philosophers, a complex family of feelings.

One moment we find ourselves pursuing traditional goals which we know we cannot reach—if only the most ancient and general philosophical goal, that of coming up with an argument that will convince everybody that our thesis is wholly right. At other moments, we find ourselves trying to slither free of the whole thing, fooling around with ingenious but suspect thoughts that lead only to more dissatisfaction. This, I suggest, is because— as in that particular type of aporia which constitutes an "antinomy"—each approach incites the other. As we crawl around Fantasy Island, seeking new things to say about its fixed repertoire of primary beings, we twist and bend our thoughts and finally thought itself, struggling to come up with something new—until we have challenged things so basic that we find ourselves off the Island, struggling about in a dark ocean. And when we swim forth into that ocean, all we have to bring with us is our memories of what we are escaping from, which grow dimmer and more misleading until they are just abstract fantasies themselves.

Philosophy's Aporia II: A Historical Account

If an aporia of the general type sketched above has in fact arisen in the case of philosophy, here is how that could have happened. Fortunately, the terms of the philosophical history I am about to recite are well-known, and so my recitation can be short. It begins by asking what the "old way" was, the one which no longer works. Socrates was a skeptic, but his faithless young friend Plato propounded that we can arrive at important truths just by arguing about them. This view was basic to philosophy for thousands of years. The rise of science threw it into doubt; for while argument is necessary to science, it is so only in the service of empirical investigation. Hence Hume, discerning that mere argument could produce nothing but tautologies, abandoned philosophy altogether and became a historian. Kant claimed to have discovered a realm for which mere argument sufficed, but this "realm"—the universal, ahistorical faculties of the human mind—was such an embarrassment that it is roundly ignored by some of today's best Kant scholarship.[2] When it comes to ascertaining the truth about the nature we live in, including our own natures, the action is all in science.

And so the old way stopped working. Philosophy ceased to be a quest for the "great truths" and settled down in the ambit of things it could deal with by argument alone —first and foremost characteristics and outcomes of argument itself, such as sentential truth, reference, and rational decision. These things ceased to be what they once were—means to larger ends—and became primary topics in their own right.

Those who did not accept such restrictions could not return to the old style of doing philosophy, for science was all around them and its superiority to mere argument in the matter of producing truth was beyond challenge. So they sought to philosophize without arguing, referring, saying true things, or deciding anything—a hopeless struggle if ever there was one.

Philosophy's Aporia III: The Path to Resolution

The devotees of Fantasy Island and the Subversive Struggle are thus opposed on the issue of whether unaided argument can yield important truths about anything. The Islanders hold that it can; since this goes against the evidence of history, they eschew history. The Strugglers hold that it cannot—but such a truth, clearly an important one, could be philosophically established only by argument. Eschewing argument, they eschew justifying themselves as well. Neither side can explain itself, then. The Islanders cannot do so because that would require taking into account things that happen off the Island, for we can only explain ourselves by referring to the histories that make us what we are. The Strugglers cannot do so because they can only struggle.

Beneath the disagreement, however, is the common view that if philosophy has any definable job to do, that job is first and foremost establishing truths by argument alone. Showing the falsity of this view is the way past the aporia and is the task of this book. It has three phases, of which one is now completed. This is the task of stating the underlying agreement of the two sides of the aporia. Merely stating that common agreement is enough to render it dubious. Who gave philosophy the job of establishing truths? Why is it the only possible job? Why should philosophy have just one function, one *ergon*, one essence—in a time in which nothing else is allowed to have one, in which "essentialism" has become a banal intellectual insult?

The second phase of the task, to be adumbrated below but accomplished in chapter 2, is to show that there is a second, very important job, which philosophy has always done and to which it can credibly devote itself now that science has taken over its first job. This, I will argue, is the task of rationally constructing situations—or, briefly, of "situating" us.[3] For human reason does not have to be either universal or situated; it can be actively situat*ing* as well. Truth, in the sense which applies to sentences anyway, is then to be viewed not as the single and sovereign goal for philosophy, but as merely one of several means to the larger end of constructing situations.

The third phase—to be broached in the final two chapters, and one which I have also undertaken in other works —is actually to engage in that sort of philosophy. For the most persuasive evidence that there is something else to do and a way to do it is just to go and do it. (Taking care, all the while, to explain yourself!)

Philosophy's Second Job

We still do not fully understand the aporia I sketched above, because we do not fully understand where the underlying agreement comes from. It will be helpful, in uncovering this, to look at an alternative view of what philosophy's job might be, and ask why philosophy does not see itself as having that sort of job—especially in view of the fact that philosophy has not only had that other job all along, but has performed it admirably.

The number of true assertions (*Sätze:* beliefs, propositions, or sentences) philosophers have succeeded in establishing by argument alone was embarrassingly small long before modern science came on the scene. In fact, it has always been close to zero. As modern philosophers like Hume and Kant point out, often and with inexhaustible glee, their predecessors were unable to agree on anything and spent much of their time on Fantasy Islands of their own, arguing about essences and quiddities. Only religious enforcement brought any kind of consensus—and that was on good days!

Suppose, however, we look at the concepts philosophers have taken up, clarified, and reshaped in the course of making their arguments—inadvertently, as it were. To do so is to stumble upon nothing less than the intellectual treasure house of our civilization. Assertions can be true or false;[4] but the concepts, or words, in which they are couched are well- or ill-shaped, often for good or evil. Truth, Beauty, Justice, Freedom, Cause, Body, Nature, Force, Right, Courage, Love, and scores of other "philosophical" concepts serve us every day. In them and through them, and only so, we articulate our aspirations, our fears, and our sense of ourselves. That is why we philosophers cannot explain ourselves in "what languages have in common"; the various languages we speak shape us to our very cores, and without them we are unintelligible, even to ourselves. It is not even clear whether the basic words we use for this are our tools, or we theirs—just as it is not clear whether or not I am, biologically speaking, a mere envelope for my DNA.

> *Hegel put it well: "we only know about our thoughts, only have determinate, real thoughts, when we [give them existence] in words. . . . What cannot be formulated in words is in truth something murky and fermenting, which only gains clarity when it is able to put itself into words" (Werke X § 462 zus.*

280/221). Heidegger puts it by adopting Stefan George's dark poetry: "Where word breaks off, no thing may be."[5] And Wittgenstein says it with illuminating intensity: "Language itself is the vehicle of thought."[6]

All three philosophers, of course, view thinking as something that takes place not in a single isolated head, but out in the open, among people. Seeing thought as public enables them to circumvent insoluble problems about proving the existence of an external world and of other people; but in order to be public, thought must be linguistic. This does not mean that thinking cannot be carried on in solitude. It can, just as sex can. But the public thought process is not founded on the private one, any more than making love is founded on masturbation.

Nor does the view that thought is linguistic deny that the diverse languages we speak may share certain universal features. I am skeptical that such a claim, with its high empirical burden, could ever be proven; certainly not all languages have been examined to date for such features. Such examination as has been carried out tends, moreover, to be inconclusive; if ancient Greek had the copula, a grammatical device which asserts mere existence and nothing more, what do we make of Gorgias's claim that "to be nowhere is not to be" (Gorgias, B.3.69, 70)?[7] But even if such universal features could be found, they would have at most an auxiliary, enabling function, for they would not include the words we use to understand our lives and explain them to others. The (empirical) proof of this is massive, and the only one possible: the meanings of those basic words vary with place and time. Aitia is not causa, and neither is Ursache.

What is clear, from even a superficial glance at the history of Western philosophy, is that each of its basic concepts has been carefully cast, recast, shaped, and polished by thirty generations of critical dialogue. None of them *simply* matches or mirrors some given fact about the world or pattern in our experience. If they do that at all, it is because, like the concept of cause, they have been *made* to do so—mainly by philosophers. Who, all the while, thought that they were doing something else entirely: establishing truths by argument alone.

There is a political point to this. Those who, in our multi-cultural era, attack "Western Civilization" for its wars, lies, and oppressions are often taken to task because they usually do so from privileged positions as professors and cultural critics. Both sides in this fail to understand the degree to which such attacks not only benefit "Western Civilization" but constitute its vital core. For the dynamic core of "the West" is nothing more than the sum of basic intellectual attacks on it—and that, in turn, is nothing other than the history of philosophy. Even the most intense critics of "Western Civilization" can be "non-Western" only in the sense of being hyper-Western, and all such hyper-Westerners, whatever they call themselves, are philosophers.

The Last God

What made philosophy's allegiance to argument so unconditional? Why was philosophy so mistaken about its own nature? Because, presumably, philosophers wanted what they thought argument could provide: truth. To what, then, are philosophers really committed by their allegiance to truth? What do they take truth to be?

I have shown elsewhere that philosophers, beneath a common surface rhetoric, have meant wildly divergent things by the word "truth" (*TD* 43–44). Plato, who established the "old way" of doing philosophy, is particularly revealing on the point. For him, to be true is to be timeless. One of his standard ways of referring to the Forms, eternal and unchanging, is as *t'alêthê*, the "true things." "True" knowledge is of these things, and so is unchanging. Plato's metaphysics of Forms has been heavily critiqued during the intervening centuries, of course. But the association of truth with atemporality has been far too slow to die.

The recent problems philosophy has had with issues of self-reference are indications of this. It seems only natural that a sentence can be about itself; "this sentence has five words" seems unproblematic. But what about "this sentence is false?" Is it true? Then it must be false, for that is its claim. But if it is false, then it correctly reports on itself and is true.

Implicit in the view that an assertion can be about itself is the idea that it can be simultaneous with what it refers to. Two things are "simultaneous," as I will use the term, if there is no time when one exists and the other does not. Anything is therefore simultaneous with itself, for there is (presumably) no time when it both does and does not exist. Thus, to say that an assertion can refer to itself is to say that reference is compatible with simultaneity.

As long as we take reference as Frege and Russell took it, early on—to be some property that assertions simply have, all by themselves—there is no obvious problem with this. But if we view reference as something that human beings themselves bring about with their utterances, it becomes problematical indeed. For it is clear that we must already know something about a thing in order to talk about it at all—to "refer" to it. And it also seems that whatever we know about "exists" in some virtual sense—as an object of our knowledge, even if not materially. Thus, Cinderella, pi, the cat on the mat, and my late parents all "exist" in the sense, at least, that they "are" possible objects of speech (as Hegel would put it, they have "being" but not "existence"). An act of referring thus, on this view, requires pre-existing knowledge of the thing referred to, and so requires that its object pre-exist the act of referring itself—at least in whatever ways objects of knowledge "exist." Since no act of reference can be simultaneous with what it refers to, no utterance can refer to itself. "This sentence has five words," for all its seeming innocence, is as problematic as "this sentence is false." For it did not have five words until I had finished uttering it (or

*you had finished reading it), at which time its "object"—itself—
was already in the past, not the present.*[8]

*My point here is not to solve problems of self-reference by provid-
ing grounds for a universal ban on it, for no such ban has been
instituted; we are still free to invent such things as "sentences"
which (somehow) exist independently of being uttered on a
given occasion, and which as thus detemporalized may be simultaneous with that to which they refer. My point here is twofold:
(a) paradoxes of self-reference do not arise unless we assume
such simultaneity, and (b) we need not assume it for the utterances we actually make.*

Atemporality shows up in the empirical world, either as
presence (of one thing) or as simultaneity (the relation between two things when at every moment in which one is
present, the other is as well). Simultaneity often functions
in philosophy as a sort of hidden philosophical imperative:
sit omnia simul. Thus, in much contemporary philosophical
thinking, an assertion, its meaning, and even (as in issues
of self-reference) its referent are all assumed to be simultaneous.

*As an expression of the imperative of simultaneity, consider
the following quote from Quine:*

> Our ordinary language shows a tiresome bias in its treat-
> ment of time. Relations of date are exalted grammatically
> as relations of position, weight, and color are not. This bias
> is of itself an inelegance, or breach of theoretical simplicity.
> Moreover, the form that it takes—that of requiring that
> every verb show a tense—is particularly productive of
> needless complications, since it demands lip service to time
> even when time is farthest from our thoughts. Hence in
> fashioning canonical notations it is usual to drop tense dis-
> tinctions. We may conveniently hold to the grammatical
> present as a form, but treat it as temporally neutral. Where
> the artifice comes in is in taking the present tense as time-
> less always, and dropping other tenses. This artifice frees us

to omit temporal information, or, when we please, handle it like spatial information.[9]

It is a fatefully short distance from this to what Peter Hylton characterizes as the tendency of analytical philosophers to see analytical philosophy "as taking place within a single timeless moment."[10]

The imperative of simultaneity, even if hidden, blocks philosophy's way to history, and in particular to its own history as the casting, polishing, and reshaping of concepts. It is the clear contemporary descendent of philosophy's ancient concern with timelessness, for eternal entities, such as Forms or propositions, are all simultaneous with each other. There is no time, for a Platonist, at which the Good exists but the Beautiful does not, or for a Christian that God exists but his Wisdom does not, or for a Kantian that the category of cause exists but the other eleven do not.

Simultaneity runs into trouble, however, when we are dealing with empirical entities, if only because after the Theory of Relativity, "absolute" simultaneity is impossible; two events are "simultaneous" only from a particular perspective. If we shift standpoints, they may no longer be simultaneous. A weaker concept is required, which I will call "contemporaneity." Two things are contemporaneous if there is some time at which they both exist. I am in this sense "contemporaneous" with the Washington Monument, and my writing this sentence is contemporaneous with various visitors ascending the monument. Contemporaneity is thus a diluted version of simultaneity (and a doubly diluted version of eternity).

The referent of a sentence cannot, I have suggested, be simultaneous with the sentence itself. It also may, as a material object, not be contemporaneous with the utterance of that sentence, as Caesar's crossing the Rubicon is not contemporaneous with my writing "Caesar crossed the Rubicon." But a sentence does have to be contemporaneous, though not simultaneous, with whatever makes us accept it for true. I accept that Caesar crossed the Rubicon because I have a memory, right now, of reading history books which I also remember as having been trustworthy. If there were no sense in which the evidence for the crossing were available to me right now, I could not accept the sentence as true.

It is very difficult to come up with a concept of truth that is not "timeless" in at least this way. It is a plain fact that to inquire whether an assertion is true, in the ordinary sense, is not to inquire about its relation to earlier or later members of a temporal sequence. Such information is sometimes extremely important; but to ask about it is not to ask after truth.[11] If I ask you whether it is true that the cat is on the mat, I am not asking how the sentence "the cat is on the mat" came to be produced on this occasion, or what effects producing it will have. (Still less am I asking how the cat came to be on the mat in the first place.) Rather, I am asking for evidence or testimony to be produced *now* that will verify the sentence: the mat with the cat on it, or an argument, or a nod of your head. And if I ask you whether it is true that the cat was on the mat last Thursday, I am also asking for evidence, argument, or testimony to be produced *now* that will verify or falsify that assertion.

In both cases, the evidence, argument, or testimony must be produced *now*. For without some sort of contemporaneous availability of sentence and evidence, the notion of verification makes no sense. And without the possibility of verification, the notion of truth makes, as far as

I can see, no sense. Even when limited to contemporaneity, then, evaluation of the truth of an assertion never carries us beyond the present tense. Philosophy's exclusive concern with truth is the limiting of itself to the present tense.

Nietzsche protested this in a particularly telling way. As he puts it in Human All Too Human,

> everything has come to be (*alles aber ist geworden*); there are no eternal facts, just as there are no absolute truths. That is why historical philosophizing is necessary from now on.[12]

This suggests that there are two ways in which something can be taken to be timeless. First, its Before and After can be denied, in which case we think we are dealing with what Nietzsche calls an "eternal fact." Or a thing's Before and After, without being actually denied, can simply be ignored, in which case we are I think dealing with what Nietzsche called an "absolute truth."[13]

When Nietzsche says that scientists "are very far from being free spirits, because they still believe in truth,"[14] *he is accusing them of deifying truth, of making it, so to speak, the last god. If "god" here is to be understood in the Augustinian sense, as that which is timeless, then philosophy which seeks truth is really seeking timelessness, a doomed quest which Nietzsche derides—with some jibes at Augustine—at* Beyond Good and Evil § 200.[15] *Philosophy for Nietzsche must in fact kill this last god; it must abjure timeless truth, i.e., the "pure truth, apart from any of its consequences" which Nietzsche even calls a "thing in itself." It must come to see truth as a "*mobile army of metaphors, metonymies, and anthropomorphisms: metaphors that have become worn out and drained of sensuous force."*[16]

Philosophy's original sin, as Heidegger reminds us (*SZ* 227), is therefore lust for eternity. Like a recurrently deceived but still entranced lover, philosophy has reinterpreted the object of its affections over the millennia, sometimes in radical ways: as Platonic forms, eternal and separate from the world we live in; as Democritean atoms and Aristotelian essences, unchanging components of a changing world; as the unchanging structures of the Kantian mind; and, finally, as linguistic entities whose only notable function is to be true or false, and which are therefore indifferent to temporal orderings.

In each case, the timelessness turned out to be an artifact of our minds—a fantasy. Plato's mistaken separation of forms from sensibles was diagnosed as such by Aristotle; Aristotle's exemption of essences from change was diagnosed eventually by Darwin; the Kantian separation of mind from history was diagnosed by Schiller; the reduction of utterances to propositions was diagnosed by the later Wittgenstein, and so forth. After Quine, we are left with no more atemporality than this:

> Strictly speaking . . . what admit of meaning and of truth and falsity are not the statements but the individual events of their utterance. However, it is a source of great simplification in logical theory to talk of statements in abstraction from the individual occasions of their utterance; and this abstraction, if made in full awareness and subject to a certain [technical] precaution, offers no difficulty.[17]

> *This point is echoed by Quine's Harvard colleague John Rawls. If such things as knowledge of one's own class, position, social status, natural assets and liabilities, and psychological propensities[18] count as temporal information—as they surely do— then it is by what Quine, in my earlier quote from him, called the "omission of temporal information" that we arrive at what Rawls calls the "perspective of eternity":*

>> Thus to see our place in society from the perspective of this [original] position is to see it *sub specie aeternitatis:* it is to regard the human situation not only from all social but

from all temporal points of view. The perspective of eternity is not a perspective from a certain place beyond the world, nor the point of view of a transcendent being; rather it is a certain form of thought and feeling that rational persons can adopt within the world.[19]

As Rawls is not the only one to teach us, such a perspective can be very valuable indeed. It results from what John Dewey called the "principle of selective emphasis," focusing on only certain aspects of a thing, rather than on its entirety. The principle of selective emphasis, for Dewey, validates precisely what Quine does in the above quote from him:

> Selective emphasis, with accompanying omission and rejection, is the heartbeat of mental life. To object to [it] is to discard all thinking. . . . Deception comes only when the presence and operation of choice is concealed, disguised, denied. (*EN* 24–27)

Philosophy is prone to such deception:

> The objects of reflection in philosophy, being reached by methods that seem to those who employ them rationally mandatory, are taken to be "real" in and of themselves—and supremely real. (*EN* 9)

Thus the genesis of what I call Fantasy Island. When we view sentences as the basic units of language, and examine them only for their truth, we place philosophy under the imperative of simultaneity. We are then thinking "universally," for what is true in English is true in French, Chinese, or Twi—if it can exist there at all. Often, however, it does not. If "the mind is identical with the brain" is true in English, then it would be true in French or German. But since neither of those languages has a word for "mind," the sentence cannot be uttered in either language.

Dewey suggests, in different places, two ways to counter this. One, which if left to itself betrays the standard failure of Pragmatists to appreciate the importance of the past, is testing what we are saying "to see what it leads to in ordinary experience and what new meanings it contributes" (EN 9). The other is to

look to the origin of what we are saying, which for Dewey is the
act of reflection which produces our selective emphasis:

> Honest empirical method will state when and where and
> why the act of selection took place and thus enable others
> to repeat it and test its worth. Selective choice, denoted
> as an empirical event, reveals the basis and bearing of intel-
> lectual simplifications; they then cease to be of such a self-
> enclosed nature as to be affairs only of opinion and argu-
> ment, admitting no alternatives save complete acceptance
> or rejection. (*EN* 28)

But selective emphasis is not only produced by conscious acts; as
I will argue in chapter 2, the languages we speak do much of
the selecting for us without our even being aware of it. Hence,
"honest empirical method" requires serious attention to how
the languages we speak guide our thoughts, and this in turn
requires us to look deeply into the histories of the words we use—
for only there can this function of language be uncovered.

Simplification, of course, is a form of falsification, and this
leaves philosophy's pursuit of truth in a final paradox. Philosophy which pursues truth *alone* treats temporal things
as if they were timeless, and so grasps falsity instead.
Truer to the spirit of Quine and Rawls is to readmit the
temporal information they only provisionally omit, if we
can do so in regulated and principled ways.

Truth Temporalized: One Step Forward

Philosophy thus has (at least) two jobs. One, which it
acknowledges but which it has performed miserably, is
producing true assertions by argument alone. The other,
which it has performed well but largely surreptitiously, is
the creation and revision of the basic concepts which inform our lives and societies—the "reshaping" of reason
itself. What has kept philosophy from acknowledging this
second job is its exclusive devotion to truth, which is itself

rooted in an ancient desire for timelessness. This desire has trapped philosophy in the aporia I have described; either it remains with the old way of trying to establish truth by argument alone, in which case it restricts itself to a self-enclosed "island" of fantastic reifications, or it struggles free and goes nowhere. In the former case, it cannot explain itself to non-philosophers, since that would require dealing with realities that are not to be found on its Fantasy Island; in the latter case, it can explain nothing at all to anyone.

In order to resolve this aporia, we need either to articulate goals for philosophical thought that do not reduce to truth, or to reconceptualize truth itself in more temporal terms. Two brilliant members of the philosophical tradition, Hegel and Heidegger, suggest that the latter is the more promising course. While I think they are wrong, they have important lessons for anyone who, like me, wants to take the former path.

In Hegel's *Phenomenology of Spirit, Wahrheit* denotes a certain sort of outcome; it is what happens to a "certainty" (*Gewißheit*) when you try to live by it. A *Wahrheit,* or a truth, is, as the *Phenomenology* uses the term, not "true" in *any* of the traditional senses philosophers are familiar with, all of which contrast with falsity. Hegelian "truth," by contrast, does not correspond more closely to reality than does falsehood, nor does it cohere any better with other things. It is not pragmatically more successful than falsehood; nor is it (and not falsehood) the outcome, even ideal, of some process of consensus formation. We know this because every *Wahrheit* in the *Phenomenology* is refuted in turn, becoming a falsehood. What is true for one section is false for the next until the book's end, when the whole game sort of dissolves.

It is tempting to say that all the *Phenomenology*'s truths, since they are later refuted, were false all along and only seemed to be true. But that is not what Hegel says. What he says, in the "Preface" to the *Phenomenology*, is this:

> "True" and "false" belong among those determinate thoughts which are held to be motionless . . . essences . . . each standing fixed and isolated from the other. . . . To know something falsely means that there is a disparity between knowing and its substance. . . . But out of this distinguishing comes their identity, and this identity that has come to be is truth. (*und diese gewordene Gleichheit ist die Wahrheit: PhS* 33f/22, translation altered)

There is nothing here about seeming truths being refuted. Rather, for Hegel, "truth" is explicitly defined in temporal terms, as an "identity which has come to be." Something is "true," then, if it has a certain sort of past. Truth, in the first instance, is a relation of a thing to its past.

> *The closest contemporary philosophy comes to this is perhaps Habermas's "consensus" theory of truth, as presented for example in his* Wahrheitstheorien.[20] *But truth is not for Habermas, as for Hegel, simply what emerges from the discussion. For the discussion could in principle concern any one of Habermas's three validity claims. When a given discussion concludes that an utterance is true (as opposed to appropriate or truthful), it is deciding, quite traditionally, that the sentence in question corresponds to something about the "objective" world.*[21]

With truth being an affair of the past tense in this way, Hegel has rendered it temporal—but in a way odd enough to lack plausibility. Some can be bestowed on it by considering Hegel's relation to Kant. In the terms of Kant's logic, the traditional view of truth as the relation of a thought to an object can be cashed out in one of two ways. First, the object in question may be taken (as the tradition takes it) to exist independently of our minds, as a "thing-in-itself." In that case, since things in themselves cannot be known, we have what purports to be a cognitive relation between two terms, one of which is wholly unknowable. That will not work, so only the other way is left: to construe the object as, like thought itself, dependent on our minds, as an appearance. Then, says Kant, we can at best compare appearances with one another.

> *This argument is found in Kant's* Vienna Logic,[22] *which according to the "Translator's Introduction" to the English edition, dates from around 1780. It is repeated in the* Jäsche Logic *published in 1800.*[23] *It is missing from the* Critique of Pure Reason, *though its traces can be found in the speed with which the discussion there moves from the question "what is truth?" to "is a criterion of truth possible?" (*KRV *B 82). The two logical passages show that we need a* criterion *of truth because we can never have truth itself, in the traditional (dogmatic) sense of the known agreement of our cognition with the world outside, or independent of, our minds.*

But here, if we read Kant the way Hegel would have read him—with more ingenuity than accuracy—something interesting happens. All appearances, for Kant, are in time.[24] The temporal form of appearances is, first and foremost, succession, i.e., that ordering in which they do not coexist but are before or after one another. This is evident from Kant's account of simultaneity.[25] That two things exist at the same time is not perceived directly, for "our apprehension of the multiplicity of appearances is always successive" (*KRV* B 225). What we actually perceive is always first one thing and then the other: A → B or B → A. A and B are "simultaneous" when the order in which we do this is indifferent.[26] Simultaneity, as well as endurance (that "endures" which is simultaneous with a succession [*KRV* B 67]), are thus not parts of the original structure of appearances, but are derivative possibilities for ordering them.

It follows that the most basic relationship any two (or more) appearances can have to one another is that of being "before" and "after" each other. Whatever other relations they have will be superadded to this one. This would hold, though Kant does not say so, for the truth-relation, if it is construed as holding among appearances only—precisely as Hegel's *Phenomenology* construes it. If truth is understood as a relation between a sentence and a fact, for example, then one of these two appearances should come before the other. Simultaneity is not an option, unless it does not matter whether the sentence comes before the fact, or the fact before the sentence. But of course it does matter; as I noted above, something which has not, in some way or other, "appeared" to us is something about which we have no knowledge and so is something we cannot even speak about. In Kantian terms, then, a declarative sentence cannot pre-exist what it is about, and the "appearance" referred to by a true sentence must precede the sentence itself.

"Phenomenological truth" for Hegel is then what happens when an object is followed by a sentence in the appropriate way. Everything now rests, of course, on just what that "appropriate way" is. I will come back to this in chapter 2. For the moment, what Hegel has done is, I hope, clear: he has imported time into the nature of truth. For something to be true of something else, it must—in an appropriate way—follow it in time. To put this differently, to be "true," in the *Phenomenology* at least, means to have a certain sort of past.

Heidegger's most important book is *Being and Time,* and the most important word in that title is, famously, "and."

Heidegger wrote the book to show (a) that the West has traditionally construed Being as atemporal, and (b) that Being cannot in fact be understood independently of time, that time is the "sense of Being" (*SZ* 1). But if *Being and Time* temporalizes Being, it is in a very different way than the *Phenomenology* temporalized truth. For Hegel, truth lay in the relation of a thing to what preceded it; but on Heidegger's account of time, the future is more basic than the past.[27]

Heidegger's discussions of truth, like Hegel's, are far too complex to treat here, and in any case I shall be making use of only a small part of them. This is the part captured by three points made in Daniel Dahlstrom's magisterial *Heidegger's Concept of Truth:* (1) truth in its most originary sense is for Heidegger the disclosure of time itself, as the "sense of being"; (2) "the basic phenomenon of time is [in turn] the future"; and (3) the future "is at bottom the 'becoming' exemplified or, better, authenticated by a resolute anticipation of death."[28] Truth for Heidegger is the disclosure of the authentic future.

We can flesh this out by noting that in *Being and Time,* death is the "possibility of no more possibilities." We do not know what death is or when it will come. But each of us knows *that* it is coming, sometime, whatever it is. Death, in short, is the final shapelessness (*Gestaltlosigkeit*) of our future (*SZ* 257–258). As such it determines, in its current absence and impending presence, the shape and scope of our lives right now. For our lives are shaped by the commitments we make, and it is the fact that we are going to die, at some unknown time, that requires us to make those commitments. If I were going to live forever, for example, I would not have to choose a life partner. I could marry every other member of the human race and live a hundred years with each—and when I had finished with that, there would be new humans to marry. Nor would I have to commit myself to a career, or to a community; I could be a Philadelphia lawyer for sixty or seventy years, then move into medicine in Houston or boxing in Marseilles for a couple of centuries, and then take up subsistence farming on the slopes of Mount Everest. It is because we are mortal that the major decisions we make require us to let some possibilities go past definitively.

Our unknown but impending future thus structures our present to its very core. Each of us, always, is feeling along the edge of something radically unknown but impending, and the necessity of that *tâtonner* is what it is to have what I will call an "authentic future." The future on this view is not something we describe or connect with, for there is nothing in it to be described or connected with. It is a gap which we *open up*. Such opening to futurity is how I cash out Dahlstrom's account of Heidegger's version of truth. It gets carried through in very diverse ways among Heidegger's many followers; I will discuss it in more detail in chapter 2.

Hegel's *Phenomenology of Spirit* and Heidegger's *Being and Time* thus offer not global "theories of truth" which compete with established theories such as correspondence and coherence, but something else entirely. Their accounts are of goals for specific forms of thought—in particular, for their own thinking—which are not reducible to "truth" in *any* of its traditional philosophical senses. Both philosophers say as much, but in a backhanded way not easily intelligible to English speakers. In accordance with much German philosophical usage, they use the word "correctness" (*Richtigkeit*) to cover the traditional senses of "true," and use "true" (*Wahr*) to designate their innovations.[29] And under this name, both *affirm* the standard views of truth. As Hegel puts it,

Philosophy must at least complain, where justified, about the false statement of the facts, and if one looks closely this species [of incomprehension] is, surprisingly, the most common, and sometimes attains unbelievable dimensions.[30]

For Hegel, then, the "phenomenological" concept of the truth of a thing as its proper relation to its past does not supplant the "ordinary" truth of sentences which state facts; it supplements it and even presupposes it (cf. *CW* 62–64). Heidegger is more succinct. *Diese Angaben der Physik,* he writes, *sind richtig.*[31]

To be sure, the disparity between Hegel's and Heidegger's innovations and the traditional concepts of truth is masked by their own repeated efforts to validate their own views as somehow more basic conceptualizations of truth than the standard variety, rather than as entirely different concepts. But in a later work, Heidegger repents:

> To raise the question of *aletheia,* of unconcealment as such, is not the same as raising the question of truth. For this reason it was inadequate and misleading to call *aletheia,* in the sense of opening, truth.[32]

And Hegel, in a spoken addendum to his lectures on logic, refers to his concept of truth as a "completely other" (*ganz andere*) meaning of the term. This expression is a telling one for a philosophy which takes nothing to be "completely other" to anything else.[33]

We now have two very different ways in which philosophers have taken truth out of the present tense. To anticipate chapter 2, the Hegelian approach seeks to reconstruct the relation of a philosophical unit—say, the notion of duty—to its past, by reconstructing a step-by-step process in which each stage solves a problem with the previous stage, and no other problems (explaining this in detail will mark my return to the issue of the "appropriate way" in which something true relates to its past). Such "dialectical reconstruction" offers us not a truthful picture of how things actually happened, but a step-by-step account of how things currently around us now could have been rationally built up; it appeals to a notion of validity other than truth. Heidegger, by contrast (and in further anticipation of chapter 2), seeks to project a future for a philosophical unit—say, the fragment of Anaximander—by putting its old words together in new ways, appealing to meanings not usually attributed to this text, etc. (for details see *MO* 240–251). Both of these approaches, like all thought, make use of assertions claimed to be true and arguments constructed of them, but neither has establishing true sentences as its proper goal. This can be made evident if we take Hegel and Heidegger a second step forward and cease to call their innovative concepts by the name of "truth." In chapter 2, I will baptize the Hegelian and Heideggerean goals of discourse "Nobility" and "Appropriateness" respectively.

Analytic, Continental

I previously presented Fantasy Island and the Subversive Struggle as two conflicting dimensions of the contemporary philosophical personality, and viewing them in that way will be important to my upcoming argument about the emergence of what I call the "new philosophy." But one very traditional way of dealing with conflicts within one's psyche, of course, is to identify with one side in the conflict, repressing the other or projecting it onto others. Philosophers who do this turn out to bear a high resemblance to what we know today as analytical and continental philosophers. This yields what amounts to a rather-too-neat interpretation of the analytical/continental distinction.

Analytical philosophy, philosophy in the present tense, is on this view an approach to philosophy which renounces time itself, and with it leaves behind our lives and experiences in order to dwell alone—on Fantasy Island. The strictly philosophical price paid for this is that such philosophers are unable to distinguish between philosophical debates that originated only recently and debates that have been going on for centuries or even millennia, and which are therefore likely to be more important. (Recall the amount of thought and ink that went into the discussion of "sense-data" around the middle of the last century, and how quickly that whole issue evaporated.)[34] This leads in turn not merely to philosophical prices, but to a personal fate. Those who do not ask themselves where their thinking can lead find, all too often, that it leads to nothing. Those who ignore the past inevitably join it and are ignored themselves.

Continental philosophy, seeking to reinstate time, discovers that it must wriggle free of the static nature of the analytical present, and comes to struggle in the following way:

Pursuing the truth of sentences, I have suggested, requires us to ignore the Before and After of those sentences. To pursue truth is then to pursue something timeless. The goal of a discourse, moreover, structures its nature in many ways (as Roger Scruton has noted in the case of truth),[35] and so is "appealed to" constantly, if usually implicitly, by that discourse. Hence, if continental philosophers pursue sentential truth, they are making a structuring appeal to something timeless. To be consistent, they cannot take such truth as their overriding goal.

But they *have* no other goal, as is shown by Hegel's and

Heidegger's inability, noted above, to use any word other than "truth" to denote their very different conceptions of the goal of philosophical thought. The extreme variance of these conceptions with more traditional concepts of truth is thus masked by the very word by which they call them. Because of that mask, those goals appear to be *competing* with truth as traditionally conceived, rather than complementing it. Pursuing either of them then requires, it appears, wholly abjuring such truth. And so even *using* the truth of sentences—by making those sentences premises or lines in our arguments, or ingredients in our descriptions—also requires us to ignore their Befores and Afters. Philosophers who accept this line of reasoning will be unable to appeal to true sentences as even the medium of their thinking. Continental philosophy so pursued is clearly going to be a most implausible enterprise, for in abandoning truth it must also abandon sentences. We are left with what Derrida calls

> a writing without presence, without absence, without history, without cause, without *archê*, without *telos*, absolutely deranging every dialectic, every theology, every teleology, every ontology.[36]

Continental philosophers do, of course, use and presuppose true sentences on every page of their writings. If it were not true, for example, that Hegel wrote the *Encyclopedia of the Philosophical Sciences,* Derrida could not deconstruct it in "Le puits et la pyramide."[37] To be sure, establishing truths like that—or of any other kind—is not Derrida's goal. But true sentences must be among his tools, if he is to do anything at all.

The problem is that neither Derrida nor any other "postmodern" philosopher, so far as I know, tells us why this is so (Heidegger laments it on one occasion).[38] If they believe that sentence structure is dispensable and wrong, and have not dispensed with it, then they surely owe us just such an explanation. In its absence, the most charitable conclusion is that they do not see sentence structure— and, hence, some version of truth—as dispensable. They take it for granted, even as they try and go beyond it.

In order to be true to our lives and experience, as opposed to pursuing "truth" within the horizon of a previous simplification/falsification, philosophy must become both postanalytical and metacontinental. "Postanalytical" in that the restriction of rationality to the present tense must be definitively ended. "Metacontinental" in that thought's necessary inclusion of things like reference and truth must be reflected upon, not merely indulged.

Philosophy in Time: Postanalytic, Metacontinental

This suggests a nicely inclusive view of philosophy. All our experience is in time, and time has three dimensions —past, present, and future. While it is possible to focus on any of these to the exclusion of the others,[39] we should allow all of them to come forth in philosophy. To do otherwise is like stubbornly proffering drawings where statues alone will do. Only an approach which unifies analytic and continental philosophy in this sort of way can be true to the fact that we, as human beings, are inescapably and to our very cores "in time."

But what is time?

This seems to be a question for physicists and for philosophers of physics. But if time is a core constituent in the way we are, we have a primary relation to time that we can neither overcome nor escape. Whatever that relation to time may be, it is one basic determinant of the way we are. An investigation of that relation is thus an exercise in self-knowledge and requires knowledge of time, not merely as it is "in itself" apart from our minds, but of time as it operates within our fundamental relation to it. The first step in uncovering that relation is to investigate our experience of time—how time appears to us. Such an investigation is "phenomenological."

It is quite possible, of course, that our relation to time, though basic to our natures, is somehow hidden from us—like the Freudian unconscious. In that case, our experience of time would disguise, rather than reveal, our real relation to it. But we can determine whether that is the case only if we first understand what time *seems* to be; we must begin with a reflection on our experience of time. Such reflection, according to Heidegger, is *the* job of phenomenology (cf. *SZ* 34–39). The next few pages will be devoted to a couple of phenomenological points about time.

One way in which our traditional way of thinking about time distorts, if not time itself then our experience of it, can be made clear at the outset. Foucault is rumored to have once said that "two sexes are not enough; we need a thousand." Similarly, to be true to the ways in which time affects our knowledge of ourselves we would need, not three tenses (or a thousand), but six; for time as we live it out, and as it constitutes us, is experienced in (at least) six dimensions. Since three of these dimensions are largely unknowable and so ineffable, our languages have understandably dispensed with them. Insofar as our experience of time is shaped by our language, our "real" relation to time is indeed disguised (and other disguises are possible, though I will not pursue them here). Still, the other dimensions are quite accessible to attentive common sense—which is another name for "phenomenology."

Two of these dimensions are commonly lumped together as "the past." My "past," in one sense, contains everything which has happened to me up to now. This past is, obviously, unknowable; to run through in memory everything which has happened to me in my fifty-nine years of life would, if performed flawlessly, take another fifty-nine years. Since it is inherently unknowable in its totality, this past approximates what Kant would call a "thing in itself,"[40] and I will call it "the past in itself."

Out of the past in itself, then, I must create for myself a "usable past," the personal history which I use to "situate" myself, to determine where I am and what I am about in my life. Common sense tells us that the usable past is simply that part of the overall past which is known, but in fact there is abundant evidence that our mind is much more creative than that in constructing our usable past. We could hardly function if it were not. Much empirical research has confirmed that memory operates, not according to norms of truth, but as what Hegel, in his *Philosophy of Spirit,* calls *Erinnerung* (*Werke* X 258–262/203–206). It produces not faithful recollections of what "really" happened, but rationalized interpretations of it. As one contemporary researcher puts it,

> The interpretive mechanism . . . is always hard at work, seeking the meaning of events. It is constantly looking for order and reason, even where there is none, which leads it to constantly make mistakes. It tends to overgeneralize, frequently constructing a potential past as opposed to a true one.[41]

Note the phrasing here. Our researcher clearly believes that the proper job of memory is to mirror the past, rather than to construct a usable past. That our mind has evolved to do the latter suggests, by contrast, that the search for "order and reason," rather than factual accuracy, is the real job of memory; deviations from the actual facts are not "mistakes" or "overgeneralizations," but merely the way memory works. What we need for our lives, and all we can have, is what our researcher calls a "potential past"; a "true" one is not an option. (The construction of a usable past, along with the specific sort of "order and reason" which philosophical memory uses to constitute this sort of past, will be discussed in chapter 2.)

The past in itself and the usable past clearly differ from each other, and radically. The one is a set of brute givens; the other is constructed by me out of a small selection from those givens. The one is a mass of facts (Caesar stepped into the Rubicon *and* his sandals got wet *and* an attendant ran across the river with a fresh pair, etc., etc.); the other is an organized construct. The one cannot be known; the other is not only constructed by me in such a way as to be knowable, but is there as a basis for cognizing other things. For I become aware of my pen when I *have decided* that it is time to write a letter; I become aware of the gathering clouds when I *have decided* that it is time to go outside.[42]

My aim here is not to clarify the nature of these two pasts in any sort of detail. (In the case of the past in itself such clarification is impossible, since that past is unknowable.) For the moment I wish simply to note that both sorts of past are there, and that temporalized philosophy must take account of their differences.

There are also two senses of "future": the predictable future and the unpredictable future. This point is an obvious one—so obvious that we spend a lot of time trying to deny it. Even when we are at our most knowledgeable about how things are likely to turn out (and enormous amounts of effort and money go into this), the unpredictable future has a larger scope than we are comfortable with. Indeed, the very laws of nature, the most reliable of constants, are increasingly viewed by scientists as susceptible to change.[43] There is, moreover, no way to be certain that the laws of logic themselves will not follow. It is quite possible that, as Nancy Cartwright has argued concerning the laws of physics, the laws of logic are really just a collection of templates for producing certain sorts of text.[44] How can we be certain that students in logic classes 1000 years from now will learn things in any way resembling today's *modus tollens* or *modus ponens*? How can we be certain that the formulas inscribed on the flaps of today's logic textbooks will not look to the thinkers of that time as Roman numerals look to us—as a collection of unbelievably clumsy and seriously misleading ways to do things?

There are thus two futures: the one that is predictable because it looks pretty much the way the present and the past have looked; and the other one, about which we cannot speak because we know nothing—the "future in itself." The predictable future and the future in itself are as different from one another as the usable past and the past in itself, and for the same reasons: we create the predictable future in order to know and do other things, while the future in itself is neither made nor known by us. A genuinely temporalized thought must respect the difference between these two sorts of futures.

The present, too, has two senses. There is the incredibly large set of things which are actually happening, just in my vicinity, at any given moment, far too large to be known and therefore constituting a "present in itself," and there is also the "presentable" present, the set of things of which I actually become aware—or had better become aware—in the course of my life.

It is clear that the presentable present is conditioned

both by the past we construct and by the future we cannot predict. What we ordinarily notice, or need to notice, are the things going on around us which are relevant to the ongoing history we are constructing with our lives, to our usable past, and to the future we have conceptualized for ourselves. As with the past and the future, the present in itself and the presentable present are radically different from one another, and the index to that radicality is truth. For the concept of truth, in our everyday employment of it, brings the important lesson that things are not always what we assume them to be.

Those assumptions are generally made on the basis of our usable pasts and predictable futures. I assume the eggs are fresh because I have gotten hungry and can predict that a nice dish of eggs will assuage that hunger. My presentable present thus includes fresh eggs. But the eggs in my refrigerator may not in truth be fresh; the world as it is, the present in itself, may not be amenable to my current projects. My need to know whether it is amenable is my need for truth. Truth so employed is not merely the excellence of cognition, then, but actually constitutes our experience of the present out of the interplay between what we would like to be the case, in virtue of our usable pasts and future projects, and what really is the case—the present understood as the Greek *ta nun,* the prevailing circumstances.

The present as we experience it is thus not a primary given, but is the product of a six-way interplay between our pasts and our futures. To appreciate this is to admit in the most radical way that we are radically temporal beings. Only a philosophy which can accommodate this radical temporality—the fact that nothing is immune from time, that everything has a Before and an After that is different from its Now—can get philosophy beyond its increasingly debilitated oscillation between Fantasy Island and the Subversive Struggle.

I suggested above that philosophy needs either to reconceptualize truth in more temporal terms or to go beyond "truth" altogether. Hegel and Heidegger did the former, but they were wrong to call their very different notions by the term "truth," as if they were offering new "theories of truth" to compete with more traditional ones. Perhaps, to be fair, that is what they thought they were doing. On my reading, however, they were broaching ways of relating to the past and future which have nothing to do with traditional senses of "truth."

The differences between the past in itself and the usable past, between the future in itself and the predictable future, and between the present in itself and the presentable present, mean that the world we live in—the usable past, the predictable future, and the presentable present— cannot be gotten at by the traditional rules of truth alone. The world we live in does not mirror some given natural reality, but is constructed out of it by various principles of selection and ordering; these principles fall under the overall heading not of faithful replication of the givens or truth, but of the regulated construction I call "situating." The philosophical application of these principles, while not restricted to truth, is not a mere struggling. When the various pasts, presents, and futures are responded to in the proper way, three different "keys" of philosophical thinking are being played at once. When they function together, each according to its own rules, a new philosophy emerges. If this philosophy cannot give us an immovable crag to cling to when the seas of life fall upon us, it can at least—as Plato said—give us a raft on which to ride them (*Phaedo* 85d).

This book will present what is, I maintain, a continuation of analytical and continental philosophy, but some aspects of it will look quite odd to philosophers trained in both of those paradigms. A brief statement of some of the oddest of those aspects, together with the rationales for them, is then in order. In all cases, the alienating factor is the role of *time* in the emerging philosophy.

Bivalence and the Present

Bivalence is the view that any assertion is either wholly true or wholly false, that there are no third possibilities and no degrees. One of the great structuring principles of traditional philosophy, it is also a crippling one—for it tells us that if we do not get things wholly right, we have gotten them wholly wrong. The number of things we can hope to get wholly right is tiny—and the number of things we can *know* we have gotten wholly right is even smaller. Fortunately, bivalence is a fantasy; it exists only as a timeless fiction. Not only is ordinary language in general not bivalent, it has no "truth valence" at all.

> *Though bivalence has ancestry going back to Aristotle, that ancestry is suspect. Aristotle's most rigorous definition of truth states that when the separations and connections of things in my mind are the same as those existing in the objects I perceive, I have attained "truth."[45] But separation and connection are matters of degree, as is sameness. In* On Interpretation *Aristotle puts the matter not in terms of sameness but in those of similarity: the things in my soul are "likenesses" (* homoiômata*) of the things outside my soul (*On Interpretation *1 16a7seq) and therefore can be more or less like them. Bivalence in its current, rigorous sense was introduced into philosophy by Russell and Frege, where it applied to—in fact, defined—those strange, timeless entities called "propositions." As definitive of propositions, it was merely asserted, not argued, to hold for them.[46]*

> *Propositions, being timeless, could not change; nor could their truth values. Each was eternally true or eternally false. But*

when propositions, the notion of which was decidedly at vari-
ance with the Empiricist allegiances of analytical philosophy,
were replaced by sentences, something rationally constructed was
replaced by something empirical. The change was momentous.
It was as if philosophers stopped arguing about essences and
started arguing about horses; though no individual horse is a
complete incarnation of what it is to be a horse, we can at least
look at empirical instances of "horseness" and get an idea of
what it is like. Bivalence ought *at this point—for example, in*
the work of Quine—to have become a matter of empirical inves-
tigation. Philosophers should have looked at a large number
of sentences and tried to establish whether they were bivalent
or not.

That no such investigation ever took place may owe something
to the politics of the McCarthy era, which enjoined philosophers
to view themselves as engaged in a "timeless, selfless, quest of
truth" (cf. TD 39–42 and passim). But it may owe even more to
the idea that bivalence was the necessary connection between
logic and language—and to the obvious point that ordinary
language, if tested for bivalence, would fail.

Few notions, to begin with, as are entrenched in ordinary language as the notion of degrees of truth. Consider, for example, such locutions as "that is very true,"
"that is quite false," "that is not true at all," "that is really
true," and "that is sort of true." Such expressions are quite
common—far more common than the simple "that is
true" or "that is false." It is hard to see why they would
exist if English sentences were bivalent. Indeed, one could
substitute "large" and "small" for "true" and "false" and
the sentences above would all make sense; so why not
see true and false as, like large and small, matters of something's position on a continuum?

This accords with our intuitions that some sentences are
falser than others. It is false to say that Lincoln was a
Christian, but falser still to say he was a Catholic, and
even falser to say he was a Nazi. Conversely, it is true that

Lincoln was an Illinoisan, but truer that he was an American. On another scale, it is true that there are more than fifteen pine trees in the Rocky Mountains, truer that there are more than a thousand, and truer still that there are more than a million.

These facts about ordinary language can be explained (away) in only two ways. If the degrees are not in truth itself, but in actual sentences, they must have been put there either on the occasions of use, i.e., by the speaker, or as standing features of the language in question. In the former case, we could say that phrases such as I adduce above do not express degrees of truth, but degrees of confidence that the speaker has in the truth of what she is saying. In the latter, the lack of bivalence can be viewed as an imperfection in language itself, to be remedied by philosophers.

Both of these approaches eventually land us back with propositions, i.e., with entities whose only job is to be true or false—for that is what will be left once we have abstracted away from things like speakers' attitudes and natural imperfections in language. But they have other problems than that.

The degrees-of-confidence approach ignores the fact that English, like other natural languages, has plenty of ways for speakers to express degrees of subjective certainty or its lack; "that's absolutely true" means something quite different from "I am absolutely certain that that is true." The imperfection-of-language approach is a recommendation for philosophers that enjoins them to make use of formal logic in dealing with their problems, and it trades on a specific notion of what a philosophical problem is.

Philosophical problems, such as the mind/body problem or the existence of God or of other minds, are generally very old; they were being talked about and wrestled with long before modern logic had been invented.[47] The terms in which they are couched are likewise very old, and most of them (like "mind," "body," "existence," "God," and even "problem") are multiply ambiguous. Before a given problem can even be stated in a logically correct language, those ambiguities must be resolved. Which means in turn that the problem itself *cannot* be solved—because we are always free to resurrect it using other meanings for its basic terms. Even if we run through all the possible meanings of each of those terms, new ones can always crop up, for words—like the rest of our world—change continually. One of the main engines of philosophical creativity, in fact, is coming up with new meanings for the words of some ancient problem—as when Saul Kripke redefined "identity" and reopened the old problem of mind/body identity, which had been relegated to the list of exhausted topics.[48]

Bivalence, then, is not tenable, either as part of an account of how our languages actually operate, or as a feature of an artificial language that would do for philosophy what artificial languages are supposed to do: restate philosophical problems in a way sufficiently precise to enable them to be solved (or dissolved). Some of the main alternatives to bivalence partake of its problems.

Trivalence, for example, is the view that there is a third option for sentences—they are true, false, or neither; it fails (or refuses) to capture degrees of truth at all. What I will call the "supervaluational" approach explicitly attempts to do this, because it assigns to each assertion a specific degree—say, 60.437%—of truth. The problem with applying this to utterances in natural language is that such determinations cannot be made.

For one thing, we do not, in conversation, have time to

make them. How would I determine the degree of truth in a sentence such as "The actions of the Roman Catholic hierarchy in covering up the abuse of children by priests are both reprehensible and stupid"? How can I even begin to determine it? What, indeed, is the degree of truth in "it's hot," or "it's 90°"? By the time I find out just how true even such a simple statement is, the conversation— even a typically glacial philosophical conversation—will have moved on. Supervaluation is a viable approach only if we forget about the timeliness of our speech.

Furthermore, if we were able to determine the exact degree of truth of a given sentence, we would be returned to bivalence; "S is 60.437% true" would be bivalently true, or false. Otherwise, we would need to assign a degree of truth to it and would find ourselves in a regress, in which in order to ascertain the degree of truth of any sentence we must first ascertain the degree of truth of other sentences, including the one which specifies the degree of truth of the first sentence, and so on. A supervaluational approach thus becomes "untimely" indeed; it would take infinite time to determine the truth value of a single sentence.

Finally, none of these approaches is adequate to one key aspect of the temporal nature of our experience: that things are constantly changing. Western thought about change is very old indeed, and there is a clear, though recently suspect, consensus that change is continuous. Something changes, that is, when it begins in state S and moves to state S′ by a continuous series of modifications. For bivalence, however, such a process reduces to two stages: S and not-S. For trivalence, it has three: S, not-S, and neither.

Bivalence cannot "accommodate" a movement from 30° to 70° because the only kind of change it recognizes is from 30° to not-30°. Trivalence could do no better. The idea that changes could be strung together so that a sentence correctly describing the first stage becomes progressively more false as the process continues does not arise for either approach. (This argument holds even if change is discontinuous, as long as a single change can have more than two stages.)

Supervaluations would give us an infinite set of values for a description of S, as S moves to being S', but that infinite set would be countable and not continuous; in between any two successive values which this approach could assign to a description of S, there would be others which would apply to the description as S changed.

No general theory of truth, of course, could hope to capture the degree to which various states of affairs diverge from the ways given sentences describe them. Nor can a given sentence itself show the precise degree of truth it claims. All we have is various ways, a few of which I listed above, by which we—not the sentence itself—can indicate in rough terms the degree of truth we are claiming for it. Nor should more be expected than this, for in the case of changes underway, which is a major example of the failure of bivalence to apply to ordinary language, the degree of truth of a sentence is constantly changing. All we can ask of a theory of truth is that it acknowledge such locutions as necessary—not that it capture them precisely.

The admission that we cannot indicate the degree of truth of our utterances other than roughly, which grows out of the problems with the supervaluational approach, leads to a final possibility. This is that our utterances have degrees of truth but that we cannot tell, with any precision, what those degrees are. I call this a "hermeneutic" view of sentential truth. It holds that true and false (to return to my previous analogy) are no more rigorously ascertainable, in a given case, than "large" and "small." It is relatively easy to tell whether one thing is larger than another; we do so all the time. But it is impossible to tell even what it would be for something to be "large" *tout court*, without respect to anything else; "large" is relative to "small."

Truth, I suggest, can be philosophically construed along such lines. Socrates did so, for example:

> . . . in every case I first lay down the theory which I judge to be soundest (*errômenestaton*) and then whatever seems to me to agree with it (*moi dokei toutôi sumphônein*) I posit as being true things (*alêthê onta*), and whatever does not I posit as not being true things. (*Phaedo* 100a)

That there are more than one million pine trees in the Rocky Mountains is truer than that there are fifteen. But there is no "truest" here; there is no number which is *the* number of pine trees in the Rocky Mountains. There are too many borderline cases, seedlings about to become trees, trees in the process of death and decay, rockslides that change the boundaries of the "Rocky Mountains," for "the number of pine trees in the Rocky Mountains" to be determined, even by God, without recourse to heavy doses of stipulation.

> In Plato's view, bivalence holds for talk about the Forms but not for talk about sensibles (cf. Timaeus 29c). This leads to a further suspicion about Aristotle: To what extent is his (quondam) advocacy of bivalence motivated by his relocation of Platonic Forms to the sensory sphere—his denial of the Platonic chorismos (Metaph I.9 passim)? Which leads on to the question: If this putative metaphysical heritage is actually the case, have contemporary "theories of truth" freed themselves from it?
>
> In his Philosophy of Logic (1970), Quine calls the view that "things are not just black and white; there are gradations"

*the "worst" argument against classical negation; literature
advocating it, he says, is "irresponsible." On the next page,
he implies that it is the "silliest" argument against the law of
excluded middle.[49] But I am not arguing that we should jettison
classical negation or the law of excluded middle, just that their
applicability is more limited than someone like Quine likes
to think. My first argument, in fact, does not hold that the gra-
dations Quine derides exist, but that the languages we speak
and in which we do philosophy—for whatever reasons—have
important resources for dealing with them.*

*To call something "silly" is not to argue against it; Quine of all
people ought to be aware (and is perhaps quite well aware here)
of the difference between rhetoric and argument. In light of this,
for him to call others "irresponsible" is remarkable. I do not
believe that I am being "irresponsible" in Quine's sense; but if I
am wrong, I will happily stand among the "irresponsible." At
Plato's side.*

To ascertain that one assertion is "truer than" others,
without claiming to know just how true it is, requires
what Socrates called, just prior to my quote above, "flee-
ing into arguments"—measuring that assertion against its
competitors rather than directly against some fact or set
of facts which it purports to capture. Such measuring may
be relevant to the overall undertaking in various ways. If
a given assertion entails something obviously false or foolish, for example, that is good evidence against its likely
being "truer than" its competitors. Even in such a case,
we are implicitly evaluating the position of our assertion
within a particular field, the field of its competitors.

Such competitive fields—the array of alternative answers to a given question—are always, to some degree,
contingent, because we can never be sure that we have in
fact formulated all the possible alternative answers; there
may be some we have not thought of, or that our language
does not permit us to express. There is thus always the
possibility that the question could be stated in ways which

would allow other assertions into the field of its possible answers. Determining whether a given assertion is truer than other assertions thus includes, in part at least, deciding how these assertions, and no others, came to constitute that particular field. I must look to the past, to the origin of the field of competing assertions. Similarly, I must not do this in a way which forecloses the future; I cannot view the field of current alternatives as the final list for all time. Truer-than, because it refers necessarily to a field of already constituted alternatives which itself may change, is thus an essentially temporalized notion.

The hermeneutic approach is the most depressing of all—as long as we believe that the only possible job of philosophy is to produce truth. If there are other considerations for philosophers to balance off against truth, however, we can relax our truth standards a bit. Just as we can tell if one thing is larger than another without (*pace* Plato) knowing anything absolutely large, so we can replace the desire to arrive at (absolutely) true things with a desire to arrive at things that are "truer than" their competitors and which do meet those other considerations.

To accept this is to stop looking for a way to say absolutely true things. We philosophically warrant what we say to be "*as* true as we can make it," and we promise that if what we accept right now should turn out to be false one day, we will rethink what we are saying. In other words, we take cognizance of the fact that our discourse, even though philosophical, takes place not in the present as such, but in the presentable present; it is inherently designed to follow on things and lead to things, rather than to get things absolutely right once and for all. In that way we can undo the restrictions imposed on philosophy by its seeking the absolute truth of bivalence without casting ourselves into a carnival of relativism in which everything is equally true. And that is, honestly, the best we can do; anything more is not rigor but fantasies of rigor.

My final argument against bivalence, then, is this: It is not true that no assertion can be anything other than wholly true or wholly false. For the sentences this book contains will be as true as I can make them—no more, no less.

Totalization and the Past

To philosophize in this way means to put truth, in any absolute sense, into our past. This introduces us to one of the other inhabitants of Fantasy Island, the notion of totality. A "totality" is something which is complete; it will not change except to deteriorate, and so what it is right now is all it can be. Totalization, as I will use that term, embraces three things: the ideas that things can actually exist in such a state of completeness; that we can know it when they do; and that we can credibly proclaim such knowledge to ourselves and others, thereby "totalizing" the thing.

In his book *Marxism and Totality,* Martin Jay traces the concept of totality through its glories and vicissitudes in the history of Western Marxism and concludes that it is today "much beleaguered."[50] The book traces "the story of the progressive unraveling" of the normative standing of totality to a point where the concept of totality could not be *either* descriptively or normatively employed. To parody Gorgias of Leontini, speaking on a slightly different topic, "totality doesn't exist; and if it did exist it couldn't be known; and if it did exist and could be known, we should not seek it anyway" (cf. Gorgias B.3.33–35).[51]

Totality so construed seems to be a thing of the past; it seems, today, to be *merely* something to wriggle away from. This is unfortunate because, as Jay puts it, "the lure of totality as a normative goal was one of the defining characteristics of the tradition of Western Marxism."[52] Indeed, totality is for Jay the key to the Battle of the Moderns and the Postmoderns:

> If one had to find one common denominator among the major figures normally included in the poststructuralist category—Derrida, Foucault, Lacan, Barthes, Deleuze, Lyotard, Kristeva, Sollers . . . it would be their unremitting hostility towards totality.[53]

This picture of "unremitting hostility" on the part of Postmoderns toward the *central* concept and norm of the *central* critical tradition of modernity is one of the starkest battle lines yet drawn between the Moderns and the Postmoderns.

We can reformulate the concept of totality in such a way as to resolve this struggle by realizing that totality not only seems to be a thing of the past, as I said above, but actually is one—and is one *essentially.* "Totalizing" is, in fact, what creates the past as a usable past; it is the process by which something becomes part of that sort of past.

Suppose a love affair has ended badly, as all love affairs end. I have broken up with my lover, or my lover has died. In order to get on with my life, I must come to see the love affair as no longer existing for me in the presentable present, as no longer offering me future possibilities. I must accept (or, more accurately, decide) that what it has already been is all it can ever be. Only when I see it in this way can it become something which, though I will not forget it and may continue to think about it and learn from it, has no ongoing claims on me. In order to free myself of my love affair, I have to be able to tell myself that what it has already been constitutes the totality of what it can be; I deny it new potential. I place it into my past. I "totalize" it.

To totalize something is to *claim* to *know* it in its *totality*, to know all that it can be. To totalize something in the present tense is, for example, to tell someone else that I know all that she can be—and that is not merely to totalize, but to essentialize. Such present-tense totalization is indeed something to struggle away from; the Postmoderns are right. To practice totalization on things that still exist at the present time, giving descriptive status to our views of their natures, is mistaken at best. To posit it in the future, as the culminating point of human society beyond which no further changes will be necessary, as a Marxist or other form of utopia, is not only mistaken but foolish— and, as history teaches, not only foolish but evil.

But when we realize that to totalize something is to place it into our past, totalization becomes the way we recognize our embeddedness in a historical tradition without making ourselves into the prisoners of that tradition. For if what I just said is right, totalizing is the means by which history becomes ours; *a* past can only be *our* past if we somehow, to some degree, see ourselves as completing it, bringing it to fruition—and, of course, also as discarding it so we can move on to other things. To totalize something then means at once to complete and discard it, and thereby to acquire it as part of our past. Intellectually speaking, totalization as the acquisition of a past is what enables us to escape the past, even as we construct it.

Any discourse, of course, is embedded in what went before; the later Frankfurt School was impossible without the early Frankfurt School, Habermas is impossible without both, the present book is impossible without Habermas, and so forth. But to recognize embeddedness as *our* embeddedness is special: it means to accept *a* past as *our* past, indeed as what I called above our usable past, and to accept ourselves as *in part nothing more* than its fruition. Such acceptance is not purely theoretical; it requires us to achieve nothing less than what Hegel, in one of his key terms, calls "reconciliation" (*Versöhnung*) with our heritage. Since our heritage is often unfortunate, such reconciliation is rarely easy, but it is absolutely necessary if we are to move on intelligently.

> *This situation is not only Hegelian, but (I would suggest) post-modern as well. Heidegger's strangely totalizing claims about the history of philosophy, or about modernity itself,[54] are clearly (if clumsily) designed to help free us from metaphysics and modernity (cf. MO 9–13). As this reference to Heidegger makes clear, "totalizing" something does not mean forgetting about it. My failed love can remain an object of concern to me; I can write poems about it and try to learn its lessons. But those activities are now optional; I no longer allow its demands to determine my actions.*

> *The idea that we can leave the past entirely behind is in fact just another form of totalizing—for it amounts to the idea that we can belong totally to the present. As such, it characterizes modernity more readily than postmodernity. Modern thought cannot easily see itself as* either *the fruition of the past or as the arrival point of an unknown future. It is standard for modern philosophers such as Locke, Hume, Kant, and Carnap to begin by dismissing everything up to now as fruitless prattle and to assume that everything from now on will merely develop, and so prolong, the truths they have uncovered. As I have suggested above, we are* not *modern in that sense, but are stretched out between a totalized past and an unknown future—a condition Heidegger calls "ecstasy."*

Universality and the Future

Totalization, when it is placed into the present tense, is something to wriggle away from; when I proclaim that X is all y *is,* instead of proclaiming that X is all y *was as far as I am concerned,* I am doing something which is not merely cognitively mistaken, but often morally wrong. It is a case of what has been called the "descriptive fallacy," that of seeing performative actions as descriptions.[55] Universality is the occasion for a similar operation, only on the future; it is claiming that what something *is* (and perhaps *was*) is just what it will always be.

The way we think of universality today tends to be muddled. We sometimes see it as what I will call "spatial," and sometimes as "temporal."[56] "Spatial" universality itself has at least two genres, leading respectively to claims that at some given time something is true either *everywhere* (such as 2 + 2 = 4) or for every*one* (such as "you are now threatened by the HIV virus"). In the former sense, universality is a beguiling but difficult notion. (How long does "some given time" last? What, after Einstein, can it even mean to think of a single "given time" that is everywhere?) In the latter sense, the beguilement is even greater; the view that certain sentences are true for every*one* gives us a picture of the entire human race agreeing on something, which is certainly a wonderful thought. But problems arise here too, for experience soon shows that there are no such sentences; people exist who will deny that triangles have three sides, and that 2 + 2 = 4. So we must restrict our community of agreement to *rational* people, and then spell out what "rational" means— an enterprise which, as feminism and race theory tell us, has a very unsavory history indeed.

It is somewhat different when we construe universality in temporal terms, so that a sentence is universally true if everyone (rational) not only agrees to it at some given time, but will always do so. Claiming such "temporal" universality looks uncomfortably like seeking to legislate to future generations. Who are we to tell our great-great-

great grandchildren that all triangles have three sides, or that people must always act from universalizable maxims? Why, indeed, would we want to? Why not just hope that they will find new and better ways in morals and mathematics, even if we cannot conceive of what those ways might be?

Temporal universality is an expression of what I called above the "modern" tendency to see the future merely as prolonging the truths we think we have uncovered. Kant's whole doctrine of the categories (to make an example of the greatest "modern" thinker) rests upon the fact that a sentence such as "every event has a cause" is *logically* distinct from one such as "every event we have learned about up to now has had a cause." The latter claims to have been true everywhere up to now. The former claims to be true always, and it is to validate making that sort of claim that the whole apparatus of the categories is brought in. Hence, what I call temporally universal judgments are not merely the goal of Kantian philosophy; they have to exist—and some of them have to be accepted as valid—if such philosophy is to get going at all.[57]

These claims ran into major trouble, however, and in short order. Schiller, in his *Letters on Aesthetic Education* (1801), suggested that the cognitive faculties themselves, though shared by all humans, are the results of a historical development. Their universality thus could not be anything more than what I call spatial. Taken up by Hegel, who called Kant's efforts at establishing temporally universal judgments "quite unphilosophical,"[58] and then by Marx, Nietzsche, and Heidegger—as well as by thousands who have thought in their wake—this view forms perhaps the most serious challenge Kantianism has faced. For it means that temporal universality can never be achieved. Claiming it is a mere mistake, not the clue which starts a new philosophy.

Conclusion: The Emergence of the "New Philosophy"

The foregoing picture of the current state of philosophy is, it may be thought, massively unfair. Certainly it is at best one-sided. Even if philosophy is beset by the institutional and intellectual problems I have sketched here, a great deal of excellent work is in fact being done on all fronts within the available paradigms; who can deny that?

That good work is currently being done in philosophy does not, however, challenge the presentation given here; indeed, it enhances its urgency. For good work is being done, in large part at least, because philosophers are already thinking along the lines to be sketched out in this book. All that is needed, but needed all the more, is to make that explicit.

Philosophy has never been a matter of the present tense only, no matter how hard philosophers have tried to make it one. Even those who, to return to the phrase of Peter Hylton cited above, see philosophy as being done in a "single timeless moment" have had to pose to themselves, if only to themselves, serious questions about what field to go into and which problems to take up. In doing so they had to consider how promising the discussion was and what contributions they could make to it; and that, in turn, required following out its history. Similarly, those who restrict themselves to philosophy's past and future— the Hegelian and Heideggerean approaches to be explained and extended in this book—have made use of argument and assertion.

Philosophers who focus on the present thus treat also of past and future; those who focus on the past treat of present and future; and those who focus on the future treat of the past and present as well. The problem is that they do so as amateurs. There is no single approach which deals with all three temporal dimensions in an explicit and systematic way. Hence, analytical histories of philosophy are often partial and impressionistic,[59] while Hegelian and Heideggerean assertions and arguments are often willful at best.[60]

The new philosophy whose emergence I am tracing here will, I suggest, be postanalytic and metacontinental. Postanalytic because the basic defining feature of analytical philosophy, which is not the use of logic and argument but the *restriction* of philosophy to these, is wholly absent. Analytical philosophy, so defined, is a necessary forerunner to the new paradigm because it developed those tools of thought beyond where they were when it began, but is not an ongoing component of it.

The new philosophy is metacontinental in that the great philosophers of continental philosophy, pre-eminently but not only Hegel and Heidegger, have ongoing roles within it—but they are transformed by being newly related to one another. Such a philosophy is not able to bring us timeless truth. In fact, it hardly brings us truth at all, but simply uses truths, many of them established elsewhere, as its means. Its results are, if not ephemeral, surely doomed, for time destroys all things—even, perhaps, itself. Such philosophy is a raft, not a crag.

2 | Enlarging the Philosophical Toolbox

Philosophers, like other workers, have what I will call their "toolboxes"—their repertoires of implements which they use to get their jobs done. Most workers have, and often prefer to have, too many tools; their toolboxes contain tools they certainly will not need for the task at hand and may never need. The toolbox of philosophers, however, has gotten rather small, and there is reason to think it should now be enlarged. In this chapter, I will discuss philosophy's current toolbox, show why it needs to be enlarged and reorganized, and suggest how that should be done.

> The largest philosophical toolbox on record is probably that of Plato. It includes not only what Aristotle would codify as the "laws of logic," but also various types and levels of myth, along with rhetorical devices ranging from ad hominem *argument* (e.g., the portrayal of Thrasymachus's doctrines as those of a

wild beast in Republic *I) to the use of onomatopoeia and rhythm (cf. Socrates' tôi kalôi ta kalá kalá [Phaedo 100e]), and even outright ridicule (e.g., of Zeno, for coming up with several different arguments that there is only one thing [Parmenides 127d]). Hence, reading Plato is a globally engaging task; one must be ready to laugh, cry, or even dance, as well as to evaluate his arguments.*

The reasons why Plato has such a complex toolbox, compared to later philosophers, are themselves complex. At least one of them is that he believes that philosophy is a communal enterprise, one to be undertaken neither alone nor publicly, but in small groups. Philosophy so understood must cope with human diversity. This requires, the Phaedrus *tells us, rhetorical means such as the above, for the universalistic procedures of dialectic apply to all people equally, and do not allow for diversity.*[1]

The problem for Plato, as Derrida has pointed out,[2] *is that the various gestures of rhetoric can be used for ill as well as for good; they can take us away from the truth as well as toward the truth. Only the "true rhetorician" can bring them under control. And doing this requires knowledge not merely of the various rhetorical gestures themselves, but of the diverse kinds of soul, for the same rhetorical gesture, says Plato, affects different souls differently.*

Unfortunately, Plato's view of diversity was by our standards rather limited. His claim (in the Phaedrus*) that the types of soul are few enough to be exhaustively known is unargued (271b), and his account of those types is little more than a mythically delivered promissory note (248d–e, 252a–253c). It is unsurprising that Aristotle, for whom philosophy was an activity of the individual soul—though only of one educated by a community—saw no need for "rhetorical" gestures within philosophy and dispensed with them, thus making the philosophical toolbox notably smaller.*

Nonetheless, down through the ages, various new tools have on occasion found their way into the toolbox: scholastic dialectic, for example, with its detailed comparisons of texts and its resolutions to problems posed by discrepancies among them;

Descartes's "analytical method"; Spinoza's "third way"; the numerous procedures referred to in Kant's various "Doctrines of Method" and developed in his Logic; the language of Schiller's Letters on Aesthetic Education, *which appeals at once to reason and to the emotions; and so forth. Most of these techniques are today relegated to the domain of the "non-philosophical." As are Hegelian dialectic and Heideggerean* Destruktion, *of which there is more later.*

Because philosophy determines its own goals, it also determines the contents of its toolbox. One way of putting what I said in chapter 1 about philosophy's task of conceptual clarification is to say that philosophy is an affair of thought, as science is an affair of knowledge. It shares its "thoughtful" quality (whatever that is) with almost everything we human beings do, for we eat, sleep, and do virtually everything else thoughtfully. We could not even be thoughtless unless we were, on a very basic level, thoughtful.

Among our many and various affairs of thought, philosophy is special because the kinds of thought it involves proceed according to definite criteria. This enables us to determine when they are performed correctly. Philosophy is not merely special but unique, however, in that it determines its standards and goals for itself. The traditional first part of philosophy was the part that set forth the criteria for successful performance of the other parts; it was usually called "logic" (in modernity, "epistemology" or "critique"). The other parts were concerned respectively with reality (metaphysics, ontology, and, in modernity, philosophy of nature), and with the proper way to live our lives (ethics, political and social philosophy). The present book follows this general arrangement.

Logic, as traditionally conceived, quickly exalted its own scope, leading to great prestige but also to major problems.

The exaltation came from those philosophers who started to see logic not merely as stipulating the conditions for success in their own undertaking—which is all they really needed it to do—but as dealing with something wider. They saw it, for example, as presenting the canons of proper thought of all kinds, or even the laws which mental activity must obey in order to be "thought" at all. Stipulations, which bind only oneself and need only explanation, thereby became constraints, which bind others and need grounding.

Logical constraints have traditionally been viewed as grounded in the nature of the universe. That thought should not contradict itself, for example, is usually asserted to hold not just because it is a good idea to be consistent—as Socrates puts it at *Gorgias* 481c–482c—but because nothing can ever possibly contradict itself. So metaphysics, though following on logic *ordine philosophiae,* came in fact to ground it. This gave rise to an embarrassing circle: thought must obey logic because all reality does, but that all reality does can only be established by argument, i.e., by logically constrained thought. Logically constrained thought is warranted, in short, because logically constrained thought tells us the whole universe works under logical constraints. The circle is hard to avoid, for we can hardly establish the necessity of logically constrained thought by using logically *un*constrained thought.

> *Aristotle avoided this circle by taking a middle way. His first argument on behalf of the principle of non-contradiction, the "starting point for all other axioms" (*Metaph. IV.3 1005b 25–34) *is "negative" in character and mainly consists in arguing that the principle is essential not to the nature of reality, but to all thought and speech. Someone who denies it can say nothing at all and is no better than a vegetable (*Metaph. IV.4 1006a 15). *The principle thus sets a standard, not for proper*

thought or even thought itself, but for that wonderfully mani-
fold "thing" the Greeks called logos, *one of whose dimensions*
was speech. To violate the principle threw you, so to speak, out
of the tribe. It made you not merely an outlaw, but a plant.

Aristotle almost immediately invokes a positive point, however,
to get on with his refutation: he premises that a word not only
(ideally) "means one thing" but that it also "refers to one
*thing" (*kath' henos sêmainei; *both views are implicit in the*
view that you can deny one thing, and so this argument is a
development of the previous one). The idea that there are units
out there in the world to be spoken of, while reasonable for some
utterances, is not true for all—otherwise there would be no
such thing as performatives. If, as J. L. Austin will argue (see
p. 94 below), all utterances have a performative dimension, it
may be that part of what we do with any *word is constitute the*
unit to which it is then taken to refer.

The current approach is closer to that of Quine, who has a very
different way of avoiding circularity in grounding logic. As I
noted in chapter 1, Quine believes that logical theory is much
facilitated by omitting "temporal information." But this move is
a mere convenience. Logical "truths" are merely very general
and successful stipulations, what I am calling "tools." Their suc-
cess is evident in their age; they are here today because they
have worked in the past and so are part of what Quine calls the
"lore of our fathers."[3] Quine thus avoids circularity in ground-
ing logic—by "grounding" it in appeals to tradition, which con-
stitutes the logically unconstrained thinking that grounds logical
constraints. Apart from my view that all parts of any tradition
are open to improvement, my main difference with Quine is
that I believe that we need to use the logical tools he discusses
together with other tools I will sketch later in this chapter.

In addition to the difficulties of their grounding, the
"laws of thought," as George Boole showed, are extremely
formal and abstract;[4] they have to be, if they are to apply
equally to everything. But what shines on everything illuminates nothing. What light do the laws of logic throw

on me when I do something *really* "thoughtful," such as send flowers to my departmental secretary, comfort a friend, or take the car keys from a drunk? How can a philosophy whose toolbox is limited to laws of thought so conceived understand human thoughtfulness?

Logic's exalted scope was extremely useful, for it gave philosophers possession of standards by which they could judge not only themselves, but other thinkers—indeed all other people—to be successful thinkers or not. But those standards cannot, it seems, be grounded by anything but themselves, and are too general to be illuminating. Prudence dictates a scope both less exalted and more concrete. I will try here to set forth the goals and procedures not of human thought itself or even of correct human thought, but of a new way of philosophizing—one which is richer, more timely, and more comprehensive than others, but which does not sacrifice rigor in its pursuit of those qualities. I will spare us the burdensome effort to put forward new laws of thought. It is quite enough to enlarge and organize the philosophical toolbox.

Nothing I have said here proves, or even argues, that the grounding problems with logic are insoluble. It may be that logical laws do in fact capture the way all things have happened since the Big Bang, and will always happen. It may even be that someone will somehow prove this. It may be that Quine is right that no proofs are necessary. What I take myself to have shown is that even if all that is not the case, it is only to be expected that some people will think and say that it is. I am too prudent to be found among them.

What Is a Philosophical Toolbox?

Viewing the forms of inference not as "logical laws" but merely as philosophical tools not only avoids a number of difficult and possibly insoluble problems, but it has another advantage as well. As long as we take the view that the criteria for success and failure in philosophy are laws of thought in general, and especially if we take the view that these in turn are grounded in very deep and universal characteristics of Being itself (large "B"), we cannot criticize or improve those criteria—for who can criticize Being? That philosophers did in fact take such a view, and for far too long a time, is indicated by the fact that Kant could write in 1787 that logic had made no step, forwards or backwards, since Aristotle (*KRV* viii).

A mere tool of thought is different from a law of logic. A law of logic (supposedly) reflects the structure of Being and is universally valid—and so above criticism. A tool, by contrast, is only a tool as long as it is useful, and it can be useful only as long as there is a specific job for us to do with it. Its validity, then, is merely relative to the current job. I take philosophers to be in possession of a set of thought-tools, which can be extended and remade when new problems and tasks present themselves. Though what I say here is compatible with more robust views of logical realism, I think it is healthier for philosophers to consider themselves to possess *only* a set of such tools—for they should allow nothing to be above criticism, especially their own criteria for success and failure.

But what is a philosophical tool? What, in fact, is a tool?

Basically, a tool is a material object that can be used to alter other such objects. Such useful objects are generally inanimate, which means that they can be reshaped by humans to serve their purposes with relative ease.

In this sense, philosophy has no distinctive tools. The material objects philosophers use—paper, pencils and pens, chalkboards, word processors—are shared with other disciplines. If we seek distinctively philosophical tools, presuming that there are such things, we must look away from the material objects philosophers make use of and toward the ways they use them, toward the intellectual gestures that constitute philosophical thought. A gesture, to be sure, is not an object—it is not enduring. But it can alter things; it can be repeated; it can have a goal; it can be performed well or badly; and—sometimes—"well" and "badly" can be spelled out.

If we construe the currently standard set of philosophical tools—the rules of inference—to be such a set of gestures, we still do not have any distinctively philosophical tools. For the rules of inference are used by an enormous variety of disciplines, in addition to which they are little short of omnifunctional in everyday life. And indeed, even enlarging the philosophical toolbox as I want to do here will not give philosophers any distinctive set of tools, tools unshared by other disciplines and not used in everyday life. What is distinctive about philosophy is not the individual tools that it uses but the way those tools work together.

And on what. A philosophical tool is a gesture of thought which alters something. What kind of thing could that "something" be? Philosophy, I suggested, is an affair of thought, so in keeping with my prudent approach, I will say that what its tools alter is just thought itself, or thoughts.

> *This also has the advantage, on the most general level, of avoiding all sorts of misplaced Berkeleyan problems about how thought can possibly affect something that is other than thought.[5] These problems have their solutions, to be sure, but it is more efficient to dispense, if we can, with both the problems and their solutions.*

Philosophy, then, is thinking which alters thinking. It may go on from there to alter minds, lives, and societies in various ways—but if it is philosophy, it can only have those further effects by changing how people think. And here, my analogy to tools finds its limit. Hammering does not have as its goal changing hammers; sawing does not aim to change saws. But in philosophy, the tool and the object on which it works are the same sort of thing. *Modus ponens,* for example, is an intellectual gesture, a way of thinking, which enables us to change the thought we are thinking into another one. The rules of inference generally are tools like this; but philosophy has, or should have, others.

What is a tool *box*?

A box is a receptacle or container, and one which contains tools is a toolbox. But a good toolbox does more than just contain tools: it organizes them as well.[6] And it does so by a *variety* of principles. In a carpenter's toolbox nails will be organized by size, while drill bits of different sizes will be grouped together according to what sorts of material they can drill and which drill they fit into. A toolbox is organized not by descriptive characteristics such as size and shape, but in terms of purpose (which may in turn require organization by size and shape, as with nails). The overall aim is to enable different kinds of tools to cooperate in doing a single job, to have one's saws and crowbars and so forth there to separate things, and hammers and nails and so forth there to join them.

There are thus a couple of problems a toolbox can have. One kind of problem is not having the right tools in it. If I have left my saws at home, I cannot take on any project that requires me to cut wood. If I have left my hammers, joining pieces of wood together is going to be difficult. And if I have left my measuring devices at home, I cannot do much of anything at all. The other kind of problem is having the right tools, but in such disorganization that I cannot find them when I need them. This, in the extreme, is as bad as not having them at all.

Whether we think the philosophical toolbox needs to be

enlarged or merely reorganized depends on how we view the current philosophical situation. The tools I think philosophy needs are all in use today in various parts of the intellectual world. If we accept (as I do) that the people using them are philosophers, then the toolbox merely needs to be reorganized. Many philosophers see things differently and believe that their own toolboxes contain all the tools of philosophy. Those working with other tools are not, on this view, "philosophers" at all. In that case, my argument can be phrased differently. It is that the philosophical toolbox needs to be enlarged to accommodate tools which, however current in other fields, are new to "philosophy." For convenience I will speak in terms of enlarging the toolbox, though its new principle of organization will also become clear.

The External Argument:
Philosophy and Self-Knowledge

There are two ways to show that a toolbox, any toolbox, must be enlarged. Internally, one can show that its tools cannot work on their own, that the tools in question cannot do anything without being conjoined with other sorts of tools. In this case, that would mean arguing that trying to do philosophy with its current set of tools is not like trying to use a hammer without a saw, but like trying to use one without nails. The other way, external, is to show that the (or a) job we need to do cannot be effectively done with just the tools that we have. I will come back to the internal issues, for they are several; right now I want to argue that the tools currently in the philosophical toolbox are not adequate to at least one properly philosophical job that needs to be done.

As I noted in the previous chapter, one very ancient task

of philosophy was formulated by Socrates in the words of the Delphic maxim *gnôthe seautón,* know yourself. Already in the ancient world, philosophy had as one of its tasks obtaining self-knowledge of an explicitly self-critical sort. (As I also noted in that chapter, and will explain in more detail in this one, philosophical self-knowledge requires us to make certain kinds of commitments and therefore is not "knowledge" at all in the standard sense of the term, but has a performative dimension. It can in act be viewed as a certain kind of construction, viz. the construction of situations. Since I cannot explain everything at once, I will for the moment continue to speak of self-knowledge as if it were knowledge in the traditional sense—the kind that does not change its object.)

Philosophy's task of self-knowledge was sharpened in the modern era, and particularly by Kant. For Kant replaced logic with "critique." The ancient concern to uncover the laws of thought thus gave way to the concern to uncover the laws of our thinking—laws such as that the categories of the understanding can only be applied within sensory experience. This is not a law of thought in general. Angels and God, if they exist, are disembodied and therefore have no sensory experience, so that law cannot apply to their thinking. It is a law for our thinking.

The demand for self-knowledge has remained an important ingredient in much post-Kantian philosophy, and some thinkers have accorded it even greater scope than Kant did, holding that self-knowledge of certain sorts is entailed by knowing anything at all. Hegel, for example, started at the converse end, maintaining that self-knowledge is never just knowledge of the self, as if I could know myself without knowing anything else whatsoever— the kind of a priori *knowledge Kantian critique aims to deliver. For Hegel, the attempt to gain such knowledge is as laughable as the attempt of Scholasticus the monk to learn to swim without* *getting in the water (*Werke *VIII 54/15). Rather, knowledge of self and knowledge of world are coordinated. My knowledge of things in general is part of me, so that to come to know anything is to come to know something about myself—at a minimum, that I know that thing.*

Something similar follows from Heidegger's concept of the hermeneutical circle. As he explicates that in Being and Time, *human Being, or Dasein, "projects itself upon" (thematizes) various practical contexts in which it already stands; it is those contexts which get "laid out" in interpretation, and which therefore constitute the "meaning" (*Sinn*) of the entity being interpreted (SZ 148–166). Interpretation is thus for Heidegger a process of* Zueignung, *or adjustment, between Dasein itself and the background knowledge or "fore-structure" it brings to the entity it interprets, on the one hand, and the practical context (significance) which that entity itself possesses as a being in the common world. Such* Zueignung *is not merely an intellectual process; when I reach for the salt shaker I relate its involvement with flavoring food to my project of eating dinner.*

Though Heidegger does not stress it, it follows that the interpretive disclosure of entities is always double; Dasein cannot interpret other entities without interpreting itself, and cannot be disclosed to itself without a disclosure of the entities that surround it in the world. We can see clearly from this, I think, why Heidegger does not view the famous "hermeneutical circle" as at all vicious. In it and because of it, we may say, we always get two disclosures for the price of one; the interpreting Dasein reveals both the entities it encounters and its own concrete situation as it encounters them. As with Hegel, and in opposition to Kant, knowledge of the self is for Heidegger always coordinated to knowledge of what is other than the self. Philosophy, if it is to provide knowledge at all, must provide both kinds of knowledge (cf. SZ 151; also 324, and my discussion at PI 113–120).

Philosophy has had as one of its main tasks to provide self-knowledge; but, as I argued in chapter 1, we are permeated by time to such an extent that our knowledge of ourselves must address our past and future as well as our present. Philosophy, if it is to do its ancient and modern job, needs to take account of that fact. A philosophical toolbox consisting merely in gestures of thought which relate to just one of these three temporal dimensions, leaving everything else over to talent, insight, and luck, will not be able to accomplish the overall task of knowing oneself.

The Inadequacy of Inference

Inference is restricted to presence in just this way. The reason, as I argued in chapter 1, lies in the nature of verification, which is the larger job of which inference is a part. An assertion must be simultaneous with whatever it is that justifies it, whether that justifying factor is a state of affairs in the world or other assertions from which it follows; otherwise it cannot be justified at all. The perceptual evidence for the beauty of Cleopatra lies irretrievably in the past; all that can justify belief in it today is the *surviving* testimony.

In an argument or proof, it is the aggregate of all the assertions made in its course that justifies the conclusion. Hence, all of them must be simultaneously available. Even on the most "computational" model of thinking, where a given assertion is justified by being a regulated transformation of the assertion just preceding it, we need to see together a statement of that previous assertion, of the new assertion, and of the transformation rule which warrants the step from one to the other.

Descartes made the "presentistic" nature of inference very clear in the Regulae:

[A] deduction sometimes requires such a long chain of inferences that when we arrive at . . . a truth it is not easy to recall the entire route that led us to it. That is why we

say that a continuous movement of thought is needed
to make good any weakness of memory. So I shall run
through [the steps in a proof] several times in a continuous
movement of the imagination . . . until I have learned to
pass from the first to the last so swiftly that memory is left
with practically no role to play, and I seem to intuit the
whole thing at once. (Rule VII, AT X 387f, CSM I 25)

He later writes, in Meditations *V, that only the existence of
God, when it has been proven to me, can guarantee the veracity
of my memory of having grasped something clearly and dis-
tinctly at a previous time, and hence can guarantee the veracity
of long arguments (AT VII 69f/ II 48).*

*Contemporary computation circumvents Descartes's need for
God by not requiring that the computer go from all the way
from the first to the last step in an argument, but simply apply a
rule to one line, thereby producing a new line. By the time the
second line is displayed, the computer may as well have "forgot-
ten" the first. The "presentistic" aspect of argument noticed by
Descartes is thus reduced, though not eliminated.*

We *could look upon a sequence of lines thus produced as a logical argument—but the computer itself, so programmed, could
not do that. For its activity would not have a stopping point. It
would not be trying to "prove" anything in particular, but just
blindly applying transformation rules. It would never know
that it has produced* an *argument for something, or that it
has successfully proved it, or from what it has proven it. Descartes's demand that all steps in an argument be simultaneously
intuited need not, strictly speaking, be met in order to verify the
conclusion. What it verifies is the statement that* this *argument
proves the conclusion.*

Causal inferences are test cases, since if event A causes
event B, A and B cannot be simultaneous; but in fact such
inferences are not exceptions to logical "presentism" at all.
Whatever the temporal relation between A and B, to infer
from one to the other requires placing both into a virtual

or imaginative present. "Harry died because he had contracted Ebola," however we parse "because," is justified only if we can determine, now, both that Harry contracted Ebola and that he is dead. Inference about past and future events thus places them into a virtual Now, just as inference about remote objects places them into a virtual Here.

Hume did the salutary job of ridding philosophy of causal powers, but because of what may be called his intellectual atomism he also psychologized causality in a misleading way. Strictly speaking, one thing never causes another; causes flock. So do effects, so that in fact whole groups of things cause whole groups of things—a phenomenon which Hume cannot see because of what Patrick Gardiner has called his "persistent tendency to construe the implications of what are logically complex notions in terms of correlations between atomistically conceived impressions."[7] The water in the test tube does not grow warm exclusively *because of the fire below it; also contributing are the container in which it rests, whatever is burning, whatever conveyed that fuel to that location, whatever ignited it, the distance between the fire and the water, the altitude, etc., etc. The fire is also heating the room and my forehead, and burns my fingers if they get too close; the fact that I cook in my room raises the cost of my insurance policy slightly, and so forth.*

What we might call the whole causal flock—totality of all the causes of some event or thing, or what Hobbes called the "entire cause"—does not precede its effect but is simultaneous with it:

... In whatsoever instant the cause is entire, the effect is produced. For if it be not produced, something is still wanting, which is requisite to the production of it; and therefore the cause was not entire, as was supposed.[8]

A Humean cause is thus a partial Hobbesian cause—a preferred member of the causal flock. What leads us to select out, from the rest of the flock, just one such component and make it the *cause? Hume is quite explicit: the impression it makes on our mind.*

> Tho' the several resembling instances, which give rise to the idea of [causal] power, have no influence on each other, and can never produce any new quality *in the object,* which can be the model of that idea, yet the *observation* of this resemblance produces a new impression *in the mind,* which is its real model. Upon the whole, necessity is something that exists in the mind, and not in objects.[9]

Hume, because of his logical atomism, finds that one thing leads (in our mind) to another; but it is easy to see that he is wrong. We arrive at causal chains *from causal* flocks. *We do so, presumably, because our observational and reflective powers are inadequate to consciously perceive or reflect upon all the causes of anything, and so we are compelled to choose just the most salient—or what Hume would call the most "forceful and vivacious"—as* the *cause, relegating the rest to the status of "conditions." But the others remain, in our experience.*

What makes something "salient," in turn, depends upon various cultural and psychological predispositions. The fire, burning brightly below the test tube, attracts our eye more than the tube itself—not least because it fits, metaphorically, with various privileges that Western culture (along with others) gives to activity as opposed to such "passive" phenomena as mere containment. To ascribe causality to a thing, rather than a flock of things, is to situate ourselves within a whole set of causes, to decide or record which of its components are salient to us. I will return to this in the next chapter.

Joining a Community

It is irresponsibly vague, however, simply to say that inferential tools, because they place everything into a virtual Now, are unable to capture the ways in which we have pasts and futures, and thus are insufficient to the task of philosophical self-knowledge. How *specifically* do we relate to our pasts and futures, and what role does philosophical thinking—in the wide sense of self-consciously critical thinking—have to play in those relations?

When Aristotle argued that what sets humans apart from other things is their capacity for *logos,* their capacity to shape the sounds they emit into conveyances for thought from one person to another, he was surely in some sense right. When he then went on as if the highest use of *logos,* the one which most fully realized its nature, was to bring us to contemplation of the eternal nature of the Prime Mover and to maintain us in that blissful state, he was just as surely wrong. Like everything else about us, language is first and foremost an affair of this world; contemplation of the eternal, if possible at all, is at most an admirable parasite. But what can more effectively realize the nature of thought, or even just part of that nature, than contemplation of the eternal and divine?

Let us accept that thought achieves its full nature, if it has such a thing, in relating us to something other than itself; and let us assume, in light of my previous argumentation and of more that is yet to come, that what it relates us to must

(a) be something which has a Before and After which are different from its Now, in contrast to such atemporal entities as states of affairs, facts, an immortal soul, or a Prime Mover; and

(b) be something to which we, as rational beings, would want to relate.

An illuminating example of such a being—and I advance it as nothing more—is a human community. Though philosophers in general still believe that thought exhibits its true nature when it relates us to something atemporal, such as a Platonic form or a "state" of affairs, my suggestion is that we can learn worthwhile things about thought by looking at how we can *thoughtfully* join and belong to a human community. Joining the community comes before belonging to it, and I will focus on that here. What sorts of thinking do we engage in when we join a human community?

Consider the case of an anthropologist studying a group of human beings. Let us take it that the anthropologist is not herself a member of the group being studied, and so her study does not illuminate her own situation. It could only provide self-knowledge if she were to join the group in question. What would that require? How would she move from being a spectator of the group to being one of its number?

Such a step would certainly go beyond merely participating in whatever initiation rites the group may choose to perform on her. One can be baptized by a priest and not situate oneself as a Catholic, and one can take out American citizenship without really becoming an American (there are American citizens who have never set foot in the United States and who speak no English). So more seems to be required than ritual participation. But what is that "more"?

It is tempting to say that the ritual participation must be sincere—I must really want to be a Catholic, or an American, if the ritual is to work. But that is not right, either, at least not always; there are people who have become American citizens under duress, who abandoned their natal citizenship with great regret and tears in their eyes, but who eventually became what anyone would regard as good Americans. The case is even clearer when the community in question is that of very special sort which constitutes a marriage, because there are many people whose marriages are arranged by their parents and who do not even know their spouse until after the wedding. They do not—they *cannot*—want to marry the person their family marries them to (other than under that very vague description alone), but they subsequently develop strong and satisfying marital relationships. Similarly, alas, in reverse, loving weddings can lead to sham marriages, and eagerly taking the oath of citizenship hardly makes one a full participant in American society. So what, other than sincere desire, is needed?

A certain interplay, I suggest, between what we adopt from the past and ignore about the future.

In order for our anthropologist to become a member of the group she is studying, she needs not merely to *feel* but to *do* something; she must adopt the history of that group as her own, must make it part of her own usable past. (When I married my wife, I adopted her history in this way; when she subsequently became an American citizen, she took upon herself an enormous panoply of glory and horror.) The anthropologist must formulate her view of where that group is coming from, and of where she believes it should go, and she must commit herself—in a way which is manifested in her subsequent actions—to carrying that development forward, rather than merely looking on as it unfolds. Adopting a history in this sense requires formulating and believing things, and so involves thought. But the thought in question, as I will argue later, is not all truth-oriented, i.e., not all of it is to be evaluated on the basis of its truth. It is in part performative; thoughtfully to join a group is to undertake something.

But adopting a group's history as one's own does not exhaust the ways in which one must think in order to move from being a spectator of that group to being a member of it. Suppose the anthropologist is studying a group of Australian Aborigines, and she knows that they need to learn about computers in order to get jobs. She knows that by working with the government she can get computer schools put onto the Aboriginal reserves. She becomes an advocate for Aboriginal computer education. She does what she can to bring it about that those schools are built and the Aborigines learn computer skills. And let us even suppose that in so doing, the anthropologist gains her identity, realizes her human mission; she *is* her participation on the ongoing history of that community. In spite of all that, I suggest that she still is not functioning as one of them, but as an outside advocate. Something more needs to become communal, to be shared between our anthropologists and the Aborigines, before she is one of them. That something is what I will call the "defining ignorance" of the group.

Any community is defined not only by its shared history, but by what it does not know; there are certain things that one cannot know and remain a member of the group. Indeed, anyone who knows anything that the rest of her community does not know is, to that extent, separated from that community. If those things are important, she is importantly separated from it. If ignorance of those things helps define the community, then her knowledge of them may actually exclude her from it.

Facts about the present or the past can be objects of such defining ignorance. In tribal societies where membership is predicated upon descent from a common ancestor, someone who discovers that no such ancestor ever existed is excluded from the group, in her own eyes, even before she announces her discovery to others—each of whom, by accepting it, would likewise be excluded. Someone from a fundamentalist American sub-culture who becomes aware of the growing body of evidence that sexual orientation is genetically determined may find herself excluded from that group, since many of them have founding beliefs that homosexuality is a sin and that all human beings know this, those who deny it being sinners.

Not all communities maintain such secrets, however, and many of the rest do not so cherish their ignorance that they will permit themselves to be defined by it. Moreover, secrets are not the only kind of unknown. There is a much greater and more pervasive unknown, an open mystery to which we are *all* ineluctably under way and which therefore helps define *all* groups as well as *all* individuals. This is what I have called the future in itself, the unpredictable future.

The anthropologist is not herself an Aborigine, however sincerely she may adopt their history as her own and try to move it along, because she knows that there is a way for them to learn about computers and that if they do learn, they will be better off for doing so; they (in our example, anyway) do not know this. She has adopted their history, but she does not share their specific ignorance of their possibilities. If she did not know what she knows, if she had exactly the same ignorance of possibilities that the typical Aborigine does—then, and only then, would she be a full member of the group.

To be a member of a community, then, is to share both its past and its future—not merely in the sense that whatever will happen to my fellows will happen to me also, but in that right now they, and I, have very specific ways in which we do *not* know what the future will bring. We build a common identity with others not merely by acknowledging a common past and accepting it as our own, but also by the questions that we ask and cannot answer, and indeed by the questions that we cannot even ask.

Asking questions is, like formulating and believing, a matter of thinking. It is a kind of thinking which helps constitute our membership in a community.

Philosophizing includes, of course, joining a particular community—that of philosophers. Every philosopher, then, engages in this sort of temporal thinking at some point or other. But its importance to philosophy goes beyond that. We not only cannot join a philosophical community but, more generally, we cannot even understand ourselves as temporal beings without understanding, at least in general terms, how it is that we thoughtfully join, and maintain, our communities. Indeed, adopting a history and opening up to the future are skills that go even beyond the very broad domain of community formation and adherence in general. They are the main ways in which we inhabit time. If philosophy is itself a way of inhabiting time (and what else, if we are thoroughly temporal beings, could it be?), these ways of thinking must be appropriated by it in one form or another.

The Stories Communities Tell
about Themselves: Criteria

Joining a community is at once a conscious act and a leap into the unknown. Both these aspects of it have norms; they are the kind of thing we can perform well or badly. To ask after the norms which govern the conscious adoption of the history of a group is to ask what criteria we should use in evaluating whether the story of a given community is one which we ought to adopt into our own usable past.

Any community's story—indeed, any story at all—passes through several stages or states of affairs. If there were only one stage to a given community's story—if

that community had only ever had one self-description—
then it would never have changed, which is impossible or
nearly so.

Like other states of affairs, those which constitute stages
of stories can be more or less truly or falsely described.
We therefore know the stages of a story just as we know
other states of affairs—by being able to say true things
about them; "An angel of the Lord appeared unto Mary,"
the traditional opening stage in the story of Christianity,
is either basically true or basically false, and it matters
which. Truth—however we understand it—is the main
norm by which we evaluate assertions about states of affairs and is therefore one part of any explicitly self-critical,
i.e., philosophical, evaluation of the story of a community.

The several states of affairs in a given story also cannot
be mutually disconnected. They must somehow be bound
together in that story—if only in order to be "stages" in
it. What sort of thing connects each stage to the next and
the one before?

It is hard to see how such connecting links could ever
be known without running up against Hume's arguments
against causal power, which apply not only to causal production (as Hume states them) but also to causal constraint.[10] Continue with my Christian example, which
traditionally runs, "An angel of the Lord appeared unto
Mary, and she received the Holy Spirit." Stage One (the
appearance) does not produce Stage Two (the reception),
nor does the telling of Stage One cause the telling of Stage
Two. However, both in the events narrated and in the telling of them, Stage One constrains Stage Two. The latter
could not have happened without the former, and given
the former, there is a specific range of things that can follow it; "An angel of the Lord appeared unto Mary and the
Cubs went to the World Series" is not an intelligible nar-

rative and certainly does not belong in the founding story of Christianity. In such cases *post hoc ergo propter hoc* is thus not, wholly, fallacious, and *post hoc ergo partim propter hoc* is not fallacious at all. But who (to echo Hume) has ever seen such "constraint"? What would it even mean to experience it?

In support of Hume, I advance a general rule that we can accept all the stages in a given story as true, and still come up with a different story. As I have written elsewhere, for example, the story of American freedom can equally well be told as a story of American hypocrisy (*TD* 151f). Similarly, the description of a given stage in a story can be rejected as false without giving up the overall story. The Bible's story of the reception of the Holy Spirit is itself famously contested, since it is the story of a virgin birth. Christians who contest it still tell the story of Christ; they just begin it differently.

Hence, the constraints which connect the different stages of a narrative are not knowable in the same way that those stages themselves are. We cannot say true or false things about them, because in order for us to do that they would have to be known in the same way the individual stages are. But, barring that, how can we evaluate them thoughtfully?

Let us return to my previous example of the anthropologist and the Aborigines. Suppose we have a number of descriptions of various states of affairs and events dating from various times in the life of a community, and we want to string these together into a narrative which can help someone decide whether she wants to join that community. What, in general terms, would we want such a narrative to be like?

First, we would want the story to be complete—to include all the known, important, and relevant facts about

the history of that community. What constitutes "importance" and "relevance" is a matter, to be sure, of contextu-
alized debate. But it is certainly a defect in the story a
community tells about itself if facts are available which
have a place in that narrative but are left out of it. The
more important and relevant the omitted facts, the more
defective is the narrative. This holds even if everything
which actually finds its way into the story is true. Thus
(as I note at *TD* 147), it was not, strictly speaking, false
for historians of the American West to focus on characters
and situations who were not African Americans; they may
have described their selected historical objects accurately
enough. But the resulting narrative failed comprehensiveness in ways which were actually morally repugnant, or
as I would say "ignoble."

Even if it does not state or rely on any untruths, and
even if it does not go all the way to repugnance, a narrative which omits important facts about a community's
history is less useful to persons considering membership
in that community than a more complete one would be.
While we cannot demand that such a narrative achieve
perfect completeness—new facts are always awaiting
discovery—we can at least require that it be as comprehensive as possible.

Second, we would want the community's story to make
sense; we would want its various stages to be in the right
order—and not merely chronologically. A narrative whose
various stages, having occurred in one chronological order, could just as well have occurred in some other one,
is not (to speak colloquially) going anywhere. It is not in
fact a "history" at all, but a series of random jumps, or
what Aristotle called mere "episodes."[11] A community
which tells such a story about itself is not one we could
join even if we wanted to, for there is no underlying de-

velopment to carry forward. It is a "community" which, by its own account, bears the unattractive visage of a group of people being yanked hither and yon by the force of random events.

We evaluate the story of a community, then, by whether it includes all the relevant and currently known facts, and by whether it presents a development which we can carry forward. That development may, of course, be one which we do not want to carry forward; the growth of the Nazi Party comes to mind. But at least the story would give us the basis for making a decision.

Narrative links are thus validated not by correspondence to reality (whatever that may be), but by the fact that they can order a diversity of material. They are organizing devices. What a narrative so organized claims is twofold: to be comprehensive and to be ordered. These together constitute what I call, though somewhat unhappily, Nobility, and Nobility constitutes the excellence of communal narratives. According to this standard, such a narrative is better if it links together more material in a more ordered way.

To be sure, Comprehensive plus Ordered does not equal True. Historical narratives are rational ways of constructing usable pasts. They cannot claim truth (though their various stages can), and one upshot of this is that competing narratives are always possible; as I noted previously, any given set of historical data can be connected into a different history. But note that the anthropologist of my earlier example, in accepting the history of her subjects, did not accept that history merely as true. She accepted it as her own. And one rational ground for committing myself to a history, to being willing to see my life as, in its widest effectuality, moving that history forward, is that the history in question is comprehensive and intelligible, or Noble.

Uncovering Defining Ignorance

Any community knows some things about its future, and so about the futures of its members. Sometimes this "knowledge" is in the form of hope. In this sense a Christian, for example, "knows" (hopes) that Christ will return; a Jew "knows" (hopes) that the Messiah will come. In any lasting religion, such knowledge goes along with ignorance; sects that predict exactly when Christ is coming, for example, do not usually outlast the failure of that prediction. Someone who "knows" when Christ is coming again can be an angel, a devil, or God himself; she cannot be a mainstream Christian, any more than someone who "knows" when the Messiah is coming can be a mainstream Jew.

Because they are ignorant of when Christ or the Messiah will come, Christians and Jews live differently than they otherwise would; they must cope with their ignorance here and now, and in important ways. This is what makes it "defining" ignorance.

As I argued in chapter 1, citing Heidegger, such impending but unknown futures define us because we are defined by the choices they force upon us. Our ignorance of the future is thus not merely an imperfection in our lives or knowledge, it is a *defining* imperfection, a void into which we are being drawn by the decisions it forces upon us here and now. Someone who knows different things about her future than we do about ours, and whose ignorance of the future is correspondingly different from ours, will have different choices to make, and so will be defined differently than we are. If those different choices are basic enough, she will not be a member of our community. Our anthropologist, for example, had to make choices about which government office to go to in order to get computer schools on the reserves, and how to approach the officials who worked in them—choices which were not available to her Aboriginal community.

The future which we do not know defines us; it is a void, but an active one. This points us to a necessary gap between the aspirations of narrative and its achievement. For it means, in the current context, that the stories communities tell about themselves are always incomplete and needful, always drawn and shaped by something beyond their own terms of comprehension. How can we respond to this thoughtfully?

I have suggested that a community's authentic future (like that of an individual) presents itself to us as a void, one toward which we are being drawn because it forces certain defining choices upon us. Clearly the presentation of this void must be indirect; sheer nothingness cannot be our anything, so it cannot be our future. An active nothing must show itself specifically, through beings that do present themselves—when those beings somehow manifest the activity of something which does not itself appear.

At this point, the manifestation of nothingness in a being sounds a bit like Brownian motion—the oscillation of small particles suspended in a liquid when molecules of the liquid, which cannot be seen because they are so small, impact on it. But Brownian motion, being random, is not an impending anything, nor is it something toward which anything can be drawn. In order to be a future, the manifestation of a nothing in the life of a community must, like a communal story, cohere over time.

In order to have coherence, we must have a plurality

of things which cohere—be they objects themselves, or qualities or motions of objects (all of which are comprehended equally in the Heideggerean term "being," *das Seiende*). Such a set of beings, or of aspects of one being, manifests an active nothing—or, as I call it, again somewhat unhappily, is Appropriate—when:

A. They belong together in such a way that none of them is adequately understood apart from the others;

B. None grounds or explains the others; and

C. No yet more basic phenomenon can ground, i.e., explain, all of them together.

So, to varying degrees, with the stories of communities. When we see something like this, either in a community or in a story it tells about itself, we know that there is something yet unknown about the community itself and about the various interrelationships that constitute it both diachronically and synchronically. We know that something is in store for that community. If the beings through which that latent something is revealed are important enough, then the community's confrontation with that latency actually defines that community. A community which is still defining itself is one which has a future—a future which might have room for us.

What draws the different stages of a community's past together into a single story is, I have suggested, what people evaluate when they ask themselves if they want to be members of that community. It is the "identity" itself of the community, and so constitutes the tie that binds the individual members of that community to each other. But this unifying force, which both connects the community with its history and draws its various members together into a single social group, cannot be fully open and understood, for then the community would have nothing further to do. It would have no future.

Thinking Past and Future Philosophically

We evaluate the stories communities tell about themselves in three ways, then. We ask after the truth of the descriptions of the individual phases in those stories: Did things take place as they say? We also ask after Nobility—the comprehensiveness and intelligibility of the arrangement of those descriptions: Is anything important left out? Does the order in which the descriptions occur manifest anything other than the brute givenness of chronology? And we ask about the Appropriateness of the story: Do its stages fit together with complete transparence, or are there things which remain to be uncovered?

This raises questions that go beyond the stories communities tell about themselves to affect a wider set of historical narratives, and in particular to affect the kind that would be appropriate for philosophy. I turn for guidance to Hegel and Heidegger.

Hegel's philosophical system, as I have argued in *The Company of Words,* is a giant narrative. It claims to be comprehensive and logically ordered, to be Noble. Seen in this way, Hegel's thought has some further lessons for us about narrative links.

The first lesson is an account of what rational transparency can be. According to Hegel's doctrine of "determinate negation"—or, as I prefer to call it, "minimal negation"[12]—each new stage in a philosophical narrative should be formed by altering just one component of the previous stage (*CW* 143–154). The fact that changes are fed in one at a time is for Hegel what gives the overall account its rational transparency. Each such change can then be seen to solve a single problem in the preceding stage (typically, for Hegel, a contradiction), and rationality consists, plausibly enough, in solving just one problem at a time. History thus *appears* as a continuum, though the continuity is an artifact of the "rationalizing" procedure.

Second, if rational transparency is bestowed link by link in this way, there need be no single overall theme or concern linking all the stages together; we can simply tell our story stage by stage and see what comes out at the end. The overall unity of the story is then an explicit product of invention (*PhS* 74/55f). It does not pre-exist the narrative (as if Hegel's philosophy, in spite of its loud pretensions to be wholly without presuppositions, somehow presupposed the existence of Spirit itself), but was constructed by it. Similarly for the smaller links which go into constituting the transitions internal to the narrative. They too, not being knowable, are inventions.

> *Hegel, as I have presented him here and argued at length in* The Company of Words, *is very different from the images most philosophers have of him. He did not believe that there was a great thing called* Geist *which was developing over time, nor did he believe that he had told the story of that* Geist *in any final way. He did not think that he stood at the end of all development—only that he stood at the end of what had developed up to then, the philosophical understanding of which could be transformed at any time. This I think is what he means when, at the end of the* Lectures on the History of Philosophy, *he offers to join his students in an ongoing community, one which will build upon his current work but not be limited by it.*[13]

The various intellectual gestures by which active nothings are uncovered and the future is thought are many and context-sensitive, but when pursued philosophically

—i.e., when pursued in a self-critical way and as directed upon thoughts recorded in specific texts—they involve four steps:

(1) Discrepancies must be registered between different doctrines stated in a text, or between different meanings of important words in it, or between what a statement actually says and the work it is supposed to do in the text.
(2) Overhasty explanations of these discrepancies— e.g., in terms of the author's sloppiness—must be argued away.
(3) The discrepancies must be followed out to show that they are enduring, not merely random occurrences like mere contradictions or momentary inconsistencies.
(4) That to which they point as their origin must be given a proper name—one which identifies it only as the origin of that particular set of discrepancies.

This conception of a defining, and therefore active, void—the Being which is not a being, or the Nichts *which* nichtet—*is, I think, one of Heidegger's most radical ideas. Heidegger's thought, like those of the "postmodernists" who follow in his wake, contains a rich panoply of conceptual gestures designed to open up the holes in our knowledge, to show where the questions are—the questions which delineate our futures. To give a couple of examples: Heidegger begins his reading of Hölderlin's poem "Andenken" by pointing out that "Andenken" means remembrance or souvenir. But the poem, at its very center (the first line of the third stanza) asks a question about where the poet's friends are now—a question which cannot be answered by memory. The last line refers to poets as "founding" something—an act which clearly bears an essential reference to the future rather than directly to the past. The "remembrance" of the title seems somehow then to be a "remembrance" of something that is not in the past. Heidegger's reading expands upon this discrepancy by arguing that the rest of the poem expands on the meaning of such future-oriented remembrance.[14]*

In Was Heißt Denken? *Heidegger considers the famous dictum of Parmenides, "It is necessary to say and to think that Being is." On the one hand, Heidegger argues, the statement is thoroughly banal, yet it is supposed to function as the crucial insight of a great thinker:*

> This assertion is not only obvious, it also remains fully empty. It really says nothing. We already know what it says. . . . Is a thinker of the rank of Parmenides supposed to have asserted triviality of this sort? Is he supposed to have asserted this, to cap it all, as that which is necessary to say and think?[15]

The rest of the discussion goes on to fill in some—not all—of the holes in our understanding of Parmenides that are opened up by these questions.

The "external" argument for enlarging the philosophical toolbox is now complete. The argument is that the tools of narrative and demarcation—actually they are families of philosophical tools, of useful intellectual gestures—are necessary to a philosophy which seeks self-knowledge while remaining faithful to the fact that we are all, in all respects, in time. For if that is the case, then philosophy itself is just another way of inhabiting time. Since the ways we inhabit time include narrative and demarcation, philosophy itself must not merely study these families of gestures but appropriate them and use them as its tools.

I turn now to the internal argument, the argument that the various tools I have sketched for philosophy cannot function apart from one another.

Philosophy Foreshortened:
The Internal Argument

Consider, first, inference. Research among non-literate peoples reported in the early 1970s raised the staggering possibility that such people were somehow alogical. When problems were posed to them which could be solved by simple inferences of one kind or another, they gave correct answers at a rate only slightly better than chance. This held for non-literate people in all the cultures studied, ranging from West Africa to Uzbekistan to the Yucatan, and was in contrast to the more expectedly "logical" results obtained from literate members of those same cultures.[16]

Further consideration of the data revealed, however, that the non-literate populations were not in fact merely alogical. Something more complex was going on. This was that unlike their literate compatriots, the non-literate subjects, in solving the problems, were not restricting themselves to the information given in the problems themselves. For example:

> *Problem:*
>> All people who own houses pay house tax.
>> Boima does not pay a house tax.
>> Does Boima own a house?
> *Answer:*
>> Yes. Boima has a house but he is exempted from paying house tax. The government appointed Boima to collect house tax so they exempted him from paying house tax.[17]

If we transpose the mood of the response from the indicative to the hypothetical (that we need to do so has lessons of its own), we see what has happened: the non-literate respondent has refused the terms not just of this problem, but of problem setting altogether. She has introduced into her thought specific, relevant "information" that was not given in the problem. Part of the game of being presented with a problem of this sort, of course, is that one is, or is supposed to be, presented with all the information one needs to solve it. Literate subjects in all cultures, expectably, understood this; non-literate ones did not. The game of problem setting, it appears, is learned in school.

The non-literate respondent in the example above has insisted on using background information to the effect that some people do not pay housing taxes because the government has assigned them to collect those taxes from others. This information, which in this case is knowledge of what I will call a cultural fact, is highly relevant to the inference the question demands, but it was not included in the premises. To deduce a conclusion from some set of premises thus requires that we learn not to feed in any other information along the way, no matter how relevant and important that information may be.

It is not that inference is somehow *merely* a game—that people really think by feeding in new premises whenever it seems good to do so. When they did not go on to adduce background information, the non-literate subjects actually made good use of standard forms of inference. Thus, there is a disjunctive syllogism latent in the answer above, to the effect that Boima either pays house taxes or he is a tax collector; he is a tax collector, therefore it is not true that he pays house taxes (it is perhaps the way this unspoken syllogism is deployed that leads to the indicative case in the response).

By rejecting the game of inferential problem setting, the

non-literate subjects highlight the contrast between how inferences arise in the particular situation of such problem setting and how they get formulated in everyday life. We see that the game of problem setting requires the problem setter to do something for the interlocutor which non-literate people insist upon doing for themselves: deciding what information is relevant to the inference, and what is not. This is a matter of inclusion and exclusion. An inference can get underway only when all the relevant information is assembled and at hand, so that further information can be excluded. The general lesson is that inference is not a freestanding activity but presupposes a certain sort of including and excluding.

The information conveyed in premises is traditionally of two types: that communicated in particular or "passing" assertions ("Boima does not pay a house tax," "Socrates is a man") and that communicated in general or standing assertions ("All people who own houses pay house tax," "all men are mortal"). If we know which general assertions apply in a given situation, to that extent we "understand" that situation, to that extent it has been defined.

"Defining a situation" is thus more than merely stating what is there to be stated. It also requires excluding all sorts of other things, also there to be stated, from consideration. Only when this *double* task is complete have we obtained the premises of a possible inference. Attempting to make an inference in an undefined situation is like attempting to glue together pieces of wood that have not been planed or sanded. The surface is too uneven to allow it.

But what are the criteria by which we can know whether a situation has been defined correctly? How do we know that the proper inclusions and exclusion have been made? The non-literate people involved in the research I have discussed used their own personal knowledge to define the situation, selecting and deploying information they already had which seemed to be useful in solving the problem. Such personal knowledge, of course, came to them in the course of their lives as members of a given culture (one in which tax collectors, for example, do not pay the taxes they collect). Situation-defining personal knowledge is thus the outcome of the interaction between an individual and her culture. In short, it is the outcome of a history.

When I adduce some item of personal knowledge, such as that tax collectors do not pay the taxes they collect, I am connecting with both my personal history and a relevant fact. The history includes how I originally came to know that fact, plus the various subsequent experiences I have had with it. As such, it requires the kind of narrative and demarcative evaluation sketched above. If that story is ever to warrant my applying the knowledge it yields on a given occasion, for example, it should exhibit the characteristics of a good narrative; that is, it should embrace different experiences, the more the better. It should also order them, not merely chronologically, but in a story of increasing understanding, on my part, of whatever facts are involved. Any such inference is thus based on a history of exclusions and inclusions which are to be judged not merely in terms of truth, but in terms of Nobility as well. (Is the set comprehensive enough to get to the conclusion we want? Is it organized enough? Are all of its members relevant?)

This is not only true of certain inferences, but indeed of assertions in general. For it is crucial to human speech (as opposed, for example, to animal signals) that it almost always offers a variety of ways to state anything. If I can say "the cat is on the mat," I could also have said "the small feline is on the small rug," or (perhaps) "the dude is on the doily." My choice of words is always a matter of excluding other ways of putting the matter, and thus is in part the product of a history.

That inference could ever have been taken for a free-standing activity now needs some explanation. In addition to the fact that we were taught that when we were young and trusting and first given school problems to solve, part of the reason is that the words we use do much of the job of situation defining for us.

At this point, a very general point about this function of words is in order. When I join a group, my "situation"—in pragmatic terms, the conjunction of all that I can and cannot do right here and now—changes. So does that of the group I join, unless it is very large. One result of the argument so far, then, is the hardly novel insight that performative thought has a capacity to constitute situations. Like other aspects of thought and language, this dimension of our words is to some degree independent of us, who use them to speak.

> J. L. Austin famously began his How to Do Things with Words *by distinguishing performative utterances, in which to say something is to do something (as when an umpire calls a batter out) from constative ones, which merely state facts. He then spent the rest of the book undermining that distinction, eventually concluding that any speech act has both constative and performative dimensions.*[18]

> As Derrida has noted, however,[19] *Austin views speech acts exclusively as performed by speakers; verbal formulas are "designed" to fulfill, if used correctly, the intentions of speakers*[20] *(hence Austin's choice of the term "performative"). But as I am arguing here, the situation-constituting functions of language are often independent of the utterer; as Wittgenstein pointed out, utterers' intentions—though he would not call them that—are themselves "embedded in situations, in human customs and*

*institutions" (*Phil. Inv §§ *337, 581). To be sure, Wittgenstein was not happy with the situation-constituting powers of language, even though he recognized them obliquely. His main discussion of them concerns the case of linguistic analogies to what "holds us captive" in metaphysics (*Phil. Inv. § *90).*

This independence can be gathered from the fact that the intentions which we have when making an utterance themselves must be formulated in linguistic terms if we are going to understand them at all. We do not stand over our actions like their sovereign lords, and (*pace* Aristotle) we do not beget them as we do children (*NE* III.5, 1113b18). We are more like the sum of them. And so the features of our language which constrain the way we formulate our intentions and express ourselves constrain us as well.

To take a repulsive example, during the Third Reich, the very word *Jude* became pejorative. The German language had always had an abundance of hateful ways to refer to Jews, of course, but when this word, which had previously had at least in some circles connotations which were neutral or proud, became hateful, no way was left to talk about Jews nicely at all. To use it openly, even if one was Jewish, was to identify oneself as a Jew hater. To use it *to* a Jew was to constitute a situation of verbal aggression against that person. To use it when speaking with non-Jews was to turn the situation into an encounter of good-old-boy Aryans. It was thus impossible, in almost any interpersonal context, for someone to make an inference about Jews on the basis of such "ethnic" qualities as emotional warmth, generosity, and wry humor. All such background information would have been excluded, not by the wishes or intentions of the speaker, but by the word *Jude* itself as used in that culture at that time.

The negative effects of *Jude* were thus independent of

the intentions and wishes of the individuals using it. In many cases, of course, those wishes and intentions conformed fully to the hateful nature of the word. But consider the case of a decent person trying to say something decent about Jews with the only resources her language had. To use the word was to crystallize the situation around hatred, and there were no other words to use. The German language itself, in other words, became coercively hateful.

Language constrains us in less extreme ways. Suppose Foldarol is a smallish horse; if I call him a "pony," it will be more difficult to get boys to ride him, because "pony" includes, in contemporary American culture, a lot of information that is appropriate to girls. Real men ride horses.

This function of language is as old as the words we use, which makes it very ancient indeed. Our intentions and the speech acts we perform to realize them piggyback on it, just as they do on the various references words have, which they also have independently of our use of them. We are left with the obvious fact that words do not simply designate observable features of our environment; it would be much simpler if they did. In fact words are multiply constrained and constraining—sometimes by such extraordinary forces as Nazi politics but also, and almost always, by their own histories. Austin calls this "trailing clouds of etymology," somewhat misleadingly, for it is often the etymological cloud that pushes the word.[21]

Though clearly an important function of language, its "situation-building," or situating, aspect has not been explored nearly as closely as its truth-telling or constative aspect—a state of affairs which has not changed from Austin's day and indeed could not, given political realities in the United States, where such exploration should have come about (see *TD*, passim). There is obviously a great deal to be done on these issues, by a version of linguistic analysis which has finally been freed from the archaic presumptions about action, subjectivity, and political innocence which plague Austin's thought. But it is not to be done here, for here I am simply talking about the philosophical toolbox.

Inference, as part of that toolbox, thus depends on a predefined situation. We define situations narratively, by connecting present givens to the story of how we came to know the world and culture we live in. If this narrative definition is often accomplished automatically, in our choice of words, that is all the more reason why philosophers should concern themselves with it.

But if inference needs narrative, philosophical narrative in turn needs both inference and demarcation. That it needs inference has already been argued, when I claimed that the truth of the descriptions of individual stages was one criterion for evaluating narratives.

Narrative also needs demarcation to open it up to the future, conceived as an impending nothing. Without the future as an unknown, impending, and therefore destabilizing force which philosophy must recognize, we wind up with a kind of thought which is entirely *too* stable. For such narrative, history has come to rest in the present; there are no unrealized possibilities to be taken account of, which means that there are no possibilities at all. The present then becomes fixed, for if it has no unrealized possibilities, it cannot change. This fixity communicates itself back to the narrative which produced it, for if a new narrative were possible, our understanding of the present situation—and thus, to some degree, that situation itself—would change. This kind of thinking thus triggers a giant reification of *both* past and present and results in reactionary quietism.

Hegelian thought is notably susceptible to such reifications. Seen without regard to the future, Hegel tells us a story of the past which comes to rest in a present which, for philosophical purposes, has no future—history has ended. The fixity of that posthistorical present then communicates itself back to Hegel's story of the past. This means that Hegel's own account of history cannot be changed, because the present in which it has resulted cannot be changed, and to change the story of the past would change that present. Hegel's reconstruction of history thus becomes the only story which, on Hegelian premises, can be told about history. The past itself, in other words, becomes present, and Hegel's philosophy becomes the totalizing of presence.

That presence can be totalized—that there is no such thing as an open future—is an absurd claim in itself, and is absurdly attributed to Hegel, who wrote an entire book—the Phenomenology of Spirit—*devoted to refuting the view that the movement of thought can be stopped. The* Phenomenology *ends, after all, with Absolute Spirit dying on the Golgotha of time.*[22]

But there is worse. The idea that there is only one story to be told about the past is not only absurd but reactionary in the strongest political sense, because when there is no future and only one past, there is no way to go forward from here. Hence the ancient caricature of Hegel as himself a political reactionary, who deified the political structures he found around him in Prussia.

Indeed, the view that reality consists in structure maintaining itself over time—whether there be one or many such structures, and even if that maintenance includes much growth and enrichment—is itself intrinsically oppressive, as I have argued at length in Metaphysics and Oppression. *It is at bottom nothing less than Aristotle's hylomorphic metaphysics of ousia, in which essential form—that in a thing which never changes as long as that thing exists—dominates matter by bounding it, ordering what is within those boundaries into working parts, and maintaining those parts in their proper relationships. There is only one basic story which can be told about a thing, which is the story of how its matter came to dominate its form—of how it grew into the thing that it is. In the case of Hegel (as carica-*

tured), this ontology of ousia is inflated into a putative monism with only one story possible, that of Geist. It is all the more oppressive for that reduction.

Sandra Harding has pointed out that

> The subject of liberatory feminist knowledge must also be the subject of every other liberatory knowledge project. Since lesbian, poor, and black women are all women, feminism will have to grasp how gender, class, and sexuality are used to construct one another.[23]

The method I am proposing here is a partial antidote to the problem Harding formulates. In order for different stories to be told about the same person in the way Harding advocates, none of the narrative threads must be allowed to dominate or be more "basic" than the others. Demarcation can ward this off by proliferating narratives and allowing them to be woven together into a larger and more complete—but still incomplete—story.

Assertion and inference thus require narratives of which they are in part outcomes; narratives require both assertions and demarcation. Demarcation, finally, needs narrative. We can see this by supposing that the past is not philosophically relevant, that only the present and future matter to philosophy. In that case, demarcation does not need narrative. Our concern as philosophers is not to connect with the past but merely to open up that future by using the intellectual gestures of demarcation, which in turn come from the myriad contortions of Heideggerean *Destruktion* or even of deconstruction itself. But what is it that we thus demarcate? Not the narratives that connect us with our past, because the past is not philosophically relevant. So all we can demarcate is the present.

To "demarcate" something means to open up a defining gap at its core, as a way of bringing about its future. But the gap, in order to be an active one, must structure a narrative, not merely a present given. Registering discrepancies within the present—pointing, for example, not to words and sentences which set up discrepancies in a temporal development and therefore suggest something as yet hidden in that development, but simply to statements that contradict themselves here and now—is an enterprise not in opening narrative up to the future, but in skepticism. When it becomes the only concern of philosophy, we are headed toward a global skepticism, one that can aim only at undermining all versions of truth and reference, and so language itself. We are pointed toward what Derrida calls, in a passage also cited in chapter 1,

> a writing without presence, without absence, without history, without cause, without *archê,* without *telos,* absolutely deranging every dialectic, every theology, every teleology, every ontology.[24]

A quoi bon? I have argued at length (in *Philosophy and Freedom*) that the emancipatory promises of deconstruction, which are very serious indeed, can only be made good by seeing deconstructive techniques as directed against what I call the oppressive "ousia" ontology, rather than the merely boring "substance" ontology. Here I am adding that the move which makes us think that presence must be deconstructed is the restriction of philosophically relevant time to the future and the present.

> *To explain the reference to ontologies here, I must take a quick dip in the history of ontology (a whole bath will come in the next chapter). There are in modernity—and not just in modern philosophy—several distinct ontologies which have not often been clearly distinguished from one another. Two of them are the hylomorphic ontology of ousia, according to which a being is composed of form and matter, with form dominating matter; and what I call "substance ontology," according to which a thing consists of a bounded substrate into and out of which*

properties flow.[25] *This ontology, like ousia ontology, stems from Aristotle, from his* Categories, *but the more important example for the moment is Descartes, who pursued the substance ontology with modern rigor and argued that an entity conceived in terms of that ontology has nothing to do with its past.*

An Aristotelian ousia must show itself via a unified develop-ment over time, a development which is directed by its form (as when an acorn grows into a tree because of the action of the form "oak" within it). Such a story is then the kind of reified, only-possible-history into which, as I argued above, Hegelian thought falls into if not corrected by demarcation. With the sub-stance ontology, things are different. The God of Descartes main-tains the world with precisely the same activity by which he created it. In effect he creates the world anew each moment, so that an entity's current state depends not on its previous states, but on God's activity alone.[26] *If philosophy is something which need not take account of the past, then the ontology of ousia is not open to it; for philosophical purposes, all is substance.*

In accordance with this, the past must present *itself, not narra-tively, but as a grand unity, all there now—not as something which was built, gradually and painfully, by people who learned from each other over time. An example of this kind of substance-ontology view of history is Derrida's view of the history of philosophy in "The Pit and the Pyramid." Referring to the philosophical history of the concept of the sign, he writes:*

> . . . breaks do occur, discontinuities regularly fissure and reorganize the theory of the sign. They reinscribe the concepts of this theory in original configurations whose specificity is not to be set aside. When taken up by other systems, these concepts are certainly no longer the same; and it would be more than foolish to erase the differences of these restructurations in order to produce a smooth, homogenous, ahistorical all-of-a-piece cloth, an ensemble of invariant and allegedly "original" characteristics. And would it be any less foolish, inversely, to overlook, not an origin, but long sequences and powerful systems, or to omit the chains of predicates which, even if not permanent, are still quite ample, not easily permitting themselves to be dis-placed and interrupted by multiple rupturing events how-

ever fascinating and spectacular these events might be for
the first unaccommodating glance? For as long as the great
amplitude of this chain is not displayed, one can neither
define rigorously the secondary mutations or order of transformations, nor account for the recourse *to the same word*
in order to designate a concept both transformed and
extirpated—within limits—from a previous terrain.[27]

*Derrida's alternative here is between a rigid identity of basic
structuring concepts on the one hand and their "interruption"
and "displacement" on the other. What is missing is the possibility that philosophy is a process in which later thinkers neither continue nor merely interrupt the work of earlier ones, but
criticize it and learn from it. This gradual improvement is, of
course, the kind of thing I mean by "narrative"; its absence
from Derrida's thought leaves only the substance ontology open
as a way to construe historical givens. Accordingly, the "long
chains" Derrida mentions function like specific substrates which
allow for a determinate set, but no more, of "secondary mutations."*

Worse is in store. Substance, as Aristotle showed in his Categories, *is intimately connected with predication. For in order to
say "S is P," I need at minimum one quality P and something
else which* is *P, some substrate S in which P inheres. If I now
try to deconstruct this, to open its gaps and fissures so that its
future can come to be, I am working against predication itself—
and rapidly reducing myself to a state in which I cannot say
anything, or do anything, or join with others in a framework
of common intelligibility. Deconstruction thus needs narrative,
at which point it becomes what I call "demarcation."*

Demarcation without narrative is empty; inference without narrative is blind; narrative without demarcation is
reactionary; narrative without inference is fiction. All
three must work together in thinking. In particular, an
effective situating philosophy, one which illuminates our
status as thoroughly temporal beings, is one which responds philosophically to the past and future as well as to
the present. In addition to the basic inferential tools of

(Quinean) analytical philosophy, it makes use of (Hegelian) dialectical reconstruction and of (Heideggerean and post-Heideggerean) deconstruction, but in such ways that those tools are stripped of their supposed truth claims and seen to be performative exercises in which we connect with the past and open up a future. Freed from the need to produce truth, dialectical reconstruction thus becomes what I call "narrative," and deconstruction becomes what I call "demarcation." Instead of competing with the standard forms of inference in a disorganized philosophical toolbox—like saws and welding torches seeking to pound nails—these intellectual tools can then cooperate with each other, making philosophy, once again and finally, responsive to time.

3 | From Metaphysics to Ontologies

Ontologies, of which the most influential constitutes what I will call "metaphysics," are produced by temporalized reason and are temporal themselves. They come and go in history, and that they do so is necessary to how they function. Also necessary, as we shall see, is what I call the "pluralism" of ontologies, the fact that there are, and will probably always be, more than one of them.

If the historicality and pluralism of ontologies are not currently recognized, it is perhaps because philosophy's lust for eternity has traditionally led so many philosophers either to ignore history or despise it. Consider this quote from Hume:

> Nothing is more usual and more natural for those, who pretend to discover any thing new to the world in philosophy and the sciences, than to insinuate the praises of their own systems, by decrying all those, which have been advanced before them.[1]

The gesture Hume discusses, that of consigning all one's predecessors to the status of mere babblers, is standard for modern philosophers from Descartes to Reichenbach.[2] Just because it is so stereotypically "modern," the gesture is widely suspect in today's "postmodern" cultural climate, for it attempts to deny the past in two ways. First, it openly claims that I (as a "modern" philosopher) do not come from the past, that I have no noteworthy predecessors. Second, it implies that I will not join the past, for I am the one who has finally put philosophy on its proper footing. After me will come only my disciples.

Decrying one's predecessors thus refuses connection to the past and denies the unpredictability of the future. Nothing could be less consonant with the temporalized view of reason I am articulating here. It is tempting nonetheless when one surveys the darkness and contradictions that make up recent thinking about metaphysics. For metaphysics and its genus, ontology, are traditionally supposed to tell us nothing less than what Being itself is; and we have reached a state where we do not even know what they themselves are. Without knowing what they are, we can hardly pursue them philosophically (for a contrary view, see the "discussion" below). Other than as New Age *pastiche,* metaphysics and ontology seem to be impossible.

The first task, then, is to sort through this confusion and figure out what metaphysics and ontology "really" are. What will be left standing after this effort, if anything, should remain an open question for now. We must *experience* the confusion before we sort it.

The Confused Confusion about "Metaphysics"

Rudolf Carnap, a logical positivist, called Hegel and Heidegger "metaphysicians." Martin Heidegger, a phenomenologist and *Seinsdenker,* called Hegel and Carnap "meta-physicians."[3] Greater confusion is hard to imagine. Only Hegel, of these three, did not succumb to the temptation to cite the other two as "metaphysicians"; but then he had already succumbed, *tout court,* long before they were born.

As a logical positivist, Carnap places himself at the opposite end of the philosophical spectrum from Heidegger, who returns the favor. Yet they call each other by the same term of opprobrium. Do they mean different things by it? Not entirely, it seems, because for both of them "metaphysics" can refer to the same object—Hegel. Perhaps "is metaphysical" just means "belongs together with Hegel."

And, perhaps, no more is necessary. Perhaps "metaphysical" is a purely emotive term,[4] one whose entire function is to express contempt for a given philosopher (by placing that philosopher together with Hegel), and to urge others to feel it as well, without having any criteria at all of what is contemptible. Certainly anyone with an ear for recent discourse knows that many contemporary followers of Carnap and Heidegger continue to use the term "metaphysics" as one of blank opprobrium and (depending on their allegiances) continue to place either Carnap or Heidegger together with Hegel (and many others) in the "metaphysical" realm.

But this emotivist view fails too, because "metaphysics" is also used today as a term of approbation. Donald Davidson, for example, is placed in the "metaphysical" camp by the admiring Simon Evnine. Jaegwon Kim and Ernest Sosa claim that after some "doldrums" at mid-century, metaphysics is now "flourishing as never before, showing that our need for metaphysics is perhaps as basic as our need for philosophy itself."[5] Carnap's antimetaphysical arguments are here dismissed as mere atmospherics (specifically, "doldrums"), while those of Heidegger go unmentioned.

Confusion is obvious, and of a confused sort.

> *Two general interest works, appearing from the same publisher around the turn of the millennium, document how deeply such confusion had gained even some analytical philosophers. In the opening sentence of the preface to their* Metaphysics: An Anthology, *cited above, Jaegwon Kim and Ernest Sosa characterize "metaphysics" as "a philosophical inquiry into the most basic and general features of reality and our place in it."*[6] *This definition, wisely, leaves open whether the features which metaphysics investigates are universal per se or merely the most universal ones apparent to us. It is also innocuous enough to leave unclear how "metaphysics" could ever have been the term of opprobrium it was in the mid-twentieth century. This, perhaps, is why Kim and Sosa are so dismissive of the antimetaphysical assaults which flourished then as to call them mere "doldrums."*

> *This characterization of metaphysics, however wise and innocuous, certainly does not capture how the term is used either by Carnap or by Heidegger. It also cannot explain an important fact about the essays the anthology contains: that none of them is an empirical inquiry. Many quite general features of "reality and our place in it" are empirical features—such as that we live within a few hundred feet of the earth's surface, or that the speed of light is around 186,000 miles per second. Yet for Kim and Sosa, the only role allotted to experience in metaphysics is to be the object of "simple intuitive reflections" which "lead us directly to some of the most profound and intractable problems of metaphysics"; experience gives rise to questions, but does not provide answers. I am not saying that metaphysics should be an empirical inquiry—only suggesting that an adequate introductory characterization of metaphysics would explain, if it is not, why it is not.*

> *A third problem with their characterization is that while "our need for metaphysics is as basic as our need for philosophy itself,"*[7] *all the essays in Kim and Sosa's anthology are by English-*

speaking authors. Apparently the need for metaphysics, and so for philosophy, is "basic" only in the English-speaking countries.

In his preface to The Blackwell Guide to Metaphysics, *published three years after Kim and Sosa, Richard Gale affirms the general confusion: all "metaphilosophical" attempts to define "metaphysics" have "failed miserably."[8] Instead of a definition, Gale goes on to provide "paradigm displays" of metaphysics. He justifies this by denouncing the "scientistic deconstructionists" who see metaphysics as "a shocking scandal because it is a history of perennial and intractable disagreements." This comes from a misguided attempt to apply scientistic decision procedures to metaphysics, where they will not work because no such decision procedure is agreed upon by all metaphysicians. If we will only refrain from such naïve "scientism," we will conclude that metaphysics is "alive and kicking"—even though its practitioners do not know what it is.*

Gale thus attempts to portray as "business as usual" what is really a highly unusual *situation. From Book IV of Aristotle's* Metaphysics, *through Aquinas's "On the Division and Methods of the Sciences," and on to Kant and subsequent thinkers, the history of philosophy exhibits nothing so much as metaphysicians who work hard to define what they are up to, as is only to be expected of a discipline which is all about knowing what you are doing (gnôthe seauton again!).[9] Calling this "business as usual" is as historically misleading as calling the antimetaphysical outbursts of the mid-twentieth century "doldrums."*

Gale's tactic exhibits a further confusion: The same argument which saved metaphysics itself can also save the practice of attempting to define metaphysics. For how could the failure to achieve such a definition manifest itself other than as a "a history of perennial and intractable disagreements?" Gale can only be applying to the practice of defining "metaphysics" the kind of "scientistic" standards of success that he rejects for metaphysics itself.

The dismissiveness, incompleteness, misdirection, and confusion in these two anthologies illustrate what I identified in chapter 1 as contemporary philosophy's refusal to explain itself adequately to non-philosophers—those who would be studying introductory texts such as these. In the face of it, it is hardly surprising that Michael J. Loux, in his much more historically informed introduction to metaphysics, should return it to its Aristotelian roots as "category theory."[10] Loux differs from my current approach in that he takes metaphysical categories to arise not from history, but from the phenomenon of "similarity of attribute agreement," which he identifies as the common root of both nominalism and realism.[11] Apart from the problems of deriving such concepts as "identity" and "substrate" from our experiences of similarity, Loux misses the fact, central to what follows, that metaphysical categories are historically active.

We can sort out the ongoing confusion about metaphysics by going back a ways into the history of that confusion. If we do, we notice that Carnap is working with what he thinks is a basically Kantian conception of metaphysics as the effort to obtain knowledge other than through sense experience. But that can be understood in at least three different ways. First, the realm of metaphysics can be *beyond* the empirical world, like the Kantian supersensible domain of God and the angels. Second, it may be *beneath* it, like the domain of Aristotelian essences, which does not show up as such within experience but somehow directly structures the things which do. Third and finally, "metaphysical" knowledge can be what Carnap takes it to be: knowledge expressed in or justified by sentences which may be about sensible objects but for which empirical truth conditions cannot be specified. This would include unverifiable statements about empirical objects, such as "the Mona Lisa is beautiful."[12]

Heidegger, by contrast, like Derrida and *his* followers, uses "metaphysics" to mean the "project of pure presence," a project motivated in turn by the view that to be is to be "present," i.e., given all at once.[13] This meaning, which associates metaphysics with exemplary givenness, seems to be completely opposed to all three of the others, for to be "metaphysical" in the general Kantian sense is to be outside the realm of possible sensory experience and so never to be given to our cognition at all.

In fact, however, there is common ground between Kant on the one hand and Derrida and Heidegger on the other. For Kant, to be outside the realm of possible sensory experience meant to be outside time, which for him is the form of all experience. For Heidegger and Derrida, to be fully present, i.e., given all at once, is to be viewed independently of what went before and what comes after and so also to be, for philosophical purposes, outside the temporal flow. This view of metaphysics as a sort of practice of atemporality would also apply to Davidson and to Kim and Sosa, for things such as logical forms and truth conditions are not in time.

> *Heidegger puts this view of metaphysics as detemporalized thinking as follows:* "*What is [viewed metaphysically (*das Beständige*)] is however stabilized (*wird jedoch zu einem Ständigen*), i.e. rendered something which constantly stands at [one's] disposal, in that it is brought to a stand through a positing.*"[14] *Derrida puts it this way in "Force and Significa-tion": to be "present" means most basically to be "summed up (*résumée*) in some absolute simultaneity or instantaneity.*"[15] *This is in contrast to the temporalized approach of deconstruc-tion, according to which*

>> Each so-called "present" element . . . is related to something other than itself, thereby keeping within itself the mark of the past element, and already letting itself be vitiated by the mark of its relation to the future element . . . being related no less to what is called the future than to what is called the past, and constituting the present by means of this very relation to what it is not.[16]

Carnap now appears as the odd man out, since for him unverifiable claims about things which are within time, such as the claim that the Mona Lisa is beautiful, can also be "metaphysical." The other side of this is true for him as well. Carnap thinks we can talk about things not in time, such as logical truth, without doing metaphysics, as long we can verify what we say (by logical argumentation). The conception of metaphysics which lies behind this is however based on a superficial reading of Kant, one which fails to see what Derrida and Heidegger see: that Kant's distinction between the knowable and the unknowable is grounded in a deeper distinction between the temporal and the atemporal. This leaves Carnap unable to distinguish between the unverifiability of metaphysical claims and the unverifiability of normative claims; all are equally "senseless." The overall result is the confused confrontation I sketched above: Carnap thinks Heidegger and Hegel are promulgating unverifiable truths; Heidegger thinks Carnap and Hegel are taking things in an atemporal way.

In fact, as I noted in chapter 1 and argue elsewhere, Hegel and Heidegger are not promulgating truths at all (in Carnap's sense), but doing something quite different. Heidegger is wrong about Hegel, though not about Carnap. Hegel in fact is Heidegger's main precursor in the project of viewing everything as intrinsically temporal.

Carnap's view of metaphysics is thus an example of what might be called a historically and discursively unsound concept. Its historical derivation, from Kant, is via a superficial reading, and it hinders philosophical discourse because it does not allow needed distinctions to be made. Rejecting it leaves us with the Derrida-Heidegger view that metaphysics is the effort to think of things as outside time and hence non-empirically (one motivation for which is the belief that they really are outside of time),[17] but some questions remain. Two of these are now pressing. First, does the putative realm of metaphysics lie completely beyond the temporal or empirical realm, or does it somehow structure it from "below"? Second, why is metaphysics so very bad? That it is a mistake, and a fundamental one, is clear enough—but how did it come to be such a preferred term of opprobrium?

The "Nature" of Metaphysics

History can guide us, at least a bit further. Recourse to Kant has already suggested that the underlying dichotomy in terms of which metaphysics can be defined is not verifiable/unverifiable, but temporal/atemporal. There is a deeper level yet. Kant considered metaphysics, the set of knowledge claims about atemporal objects, to be pursued in his day mainly by the philosophers we call "rationalists" (and whom he called "dogmatists"), such as Descartes, Leibniz, Spinoza, and Wolff. If we ask why the supersensible realm became so important to these philosophers, we find that it is because they were trying to maintain the capacity of an older, indeed premodern structure to offer the supreme criterion by which to judge ethical, social, and political realities (cf. *MO* 105–127, 194–202).

That structure was first articulated philosophically as the Aristotelian concept of *ousia*. Understanding it will not give us a complete understanding of everything philosophers have pursued under the name of "metaphysics," for ousia is the fundamental concept of only one form of that pursuit. Because it is both basic to several other forms and of supreme historical importance in its own right, however, I will shortly come to identify it with "metaphysics" itself, reserving the term "ontology" for the whole family of accounts that purport to tell us what it means to be.[18]

Kant suggests a genus-species relationship between metaphys-
ics and ontology when he identifies ontology as the discipline
which deals with the concepts and principles by which we
think of objects, whether those objects are sensually given or
not (KRV B 873f); metaphysics is restricted to one class of such
object, the supersensibles. Though I will define the genus just as
differently as I have defined the species, my usage will remain
true to this basic stipulation of Kant's: ontology is the genus of
which metaphysics is a (particularly bad) species.

Ousia ontology, i.e., "metaphysics" *sensu proprio mihi,* works out to the view that any being has a form which is or should be responsible for the boundaries, internal order, and outward effects of that thing. Its form thus, in Aristotle's own term, "dominates" (*kratei*)[19] that thing by exercising over it the three functions which I call "boundary," "disposition," and "initiative." It determines the *boundaries* outside of which no part of that thing may be found; it *disposes,* i.e., generates and/or orders, everything within those boundaries; and it takes the *initiative* in dealings with the outside world, all of which should be directed by the form.

Such ousiodic structure can be found, I have argued, in social arrangements as diverse as the ancient family (where boundary, disposition, and initiative are exercised by the *pater familias*), the Hobbesian state (where they are exercised by the sovereign), the slave plantation to which Frederick Douglass is taken as a youth, and even the modern classroom (see *MO* 62–66, 128–144, 180–193). So viewed, metaphysics is anything but a set of doctrines about some realm other than the one we live in and must cope with. Rather, it purports to teach us about the "deep structure" of experience itself. The "metaphysical realm" is not "beyond" but "beneath" the empirical world.

Ousia's title to organize such a diverse variety of social

structures was originally bestowed on it by its status as the paradigm of nature itself. As Aristotle put it,

> In all things which are composed out of several other things, and which come to be some single common thing, whether continuous or discrete, in all of them there turns out to be a distinction between that which rules, and that which is ruled; and this holds for all ensouled things by virtue of the whole of nature. (*Politics*. I.4 1254a 28–32)

Ousia is then the concept of nature that metaphysics delivers to us; it is the "nature" of metaphysics. Ousiodic structure is "natural," and this installs domination as the central factor in human relationships.

The rise of modern science, centuries ago, showed that the idea that natural beings exhibit ousiodic structure was a fantasy. But even in the ancient world, not every being actually exhibited this structure equally. Parts and properties, for example, had Being only in a secondary sense, due to their participation in true ousiai such as humans and horses.[20] Ousiodic structure in its plenary form was thus never considered to apply to all things in equal degree. To claim it as basic to all of nature was, as Heidegger points out, the result of an odd kind of generalization which medieval philosophers called "analogy."[21] In the most relevant version of this, which even today remains Aristotle's, beings which exhibit the traits of boundary, disposition, and initiative to the full—living beings, and in particular (for Aristotle) the good citizens of Athens—are the plenary exemplars for everything else.

So understood, metaphysics consists of two parts. One part claims to be descriptive, not of all beings but of a certain privileged subset of them. I will call these the "plenary examples" of Being for that metaphysics. The second part is a recommendation that this description be used to structure our thinking about beings in general. This general recommendation may then be fleshed out with various concrete programs for doing so in various cases, as with Aristotle's thoughts about social arrangements.

The plenary examples of ousiodic metaphysics were, again as the above quote from Aristotle makes plain, natural beings; ousia had standing to order the human realm because it was descriptive of the natural realm. Once it was discovered by modern science that ousiai of that type do not exist in or by nature—once nature was categorized as merely matter in motion, rather than as a domain of what medieval philosophers had tended to call "substantial forms"—another place had to be found for ousia, a place from which it could still serve as the standard for arrangements in the social realm. The rationalists therefore assigned ousia to the divine or supersensible realm, and that is why it was so important for them that we have knowledge of such realms. It was partially in response to the ejection of ousia from nature by empirical science that the rationalists needed to anchor ousiodic structure in a "supersensible" world.

On its deepest level, then, metaphysics is concerned not so much with knowledge of some non-empirical realm, beneath or beyond the empirical realm, as with the structure and status of ousia. True to its Aristotelian origins, the concept of form-in-matter serves less to mirror reality than to structure thought. Deployed metaphysically, it sets boundaries to what we are to regard as "beings" at all, and it orders the way we think about them. This suggests an underlying reason why metaphysics is in ill repute today, for in the eyes of moderns the structures it sanctions are not givens of nature but structures of oppression.

The Heidegger-Derrida version of metaphysics recognizes that metaphysics is not just a philosophical mistake, but a profound social evil. However, as I have also argued (in *PF*), the Heidegger-Derrida critique of metaphysics rests on a confusion of its own, in which the dominance-oriented structures of ousia are confused with presence itself. The result is the welter of aporias, often fruitful, known as "postmodernism."

My conclusion is that *all* of the currently accepted meanings of "metaphysics" fail in two specific ways to capture what really goes in metaphysics. First, metaphysics, from its beginnings until the present day, has been deeply concerned—almost obsessed—not with giving an accurate account of beings in general, but with maintaining the status of one particular account of them, with "ousia ontology." Second, the reason for that obsession with ousia is that metaphysics is anything other than what it is traditionally understood to be: an abstruse exercise in conceptual argumentation, of significance to no one and of interest only to philosophers. It is instead an important, perhaps the most important, feature in the shaping of the West. Beneath the breathtaking diversity of its religions and cultures and of its manifold economic, social, and political systems, the West has always had a metaphysical unity. Like honeybees building their six-sided cells, Westerners are always and everywhere hard at work, consolidating and contesting ousia ontology.

Types of Ontology I: Four Limit-Case Ontologies

If metaphysics is definable specifically as an ousiodic account of Being, then it belongs to a genus and other accounts of Being are possible. Metaphysics, as I have presented it here, furnishes a basis for understanding them.

It is only to be expected, then, that a number of different ontologies should be found articulated in Western thought. A short and unrefined list of them, taking the ousia ontology to be (1), would include the following:

(2) *Substance ontology,* according to which beings are compounded of a substrate plus various properties, some of which—the accidental ones—move into and out of that substrate, while others—the essential ones—remain in it as long as it exists. In contrast to an ousiodic form, a substantial substrate is passive (I briefly discussed this ontology, like the ousia ontology, in chapter 2).

(3) *Pantheist ontology,* according to which all beings are really just a single thing, of which everything else is a mode (configuration) or property, etc.

(4) *Force ontology,* according to which a being is something which expresses itself through action on other beings and, perhaps, requires such expression in order to exist.

(5) *Node ontology:* to exist is to be nothing but a site of transfer, a sort of crossroads where various movements and forces intersect.

These four ontologies have many differing versions, and each has a complex history of its own. Substance ontology received its first adequate formulation in Aristotle's Categories *and was articulated in a different way by the atomists (who posited many very small substrates). Aristotle later abandoned it in favor of his ousiodic view of the underlying nature of a thing as constituted by an active form, rather than a passive substrate.*

Once modern science had disposed of the view that such active forms actually existed in nature, substance ontology with its inert substrates made a massive return and came to occlude the ousia ontology (see MO 105–202, esp. the summary at 105–108). This led Heidegger, and following him Derrida, to their chief error: they saw the problems with ousia ontology, but not that ontology itself as such. Instead, they attributed those problems to substance ontology, with its reliance on the inert presence of the substrate (MO 205–251; PF 20–48).

But substance ontology had already encountered problems of its own—pre-eminently that of how substrates were to be known, given that (a) only properties were determinate enough to be objects of knowledge, and (b) they were not identical with the substrates in which they inhered. From these two assertions it followed that we could know properties but not substrates. This vexed Locke enough that at one point he characterized the assumption of an explanatory substrate as a mere matter of "custom" and "supposition," which suggests that the idea of substance could be entirely dispensed with. But when challenged on this ground by Stillingfleet, who thought that Locke was making substance an optional concept, Locke responded that any other explanation for the subsistence of concatenated ideas is "inconceivable."[22] Berkeley pushed on and argued that the idea of an unknown material substratum for the concatenated ideas we actually perceive is untenable—a main thesis of his "subjective idealism."[23]

Descartes and Spinoza, for their part, fell back toward the idea that in truth there is just one real being: God. Descartes's view that all natural motion is directly caused by God, for example, follows from his rejection of substantial forms conceived on the analogy of souls. As Daniel Garber puts it:

> Descartes rejects the tiny souls of the schools only to replace them with one great soul, God, an incorporeal substance who, to our limited understanding, manipulates the bodies of the inanimate world as we manipulate ours.[24]

This assimilation of forms to souls was grounded in the fact that the substantial forms of traditional philosophy were conceived on analogy to immaterial substances, and in thus conceiving of those forms we attribute to material objects a sort of soul. As the above quote suggests, the form-in-matter is for Descartes an illegitimate generalization from the soul in the body:

> . . . I confess that the only idea I can find in my mind to represent the way in which God or an angel can move matter is the one which shows me the way in which I am conscious that I can move my own body by my own thought.[25]

The rejection of such "animistic" forms leads to pantheistic ontology, to the view that the universe is, as it were, a single giant body, which God moves as if it were his own. Descartes is clearly uncomfortable with this view, but he is propelled toward it, in part, by his inability to conceive any other way in which God could order the universe.

For Spinoza, God is not, as he is for Descartes, the only true substance. He is the only substance at all; finite substances cannot even be conceived.[26] Every other thing that exists, whether thinking or extended, somehow inheres in this single divine substance, either as an attribute or as a mode. Pantheistic ontology is in full bloom.

Force ontology was prominently, though elusively, articulated by Nietzsche:

> My idea is that each specific body strives to become master over the whole of space, and to spread out its power—its Will-to-Power—repelling whatever resists its expansion.[27]

Here, we have a body which, on its most basic level, exists by exercising a force, in an effort "to spread out its power." Arthur C. Danto has rightly noticed the affinity of Nietzsche's "idea" with the substance ontology:

> It is hardly avoidable that we think of Will-to-Power in exactly the terms in which men once thought of substance, as that which underlies everything else and was the most fundamental of all. For Will-to-Power is not something we *have*, but something we *are*. Not only are *we* Will-to-Power, but so is everything, human and animal, animate and material. The entire world is Will-to-Power; there is nothing more basic, for there is nothing other than it and its modifications.[28]

> *Force, the effort of a body to "spread out its power," is here con-*
> *ceived as the most basic, or even the sole, reality. It then becomes*
> *hard to see, however, how force could be something exercised by*
> *a body, since at bottom that body itself can be nothing but force.*
> *Denying that would, however, make it difficult for Nietzsche to*
> *maintain the* moral *import of such important distinctions as*
> *that between active (healthy) force and reactive (unhealthy)*
> *force—for how can a force, except when related to a body, be*
> *healthy or unhealthy?*[29]

> *The status of body is thus a problem for force ontology. Node on-*
> *tology speaks to this issue. It decisively eliminates from the body*
> *everything except force, so that a body is simply a contingent con-*
> *geries of forces. It also, as with the middle Foucault, abandons*
> *all moral import. Bodies become what* The Archeology of
> Knowledge *refers to as "discursive formations," contingent—*
> *and,* contra *Nietzsche, amoral—intersections of forces. They are*
> *not themselves dynamic, but are "subjects" of power.*[30]

This plurality of ontologies is only enhanced when history makes the ontologies listed here into whole families of on-tologies, each of which is formulated, reworked, criticized, damned, and saved again by generations of philosophers.

What, in the face of all of this, are we to do about on-tology? Should we convince ourselves, yet again (and yet again falsely) that we have somehow gotten beyond it? Should we give over to the hope that no overall views of what it is to be structure our lives and societies? Shall we simply choose an ontology from the list above? Invent a new one? On what basis would we do either of these?

It can be shown that all four of the ontologies listed above are limit cases of ousia ontology, in the sense that in each of them one or more of the three features central to that ontology is simply suppressed. Roughly speaking, substance ontology (2) denies disposition and initiative; a substrate has boundaries, and nothing more. Pantheistic ontology (3) keeps God as the ordering principle in the universe, thus retaining disposition, but his boundaries are those of the entire universe, and there being nothing outside it, he exercises no initiative at all. Force ontology (4) makes initiative basic, which means that it contests both the boundaries of individual beings and the disposition of any sovereign component within them. Node ontology (5) goes one step further, denying even boundaries (a view to which some assimilate Spinozistic ontology).[31] None of these four competing limit-case ontologies, then, is a radical challenge to the ousia ontology.

Types of Ontology II: Two Contestatory Ontologies

One purpose of ousia ontology, as Book II of Aristotle's *Physics* makes clear, was to solve the "paradox" that change implies stability; in every change a thing undergoes, something must remain unchanged. Otherwise the thing does not change but passes out of existence altogether, to be replaced by something else. One way to resolve this paradox is by way of Otto Neurath's famous example of a ship at sea, which must be repaired plank by plank until it is composed of completely different wood;[32] but Aristotle takes a more fateful path. His solution is to claim that there is one component of a thing that can *never* change, that persists through all its possible transformations and constitutes its identity. This is its form. Form relates to the rest of the thing via the three axes of domination I have mentioned: by setting the being's boundaries, by ordering what happens within them, and by relating to the world outside them. Ousia ontology thus removes change from the basic identity of a thing, for the immanent principle of identity in a thing, its form or essence, does not change.[33]

The limit-case ontologies I have listed accept this divorce of being from time. None of them locates change within a thing; change always comes from outside. Force ontology, which comes close to seeing change as immanent to things, still has bodies which exercise force, meaning that they are (somehow) not just forces themselves. Even node ontology, which comes still closer, retains the idea that change comes from outside; it just claims that beings, since they are merely nodes, have no "insides." The most important Western ontologies to insist that to be is to be intrinsically dynamic are what I call "negation" ontology and "diakenic" ontology. It is they which move far enough beyond the ousia ontology to be able actually to *contest* it:

(6) *Negation ontology* posits change at the core of individual beings in a twofold way: On the one hand the being exists, Neurath-fashion, as an unfolding of components, none of which persists unchanged throughout the whole development. On the other, this process of unfolding is itself unstable and so, eventually, reveals itself to be a process of dissolution.

Hegel concludes his Encyclopedia *by equating his book with nothing less than Aristotle's God, the Prime Mover—and the prime instance of Being itself. Hence, it is not farfetched to take what Hegel attributes most basically to his own system for what he would, in his own ontology, ascribe to Being itself, and this is its ongoing, radical self-transformation. The famous analogy of the flower at the beginning of the Preface to the* Phenomenology of Spirit *is an example:*

The bud disappears in the bursting-forth of the blossom . . . similarly, when the fruit appears, the blossom is shown up in its turn as a false manifestation of the plant, and the fruit now emerges as the truth of it instead. These forms are not just distinguished from one another, *they also supplant one another as mutually incompatible.* Yet at the same time their fluid nature makes the moments of an organic unit in which they not only do not conflict but in which each is as necessary as the other; and this mutual necessity *alone* constitutes the life of the whole (*PhS* 10/2, emphasis added).[34]

(7) *Diakenic ontology* posits an active core at the heart of every being, much as do the ousiodic and negation ontologies. It denies, however, that such a core has any determinate nature. The core is thus an emptiness or a nothing, but an active one, which gathers and shapes beings— properties, materials, figments of the mind— around itself.

The diakenic ontology is Heideggerean. In his 1951 essay "Das Ding," Heidegger writes, concerning the hollow core of a jug,

> The emptiness is what does the jug's holding. The emptiness, this Nothing in the jug, is what the jug is as a container which contains . . . [From this perspective, the potter does not instill a plenitude of form into clay, but] "shapes the void."[35]

The defining emptiness in the jug is specific to it: its *own void. This individual void is active; it is what holds the jug together as a thing and places its other features—sides, bottom, spout— into what I call a diakenic interplay.*

These ontologies, too, have their plenary examples. Hegelian negativity hardly applies to something like a mountain range; its plenary example, as I suggested above, is thought itself. Heidegger explicitly says that diakenic ontology is not supposed to refute other ontologies but simply to displace them by providing an alternative to them (diese Angaben der Physik sind richtig, cited in chapter 1).[36]

Evaluating Ontologies

We now have seven different ontologies: the basic ousia ontology, four of its limit cases, and two contestations of its basic principle. Which of these ontologies is right?

The issue is going to be tricky. In its rawest formulation, which is the one I just gave it, the question presupposes that only one of the seven ontologies I listed *can* be right, while the others all have to be wrong. This way of putting the issue thus presupposes bivalence, the general problems with which I discussed in chapter 1. A specific problem arises here as well, for ousia ontology itself is not bivalent. It allows, as I have noted, for degrees of Being; not all beings exhibit boundary, disposition, and initiative in plenary ways. In addition to its plenary examples, ousia ontology also has what I will call "weak" examples, i.e., it allows for things which, in different ways and to varying degrees, do not fully exhibit the characteristics that it identifies with Being itself. Ousia ontology thus does not claim it to be true that every being exhibits boundary, disposition, and initiative. It claims only that it is more or less true that all of them do (or otherwise participate in ousiodic structure, an issue which can be left aside here). Its central claim, the claim that to be is to exhibit boundary, disposition, and initiative, thus has degrees of truth.

Everything which is a plenary example of the characteristics assigned to Being by the other ontologies can thus count as a weak example for ousia ontology. Moreover, all the various "definitions" of Being that the other ontologies advance also, like that of ousia ontology, have both plenary examples, to which they claim to apply fully, and weak examples, to which they apply only to a degree; none is (bivalently) true of everything. But that hardly makes them mutually incompatible. We are free to say of any given thing that it is a good (or even plenary) example for one ontology and a weak example for the others. There is no more incompatibility here than if I say that Betty is both an excellent physicist and a fair swimmer.

And yet there is incompatibility; these ontologies do compete with one another. For each offers an account, not of just any properties, but of what it is most basically to be a thing, so that if something—anything—is most basically an ousia, it cannot be most basically a force or a node. Ousia ontology (and, *mutatis mutandis,* the others) must therefore claim that even weak examples of ousia are still most basically ousiai.

There is thus a theoretical gap between what each of these ontologies is true of—namely, its plenary examples —and what it applies to—namely, everything. That gap is filled, traditionally, by reams of writing about such things as the "analogy of Being." But those writings cannot even address the actual issue raised by the fact that there is a plurality of ontologies. That question is not "how can something be most basically an ousia (for example) and still be only a weak example of ousia?" which is the basic question of the analogy of Being. Given the plurality of ontologies, the real question has to be "what is there about a weak example of ousia (for example) that requires us to call it an ousia rather than a node, or a force, or by some other ontological name which may in the event fit it better?"

If other ontological names really do fit better, the answer can only be—nothing. Our decision about which ontology to apply to a thing is not dictated by any features of that thing, which means *that it is not decided theoretically at all.* The gap in question can only be filled practically; each ontology must make a covert *recommendation* that we apply it to beings of which it is not strictly true. Each of the ontologies I have listed thus recommends itself as the sole model for understanding all beings, even those which exemplify it only weakly. It makes such a directive because that is the only way for it to get from its plenary examples to everything else—the only way, then, for it to be an "ontology" at all. I will call this kind of directive an "ontological recommendation."

All of the ontologies listed above must, it would seem, make ontological recommendations. This appears to be the only way to make sense of the facts that:

—there is a variety of ontologies in the West;
—there is no theoretical way to decide among them; and
—such decisions get made.

Let us look a bit more closely, however, at exactly what sort of recommendation an ontological recommendation is. We are recommended to take a certain set of beings as "plenary examples" of Being itself, which means that we are to take certain properties of those beings as present, if only to a weak and attenuated degree, in all beings whatsoever. The problem of deciding which ontology is right has now become the problem of evaluating the ontological recommendation made by each of them. How can we evaluate the merits of such a recommendation?

There are, of course, certain standards that any recommendation as such ought to meet, such as clarity sufficient for us to know when it is being properly carried out. In addition, a philosophical recommendation ought, like some but not all recommendations, to have good reasons behind it, and these can be expected to fall into two groups: the recommendation is either justified in itself, i.e., deontologically, or it is justified in virtue of the consequences of following it, i.e., consequentially.

How clear, to begin with, are ontological recommendations? How are we to know when we are "taking something as" having a specific set of ontological characteristics? What, in fact, do we mean here by "taking as"?

The philosophical tradition (as I argue throughout *Metaphysics and Oppression*) shows two main senses of this. Ontological recommendations can be understood

I. *Hermeneutically:* any being should be interpreted, to the greatest degree possible, as having the properties specified by the ontology in question. On this level, an ontological recommendation recommends that we use those properties as the *hermeneutical basis* for interpreting anything whatsoever.

An example of the hermeneutical version of an ontological recommendation is at the beginning of Book II of Aristotle's de Anima:

> We say that (*legomen*) one genus of what is is ousia, and that in several senses, (a) in the sense of matter or that which in itself is not "a this," and (b) in the sense of form or essence, which is precisely that in virtue of which a thing is called "a this," and thirdly (c) in the sense of what is compounded of both. . . . Given that there are bodies having life . . . the soul cannot be a body; for the body is the subject or matter, not what is attributed to it. Hence the soul must be an ousia in the sense of the form of a natural body having life potentially within it.[37]

The argument of this passage, which I have severely truncated, can be loosely summarized as follows: We recognize that all ousiai contain matter and form; natural bodies are ousiai, and so contain matter and form. Matter and form, validated here by what "we say," thus provide the conceptual alternatives in terms of which we can understand the nature of soul. They are

the *"hermeneutical basis" for determining what that nature in
general is. The body is matter, and so the soul must be, in Aristotle's definition, "the form of a natural body having life poten-
tially within it."*

II. *Practically:* things should be made, where feasible
and so far as possible, to exhibit those properties.

*This sort of practical ontological recommendation applies to
human beings as well as to things which human beings can
shape. One place to see it exemplified is in the moral hierarchy that, at the beginning of* Nicomachean Ethics *VII.1, spans
the realm between gods and beasts. The human extremes of
this hierarchy are the "good" or "virtuous" person and the "un-
hindered" or truly evil person. The middle states mark the line
between the good and the bad; the "continent" person is the
lowest form of good man, while the "incontinent" person is
the highest form of bad man. Most important, however, are the
Greek terms Aristotle employs for these two states, respectively*
enkratês *and* akratês, *the person "in" dominance and the person "without" it. The same Greek word,* kråtein, *was used in
Aristotle's discussion of females and monsters, where it explicitly
referred to the capacity of form to shape the matter of the fetus.*[38]

*It is not the whole "person" who has mastery here, but her rea-
son. "[T]he continent and the incontinent person are so called
because in them reason dominates or does not,* reason considered as being the person herself . . . " (NE *IX.8 1168b 31–
1169a 1, emphasis added). Reason is our human essence; if it is
not in control of our lives then "we" are not in control of our
lives, but if it dominates then "we" dominate. It is thus the
domination of reason over desire, as form over matter, which
makes one's actions one's own and one's life a good one. Where
it is not present it should be installed.*

A general formulation of what an ontological recommendation recommends, for a given ontology *O,* would
run as follows:

All beings should be interpreted as if they exhibited the properties of Being specified by *O*. All beings which cannot be interpreted as exhibiting those properties should, if possible, be remodeled so that they do.

This leaves us in the dark, however, as to what it means to "interpret something as if" it exhibited properties specified by a given ontology. We are also in the dark about what it means to "remodel" a being in accordance with the recommendation. Spelling these things out is not the point here. Rather, in its appeal to the very general notions of "interpretation" and "remodeling," the formulation shows how complex and multifarious ontological recommendations are, embracing not only all the ways we seek to understand things but all those in which we strive to make ourselves, and others, better.

Ontological recommendations are thus intrinsically vague. Like such injunctions as "be fruitful and multiply," or "be happy," any such recommendation is so broad and supple that we cannot, in general terms, state what it recommends with sufficient precision to know once for all what would count as carrying it out; that must be decided on a case-by-case basis. What would justify an ontological recommendation is also vague, then. What it recommends is certainly too unclear for it to have a "deontological" justification—one which would show that following some given ontology's version of it is always the right thing to do. How could something so vague be shown to be right?

It appears that the only kind of justification open for ontological recommendations, then, is a consequentialist or pragmatic one; we are to justify adopting one ontology over others in virtue of the beneficial results such adoption brings to us. The reason this option is still open, however, is also the reason why it will not work as a basis for deciding among ontologies in a once-for-all way: because it preserves the complexity and variety of the recommendations themselves. What is, and what is not, a "beneficial result" must be decided on a case-by-case basis. So here, too, we find ourselves unable to rank the various ontologies, or to decide the issue of which of them is right. Ontological recommendations, on their own overall terms, are inherently unjustifiable.

They can, however, be justified as I have suggested: on a case-by-case basis. Choosing an ontology is not something we can do once for all—as if an ontology were a *theory* of Being whose truth or falsehood could be decided by argument. An ontology, properly understood, is of local validity, like the "prototypes" studied by Eleanor Rosch and others.[39] Some work on some occasions, and others on other occasions. Sometimes one works best, but none is always best. The problem with ontological recommendations, it now appears, is that they presuppose that some single ontology—the one they recommend—is right for *every* occasion. This ignores the fact that ontologies are inherently plural—that there is never just one of them in play.

There are of course many kinds of prototypes; any analogy propounds one. But ontologies, as we now understand them, differ from other kinds of analogy in that their recommendations are unrestricted. We are allowed to try a given ontology on anything whatsoever. This is the difference between "think of France as a hexagon," which specifies a one-object domain to which hexagonality is to be applied, and "think of anything whatsoever as a hexagon," which is a very unpromising ontological recommendation.

Ontological *recommendations* are more usefully construed,

in fact, as ontological *invitations*. An ontology, properly understood, is unrestricted, rather than universal, in its applications. It has a specific domain of entities of which it is true—as it is true of Socrates that he exhibited boundary, disposition, and initiative (cf. *PI* 178–182). It invites us to view anything whatever as similar, in its most basic nature, to those entities. So understood, an ontology is non-exclusionary; it does not even exclude other ontologies. It simply suggests that we use its model on whatever we come across, which does not entail that some other ontology, on a given occasion, might not work better. What has traditionally seemed to be "the universality-claim of ontology" is, I suggest, merely a refusal to restrict the domain to which various specific ontologies might apply.

Ontology-Independent Properties

Consider now what it means, not to "choose" an ontology in general, but to "adopt" one in a specific situation, to decide, with respect to some given being, that one or another unrestricted ontology best applies to it here and now. No such ontology has more intrinsic merit than any other (it is difficult even to imagine what such "merit" might consist in), so we must make such decisions, it appears, with respect to the consequences of adopting some particular ontology rather than any of its competitors. The rational side of making that decision is a procedure I will call "pragmatic evaluation," which I will characterize only roughly here as the attempt to measure out the consequences of adopting a particular ontology for our interaction with a particular being on a particular occasion.

> For a canonical account of the kinds of thing we do in pragmatic evaluation, see Aristotle's accounts of deliberation in Nicomachean Ethics *III*, of practical wisdom in

Nicomachean Ethics *VI, and of the ways knowledge guides
action in* Nicomachean Ethics *VII.*[40] *Basically, practical reasoning begins with the end, which in general is happiness; takes account of the main ways in which my current situation diverges
from that state; examines various possible ways of reaching that
good; and ends when it reaches an action which I can perform
right now. This model can be usefully applied to the adoption of
an ontology on a particular occasion, but it is not the only
model for such adoption and I will not pursue it here.*

It is not only the general consequences of adopting an
ontological prototype that we take into account in such a
case, however. We can only evaluate the applicability of
an ontology in light of the various concrete possibilities
which adopting it on that occasion opens up to us. And
our deliberation concerning those consequences and possibilities must, in turn, be guided by certain characteristics the being has independently of the various ontologies
we are considering adopting for it—otherwise we could
take any being in any way, arbitrarily, and our prototype
would not be a prototype *of* anything.

Which ontology best captures features of the thing,
which of its features are the ones we want to capture, and
to what purpose we want to capture them are all considerations that we must allow into our deliberations. All of
these considerations appeal to properties which the thing
has *prior* to the choice of an ontology for it and so independently of any such ontology. Whether an enraged lion
is a substance, an ousia, a body exercising force, or a node
of forces, it is *first of all* extremely dangerous.

*The idea that ontologies can be adopted in rational ways is im-
plicit in the final words of Quine's essay "Speaking of Objects":*

I philosophize from the vantage point only of our own
provincial conceptual scheme and scientific epoch, true; but
I know no better.[41]

From which we conclude that Quine does know worse, and has not chosen it.

The contrast is with Heidegger, who recognized the plural nature of ontologies but for whom an ontology is not at bottom an object of choice. "Regional ontologies," which concern kinds of being that we are not, are each coordinated to a particular domain of being (Seinsbereich) *and so do not compete—except, possibly, when a being belongs to more than one domain. The "pre-ontological" understanding which provides the basis for such explicit regional ontologies, and which Heidegger seeks to articulate conceptually in his own project of "fundamental ontology" (SZ 8–15), is a unitary condition of experience, not pluralistic. For Heidegger, an ontology—in the sense of an understanding of Being, however inexplicit—is already in place* before *we can say anything at all about a given being. Being is "that which determines a being as a being; [it is] that with respect to which a being, however it is then discussed, is always already [* je schon*] understood" (SZ 6; also cf. 150). In the later Heidegger, this priority of ontological conceptuality over concrete experience is virtually absolutized:*

> In metaphysics, meditation on the essence of beings and a decision concerning the nature of truth are brought to completion. Metaphysics grounds an age in that it gives it the ground of the *form of its essence* via a determinate interpretation of beings and a determinate comprehension of truth. This ground thoroughly *dominates* [*durchherrscht*] all the phenomena that distinguish the age.[42]

In my terms, Heidegger sees correctly that an ontological recommendation cannot be theoretically justified, but he does not see that it really has the status of a mere invitation. Instead he takes ontologies to be imposed on us, somehow, by history or by what is beyond history. The result of this is Seinsgeschichte— *a project Habermas rightly charges with decisionism.*[43]

Conditions of Pragmatic Evaluation

It is at this point, where ontology seems to have dissipated into a welter of occasional judgments which do not even consider all the properties of a being, that the way to pursue it becomes clear. For not only must any being have certain properties which are ontology-independent in this way, there are certain properties it must exhibit if it is to play into a case of pragmatic evaluation at all. We can come up with a model of Being of greater generality than those which I have listed above if we ask what a being must be like in order to be evaluable pragmatically— i.e., with respect to the consequences of applying any of the traditional ontological models.

> *This kind of recoil back from the question of what a thing is to the question of how we constitute it as the thing that it is was a specialty of Kant's; instead of asking what causality was, for example, he asked how our mind constitutes causes. But it is much older than Kant. Aristotle's answer to the question of what happiness is, for example, is that it is the (rational) activity of the soul in accordance with virtue. But the action of the soul in human life is deliberation, the process of rational choice by which we make ourselves happy (NE I.7, 1098a 17–19, III1–3 passim). True happiness, in other words, is simply the developed capacity to constitute yourself as happy.*

> *This reference to Kant should not, therefore, be taken to mean that I am endorsing his project or attempting to reinstate the occasionally lamented "subject" by grounding ontology in it. The "subject," for Kant, was capable of operating with perfect self-transparency, which meant that its inner realm was unaffected by any laws from without. None of that applies here, as will be seen.*

In order for us to evaluate a given thing or event with regard to the consequences of adopting a particular ontology with respect to it, that thing or event must have consequences, i.e., causal effects (otherwise no one could ever notice it in the first place). It must therefore have a role in what I called, in my discussion of Hume in the previous chapter, a causal flock. That role is, clearly, to be responsible for various changes in the causal flock in which it stands.

The term "cause" here plunges us into some of the perennial issues of philosophy, for philosophers since Plato have been ferociously eager to figure out what it means to say that "x causes y." I will use the notion of causality only as a momentary makeshift, because my topic differs from that of causality in two respects. The first of these is that causal relations exist independently of us—there were causes and effects long before there were humans. Pragmatic evaluation can take account only of effects known to us. Moreover, the kind of "cause" I will be talking about does not operate in our absence, for its operation consists in getting us to do something—to adopt one ontology rather than another. The relation between "x" and "y" that I want to talk about, unlike the relation of causality, is mind-dependent.

Second, philosophers generally view causality as a relation between an effect and its cause—whether the latter be a single event or object, as with Hume, or a whole set of them, as with Mill.[44] Causation enters into pragmatic evaluation in a very different way, as a relation between a single cause and the whole set of its (currently knowable) effects. Where traditional accounts of causality presuppose that we have identified the effect and want to know what it means to say that something caused it, in pragmatic evaluation we identify something as a cause and then seek to understand what its effects are or may be—as we do in practical evaluation in general. "Causation" here would be the relation between an object or event and everything it caused, a relation which has not been central to the philosophical discussion of causation.

In pragmatic evaluation, then, we look to the conse-

quences of our adopting one ontology or another with respect to a particular being on a particular occasion. We
take it that our single act of adoption has multiple effects,
and this means that the being in question on that occasion
also must have multiple effects—since it is itself part of
what "causes" our adoption of some ontology or other to
cover it.

The changes set in motion by a given event or thing
tend to ramify over time, until they fade into the ongoing
background. Thus, the entry of a bullet into the brain
of Abraham Lincoln on the evening of April 14, 1865,
caused, at first, the destruction of an ounce or so of brain
tissue. But that led to the failure of several other vital systems in Lincoln's body, which led to the end of his presi-
dency, which ended his efforts to reconcile the North with
the South, which debilitated all such efforts—which led
to Reconstruction, to Jim Crow, to the civil rights movement, and onward to so many facts and aspects of American, and indeed world, culture today that no one could
even begin to list them.

We now have the picture of a causal flock which begins
with a single thing or event and ramifies outward, having more and more effects at each subsequent temporal
stage. Still using the language of causality, I will call this
a "causal delta." The example of Lincoln's assassination
suggests two things about such deltas. First, as they ex-
pand they fade into the background. It is very hard, for
example, to say that if Lincoln had not been assassinated
there would have been no Jim Crow. The argument is
strong that the South was simply not ready to accept de-
feat and that some version of the perpetuation of slavery
by other means was inevitable. To say that Lincoln's assassination changed the nature of today's American society

hardly even makes sense when we try and specify it. The members of the causal delta of a given event, *e,* cannot therefore be completely listed. Neither can those of a thing, which (however we think events and things are related) participates as such in a number of events.

Because of this, we can identify the members of a causal delta only comparatively; we need the help of a template which will enable us to distinguish the effects of *e* (or of the thing in which *e* participates) from everything else that subsequently happens. In order to isolate these, the details of that template must be similar to what actually happens except in one respect: the absence of *e.* The general form of such an identification of the effects of an event would run something like this:

- From a situation of type A, a situation of type B is generally produced (this is our "template").
- Situation *a* was in fact of type A, except for the intrusion of event *e;*
- Situation *b* followed causally from situation *a;*
- Characteristics {1 . . . n} of *b* differ from those of B;
- Therefore, {1 . . . n} are consequences of *e.*

The actual course of events is compared here to the move from A to B. Since A and B are *types* of situation, our knowledge that situations of type A tend to produce situations of type B is general knowledge that we have garnered from previous experience. It will differ from person to person and from culture to culture (even if situations of types A and B occur in different cultures, actual situations of those types may not tend to produce one another in all those cultures). In the absence of such knowledge, it is not possible for characteristics {1 . . . n}, the effects of *e,* to be separated from other characteristics of *b.* Someone who did not share our knowledge of types of situation could not identify them as distinct from the rest of the flock—so for purposes of pragmatic evaluation they are not, in fact, distinct from it.

The members of a causal delta thus do not carry on themselves any mark of that membership; they can be identified as members only through our activity. To that extent causal deltas are our doing. More basically, it is we who identify *e* as the beginning of a causal delta; of itself it has no such status. The causal delta that I sketched above with respect to Lincoln *could* have as its beginning the entry of John Wilkes Booth's bullet into Lincoln's brain. But it could also have begun with the bullet bursting Lincoln's skull; with Booth pulling the trigger; with Lincoln taking his seat in Ford's Theater; with the president's policies, which so enraged Booth; and so on. Similarly, the collapse of efforts to reconcile North and South could have been a result of various things and events which were in no causal relation to Lincoln's murder, such as the punitive mindset of Congress, anger toward the South in the hearts of Northerners in general, the difficulty and expense of such reconciliation as compared to the opportunity to exploit the fallen Confederacy, and so on. The beginning of a causal delta in other words, is not a given. It must be separated out both from its own causal antecedents and from other contributing conditions, and that separation requires our efforts. The second contribution that we make to a causal delta is thus the identification of its beginning.

The concept of the beginning or origin of a causal delta is intended to rethink the meaning of the Greek word archê, *usually*

translated as "origin," the point where you look for the begin-
ning of something. It is not the cause of that thing, partly
because (as I have been repeating) there is no single cause to
anything, and because the beginning of a causal delta is, conse-
quently, fixed by us; it is where we *look for the beginning of a*
thing.

If we try and locate origins independently of this, we run up
against the aporia documented by Derrida in his account of
Rousseau's attempt to think the origin of language: An origin
must be complete in itself, independent of what it originates and
so exempt from whatever goes on in what it originates. But if it
were truly complete in itself, it would not have to give rise to
anything else; that it originates something points to a deficiency
within it, which amounts in turn to saying that the origin is
contaminated by what it originates.[45] *As I would put it: Since it*
is we who identify events as origins, they exist independently
both of us and of what they originate—but as events, not as
origins. Such an externally bestowed origin can be the source of
no essential privilege.

The Hegelian dialectics of origin are also disarmed: A being or
event is not an origin until it has effects, and so its effects are the
origin of the origin qua origin, etc. (Werke VI 102–113/461–
469). The origin of the origin is our bestowal of originary status
on something, a bestowal which has explanations of its own.
Donald Davidson puts the matter well for the specific case of
reasons: "What emerges, in the ex post facto *atmosphere of*
explanation and justification, as the *reason frequently was, to*
the agent at the time of action, one consideration among many,
a reason.[46]

Causes thus come in flocks, not deltas. Nothing has a
unique object or event as its sole cause. To say that some
earlier event *e* was *the* cause of some later set of events is
always partial, but that is just what the concept of the
causal delta pushes us to do.

We thus make two contributions to causal deltas. We

discriminate what is in them from other things going on, and we posit their beginnings. These contributions, of course, need not be conscious. As I will put it, a causal delta can be *recognized* without being explicitly *known*. It makes a great difference, to be sure, which is the case. We perform most actions, including those which go into constituting causal deltas, differently when we know that we are performing them.

> *That kind of knowledge—knowing what you are doing, and even perhaps knowing why—is an important part of what philosophy has, since Socrates, undertaken to provide us. That philosophy does not produce wholly new knowledge, but only renders explicit what we already know or do, goes together with the recoil from things to our constitution of things which I discussed above. For if constituting things is something we already do, it is something we already know how to do; the "recoil" consists in identifying our main job as explicating that knowledge. That philosophy does this was first argued forcefully in Plato's* Meno *as the solution to Meno's paradox:*

>> Meno: But how will you look for something when you don't in the least know what it is? How on earth are you going to set up something you don't know as the object of your search? To put it another way, even if you came right up against it, how will you know that what you have found is the thing you didn't know? (*Meno* 80d)

> *The way Meno phrases this means that Socrates cannot suggest a model of inquiry in which we know some facts about something and undertake to discover other facts. For in such a case, the paradox will apply to those "other facts." If I know how old George is, and seek to investigate how tall he is, I must know something about what "height" is, and indeed about what his height is (otherwise I might try and measure it in yards, or even light years). The very same object must be known at one way at the start of the investigation, in another way at the end—from which Plato argues, unconvincingly to be sure, that the investigation itself is a recalling of what we already know.*

Kant's version of this view is why each of his three Critiques
*begins with, and seeks to legitimate, a feeling—the feeling
of necessity and universality for some of our judgments in
the* Critique of Pure Reason, *the feeling of moral obligation
in the* Critique of Practical Reason, *and the feeling of
disinterested pleasure in the* Critique of Judgment. *Hegel
follows Kant here, remarking in the Preface to the* Phenomenology of Spirit *that "what is familiar (*das Bekannte), *just
because it is familiar, is therefore not truly cognized (* Erkannt)"
(*PhS 28/18). That insight, in turns, underlies Hegel's earlier
(and later) claim that "everything turns on grasping the True,
not only as Substance but as Subject" (*PhS 19/10), *by which
he means that it is the job of philosophy to convert our "feel"
for the societies and cultures within which we live into explicit
knowledge.*

For Heidegger, who here alludes to the Meno, *Being is given to
us in our "pre-ontological understanding of Being," i.e., the
"feel" we have for Being, which it is the job of phenomenological ontology to explicate with the aid of a developed concept of
Being (SZ 5f).*

*As often, Wittgenstein said it best: "The work of the philoso-
pher consists in assembling reminders for a particular purpose"
(* PI, § 127).

*In virtue of the names cited here, it need hardly be said that
rendering practices explicit does not preclude criticizing them on
various grounds.*

What I have been calling causal deltas are thus not present as such in the world when we are not around; they
are a way we have of organizing experience. Because of
this, it is not very perspicuous to call them "causal" at all.
The point of organizing experience in terms of such deltas
is not to provide a faithful representation of the facts, but
to enable us to orient ourselves, to see processes underway
as like other processes with which we are already familiar
and as having had specifiable origins. In this respect, the

"causal" deltas that surround us at any moment, in various stages of their unfolding, guide us; and I will henceforth call them "guiding deltas." The guiding delta is thus a condition for pragmatic evaluation; unless a being is part of such a delta, it cannot be pragmatically evaluated. If it is, it can.

Guiding Deltas and Ontological Foundations

The concept of a guiding delta is still an obscure one, and there is obviously a great deal to be done before that changes. Not all of it can be done in this book; but it is already clear that the concept of a guiding delta is fundamental to ontology, in the sense which I have given to that. For we cannot evaluate the consequences of adopting, in a particular situation, one or another of the ontologies I have listed unless such adoption has consequences, unless it is the origin of a guiding delta. And any being thus evaluated must also have delta-changing properties of its own, for otherwise we would not be approaching it with a pragmatic evaluation at all. Indeed, as I noted above, our pragmatic evaluation of a thing presents itself as following upon the thing, and so as being part of the guiding delta of that thing. The concept of the guiding delta is thus fundamental to the emerging ontology.

Guiding deltas have a number of characteristics which could be the objects of further study. Among them are:

(1) *Rate of proliferation:* Some deltas are very narrow, i.e., their behavior-guiding effects do not multiply quickly. An example would be the publication of a book which, like Hegel's *Faith and Knowledge,* has endured but has had relatively circumscribed influence. Other deltas are broad,

in that their effects spread almost instantaneously over vast reaches of behavior. An example would be the second plane hitting the World Trade Center on September 11, 2001. (It is obvious from that example that contemporary media generally have the effect of explosively broadening guiding deltas.)

(2) *Constancy of proliferation rate:* Some guiding deltas spread at an even rate; others begin by spreading narrowly, and later widen more quickly. The works of Aristotle, for example, were not nearly as influential as those of Plato until the nineteenth century, but since then have become so. Other deltas start off broad and then narrow, as in the restoration of an equilibrium.

(3) *Speed of development:* Some deltas develop quickly, going through a large number of discernible changes in a short time; others develop more slowly.

(4) *Transparency:* Some deltas are more comprehensible than others in their development, and this in two distinct ways:

   (a) Each stage can be seen to follow the previous stage of the delta according to some more or less determinate rule;

   (b) The overall development of a delta can be shown to have a unity, so that it is the development "of" some (relatively) unified thing.

(5) *Relative arbitrariness of origin:* The origin assigned to any delta is, I have argued, to some degree arbitrary; other origins could have been assigned. The degree of arbitrariness varies from case to case. There are reasons why the Japanese attack

on Pearl Harbor is considered to have begun
World War II; there is less reason for what we
posit as the first moment in the Great Depres-
sion.

(6) *Endurance:* Some deltas are relatively short-
lived, such as that generated by my turning on
the coffeepot this morning. Others persist for
enormous periods of time, as with the Big Bang.

(7) *Persistence of origin:* Some origins are punctual
events, which happen and are then over with
while their effects continue, like the assassination of Archduke Ferdinand. Other origins persist as things and continue to generate effects at
the core of their deltas, as the works of Plato
continue to generate interpretations and debate.

(8) *Containment:* Some deltas are confined to relatively bounded areas; an inflammation, for
example, is confined to a single body. Others
spread their effects into a variety of spheres, as
did the assassination of Lincoln.

Some of these properties make a given delta more amenable to one or another ontology. An uncontained delta
without a persistent origin can hardly count as an ousia,
for example; one which is in no way transparent will not
be good ground for the negation ontology. The point is
not that we are free to assign any ontology to any being
at will. It is, rather, that whatever beings any of these
ontologies are applied to must participate in the overall
structure of a guiding delta.

Some of these eight properties of guiding deltas may be
related in ways which themselves call for further investigation. It stands to reason, for example, that a broad delta,
or one whose rate of proliferation varies greatly, will be

less transparent than one which progresses at an even rate. A delta which develops more slowly may endure longer than one which develops quickly, and so forth. I will leave these issues over to future research, partly for reasons of space and partly because it is unlikely that a general theory of guiding deltas would be of much immediate use. The important deltas, the ones that affect us most often and deeply, are individuals and must be studied as such—i.e., in terms of their histories, not in those of a general theory. As Davidson says regarding the weather, "the descriptions under which events interest us . . . have only remote connections with the concepts employed by the more precise known laws."[47]

Situations and Parameters

Further reasons why a general theory of guiding deltas is likely to be of less use than regional theories of the various types of such deltas will emerge if I clarify two further concepts of the emerging ontology: those of "situation" and "parameter."

The concept of situation is important because there is more than one guiding delta—indeed, there is *always* more than one. The broader it gets and the longer it proliferates, the more likely a guiding delta is to intersect with other deltas.

At any given moment, then, we stand at the intersection of an indeterminate number of guiding deltas, developments which began in the past and which are now unfolding around and even through us. The intersection of a set of guiding deltas is what I call a "situation." When we are located at that intersection, that situation is *our* situation. In the diagram below, person α is at the intersection of deltas A–D:

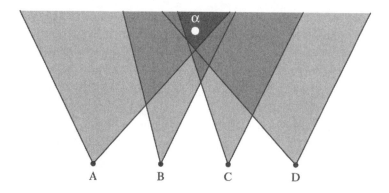

From the position of α, A, B, C, and D will all appear to be converging on α. They make up the "situation" of α.

The intersections of guiding deltas—the situations in which we find ourselves—are highly contingent, even if the deltas in question are ancient ones. Catholicism and Protestantism, two components of the overall story of Christianity which themselves qualify as guiding deltas, are both ancient and not particularly contingent; given the basic nature of Christianity, it can be argued that it was likely to develop into these two main forms. That they intersected in such a way that I found myself with a Protestant mother and a Catholic father was clearly far more contingent than either. Though intersections of guiding deltas tend to be more contingent than those deltas themselves, they also tend (in line with Davidson's remark quoted in the "discussion" on p. 139) to be of more importance to us. Because of this, the nature of an individual situation cannot be deduced from a general theory of the types and properties of guiding deltas. More appropriate, once again, is the study of such deltas as individuals, i.e., in terms of their histories.

The idea of an intersection of guiding deltas suggests

two further properties which they can have relative to one another:

(9) *Weight:* The "weight" of a guiding delta is, very roughly, how much of a given situation it determines. A "weighty" delta determines more of my situation than a less weighty one. It can do this in two ways:
(a) by influencing the development of neighboring deltas, as when growth in the economy leads to a decline in religious attendance;
(b) by actually containing other deltas within it as sub-phases, as the overall story of Christianity contains Protestantism, which in turn contains, for example, Presbyterianism.
(10) *Tractability:* Some deltas are relatively easy for me to change; others are more difficult. The coffee I drank this morning has made me mildly jumpy for a while, and I can easily deal with that, but I will surely spend the rest of my life coping with the guiding deltas that originated in the religious disagreements of my parents.

Codifying the nature and respective weights of the guiding deltas that constitute the situation of some person or group is a thus concrete, complex, and often difficult enterprise. It is carried out in very different ways by such disparate fields as art and psychotherapy. Cubism, for example, visually codified the increasing abstraction being worked into natural forms by technology, especially mechanization. Rap verbally codifies the anger of young men. A standard course of Freudian psychotherapy aims at revealing to the patient the ongoing proliferation of effects originating in a traumatic event of childhood. Historians of all sorts trace the development of guiding deltas for whole societies. There is thus no unified study of guiding deltas, and no clear path to establishing one; even a general theory would not get us very far.

The topic of guiding deltas seems now to have devolved into a welter of disparate, occasional, and even personal judgments, much as ontology briefly did earlier. That it has not quite done so can be seen from the final basic concept of this emerging ontology: that of a parameter.

To understand this concept, we note that the relation between types and tokens of such deltas is an unusual one, for here there can be no token without a *recognized* type. It is evident from their mating behavior that horses are members of the species *equus caballus* independently of the fact that humans classify them in that way (or in any way). Guiding deltas, by contrast, do not exist independently of our recognition, however inexplicit, of their existence. And that recognition, I argued above, requires that we refer to types of such deltas, to our knowledge of the standard ways in which one state of affairs leads to others. That standard way is what I call a "parameter" (the "templates" I referred to in the specific context of pragmatic evaluation are one variety of parameter). A parameter thus has two fundamental components: the description of an initial being or state of affairs and a set of predictions/guidelines for how that original state is to develop into other states. What I call the "predictions" simply tell us that a situation of one type will be replaced by one of another type; the "guidelines" tell us what we must do, if anything, to make that happen. The balance between predictions and guidelines varies with the parameter in question.

Consider what happens when you hear someone cry

"fire!" (and not merely say "fire," or whisper it, or sing it).
You should:

1. Locate the fire and determine its size.
2. Determine whether you are safe.
3. If not, make yourself safe by moving away from
   the fire.
4. Once you are safe, see if others are safe.
5. If they are not, help make them safe
   a. By crying "fire!" to them;
   b. By physically moving them away from the
      fire;
   c. By otherwise facilitating their movement
      away from the fire;
   d. By calling for help in getting them away from
      the fire.
6. If all others are safe, try and put the fire out:
   a. By smothering it
      i. With a covering;
      ii. With water;
   b. By depriving it of fuel;
   c. By calling for help in putting out the fire. . . .

And so on. This is a much simplified formulation of
what I will call the "fire!" parameter. That we can in-
voke it as quickly as we do when we hear someone shout
"fire!" testifies to our facility with guiding deltas in general, and to the naturalness with which we think "in" parameters. That we can remember having been taught that
parameter, or parts of it, indicates that at least some guiding deltas are culturally specific.

> This kind of complex response to an utterance, like less "pro-
> grammed" kinds, includes a good deal of inferring, broadly
> defined. If I determine that I am not safe (step 2), I can be said

to "infer" that I should move away from the fire (step 3). The response also includes a good deal that is not inferring, such as actually moving away from the fire. If we limited our statement of the fire parameter to just the inferences that it contains, we would get something resembling what Robert Brandom calls an "inferentialist" account of the meaning of "fire!" Common with Brandom is the view that

> Expressions come to mean what they mean by being used as they are in practice, and intentional states and attitudes have the contents they do in virtue of the role they play in the behavioral economy of those to whom they are attributed.[48]

The contrast with Brandom lies in my not restricting "practice" to inferring. Such restriction is often, as here, quite artificial; the inferences we make are deeply enmeshed in the rest of our behavior, and separating them out is rather like trying to play a concerto with just your ring fingers. As Wittgenstein put it,

> An inference is the transition to an assertion, and so also to the behavior corresponding to the assertion. I "draw the consequences" not only in words, but also in actions. (*PI* § 486, my translation)

One reason for making that separation is in order to do what Brandom does: to show that logic is best understood as the way we make explicit certain of our very basic linguistic practices, and so is a "sophisticated, late-coming sort of propriety of inference."[49] Rooted in specifiable practices rather than the "nature of things," logic is a very special tool in our toolbox.

Each guiding delta is an individual, and its intersections with other deltas are not only individual but highly contingent and therefore likely to be unique. The parameters which we require in order to recognize such deltas, and thus for them to exist at all, are by contrast types. Though they exist psychologically as stereotypes, and so vary to some extent from person to person, many of them also exist intersubjectively, and indeed are conditions for intersubjectivity. The "fire!" parameter sketched above, for example, does not consist simply in various sequentialized activities of my mind, or even of my mind and body together. It is materially codified in the positioning of doors, fire escapes and extinguishers, telephones, windows, and so on. Similarly, the "restaurant frame" of Shank and Abelson (which I would call a "restaurant parameter") gains material, and so intersubjective, codification in the design of restaurants.[50] Indeed, (almost) any encounter that we have with others unrolls as an instance of a type of encounter, i.e., of a parameter, and depends on common definitions of various other aspects of the situation.

The concept of the guiding delta is intended to capture, with two qualifications, the common ground of the two "contestatory" ontologies listed above. In chapter 2 I noted the way Dasein, for Heidegger, "projects itself upon," thematizes, or interprets, contexts of involvement. Such contexts are not themselves pure products of interpretation; they pre-exist it (though Dasein's self-projection onto a context of involvement may change some things about that context). Thus pre-existing the projective/interpretive/thematizing activity of Dasein, these contexts are what Heidegger, earlier in Being and Time, *calls a "totality of involvement" (*Bewandtnisganze: SZ 66–88t).

*Such a "totality" is structured purposively, or in terms of what Heidegger calls the "in-order-to" (*um-zu), *meaning that to encounter any being as having "involvement" is to encounter it as appropriate (*geeignet) *or inappropriate (*ungeeignet) *for various projects already underway. The qualities which give a being such appropriateness or inappropriateness are its currently salient ones (*Eigenschaften—*or, as we might say,* Eigen-schaften). *Other beings to which it relates via its* *appropriateness—as a hammer relates to nails and wood—are themselves appropriate for some things and not for others. A totality of involvement is thus a set of purposively structured relations among beings which can be used together to achieve an end; as the phrase "in-order-to" suggests, the relations are temporal ones. To rephrase an example of Heidegger's (SZ 84), I pick up the hammer and nail simultaneously; I then position the nail; I then strike it with the hammer, so that two pieces of wood will stick together, so that I can eventually build a roof, so that somebody, finally, can dwell beneath that roof.*

Such a set of "in order to's," for Heidegger, always ends with a way in which I and others can exist, with what Heidegger calls a "possibility of Dasein's [our] being." The purposive structure which constitutes totalities of involvement thus ends in our *purpose. All totalities of involvement converge ultimately upon Dasein:*

> Whenever something has an involvement (*Bewandtnis*), *which* involvement it has in each case been traced out in advance in terms of the totality of involvement [in play . . . which] is "earlier" than any single item of equipment (*Zeug*). . . . But the totality of involvement itself goes back ultimately to Dasein, a "towards-which" in which there is *no* further involvement: this "towards-which" is . . . an entity whose Being is defined a Being-in-the-world. (*SZ* 84)

*The various possibilities of Dasein's Being also converge, this time on its "ownmost" (*eigenste*) possibility of Being, which is death (SZ 258f). The global totality thus constituted is what Heidegger calls "world."*

This is as far as I will follow Heidegger's discussion of world. It is clear that in spite of the many variations in the concrete projects and contents that make it up, world for Heidegger has a structural unity provided, ultimately, by the convergence of "in order to's" on a final end, which for Heidegger is not a goal but death itself. It is not difficult here to see a rethinking of Aristotle's portrayal of the human world, at the beginning of Nicomachean Ethics, *as a hierarchy of ends—all aiming at, and bound together by, not death but the ultimate goal of* eudaimonia, *happiness or flourishing. Even the words Heidegger*

uses to convey the purposive structure of totalities of involvement—
um-zu—*read like a translation of Aristotle's standard phrase*
hou heneka.

*The concept of the guiding delta aims to purge totalities of in-
volvement of this residual teleological structure. Guiding deltas
do not all lead to "possibilities of Being," and they do not all
converge on death; mostly they just fade away. Their unity with
other contexts does not constitute a single overarching "world"
as the ultimate horizon for all meaning, but is a matter of
largely contingent intersections.*

*Connecting guiding deltas with Hegel is simpler and can be
done via his concept of mediation, which as he characterizes it
in the* Encyclopedia *is "a having-advanced (*Hinausgegangen-
sein*) from a first to a second, and a proceeding forth from
things that are distinct."*[51] *Mediation as the passage from one
thing or state to another (from an "immediate" beginning to a
"mediated" ending) applies to everything in the world for Hegel,
and in particular to Being itself, which at the beginning of his
Logic passes over into Nothing and eventually into the "mediated" moment of becoming. The developmental character of guiding deltas is thus captured by the negation ontology; to posit a
thing or event as the beginning of such a delta is to render it
"immediate" in Hegel's sense and the further development of
the delta is one of mediation.*

*However, Hegel's phrase "proceeding forth from things that are
distinct" suggests the opposite, for it suggests that mediation for
him is a unification rather than a ramification, in the sense that
several distinct things give rise to a single process. Not only is the
ramifying of guiding deltas absent—it seem to be replaced by its
opposite.*

*A process which comes to rest in something unified is, in tradi-
tional parlance, a "teleological" process, and so we see that Hegel
has the same problem with intrusive teleology as Heidegger has.
If we subtract that unified ending from Hegel's conception of
mediation, thereby losing the "second" element in his above
characterization of it, we have mediation as merely an advance
from a "first," with no end in view. This "meta-Hegelian" con-*

ception of mediation, though it does not mention ramification, can tolerate it.

Hegel's contribution here is a way to evaluate guiding deltas, and with them parameters, as rational. As I argued in chapter 2, such evaluation comes about by applying another "meta-Hegelian" concept, that of minimal negation: When the difference between one stage of a delta and the stage following it is merely a single change, then the delta (or parameter) develops rationally. Teleology is not a necessary condition for such rationality.

The ontologies offered by Hegel and Heidegger both need to be purged of their intrusive teleology, and this is one qualification on my reception here of their thought. The other qualification arises from the fact that neither of them explicitly distinguishes guiding deltas from parameters; neither distinguishes the types from the tokens. Since guiding deltas, as I have argued, cannot exist unless they are recognized, and cannot be recognized except from types, the distinction is an important one.

Hegel's rejection of it is principled. It is argued via his account of concrete individuality as "determinate universality," i.e., as a being which can be completely captured in predicates, and hence in universals (Werke VI 296–301/618–622). As Kierkegaard argued often and well, this identification of concrete individuality with determinate universality means that Hegel cannot account for the uniqueness of individual beings (especially human ones).[52] Hegel's unfortunate move here is itself motivated by his doctrine of the unity of thought and being, which as I have unpacked it elsewhere is in turn motivated by a rejection of the ineffable: If we cannot talk about something, it does not exist for us (CW 235f). For Heidegger, in the passages cited, there is simply a failure to address such issues as: If two people are hammering nails to make two different roofs, are they involved in the same totality of involvement? Some of his statements (one of which is quoted above) suggest that the context of involvement is prior to my use of the tools which belong to it, which would mean that he believes this is indeed the case. But the point is not made explicitly.

Conclusion: Ontology and the Enlarged Toolbox

"Ontology" is best conceived, then, as an effort to put forth a model for the basic structure of individual things without specifying the domain to which that model is supposed to apply. What bivalent thought has traditionally seen as ontology's universality claim is better viewed as a refusal to make any claim at all with regard to scope. This explains why several ontologies have, in practical terms, coexisted in the West from its beginnings. Philosophy's obsession with truth explains why that coexistence, so crucial to the nature of ontology itself, has not been noticed other than as a sorry state to be overcome by argument.

Because they specify no domain for their application, the various available ontologies cannot be given overall acceptance or rejection, nor can they even be given overall rankings. Decisions as to their merits must be made on a case-by-case basis as we evaluate how, on the most basic level, to take individual beings. This, I have argued, can only be a pragmatic decision, based on the consequences of adopting this or that ontology. The pragmatism of ontology is in itself is a salutary feature, for it replaces the coercion normally associated with philosophical theories (argument is the "tether" that turns true opinion into knowledge, *Meno* 97d) with the more benign idea of invitation. By not specifying a domain of application, each ontology invites us to use it as often as possible.

But if adopting this or that way of taking a being is an option, then that being must have at least some properties which are knowable independently of such adoption. If the adoption has consequences, moreover, the being itself must have a certain sort of causal, or "guiding," property as well. This suggests a new ontology, one which is keyed to the features that any being must have in order that we can decide which of the available ontologies applies to it. This new ontology will be more general than the others, then, for it applies to more beings than any one of them—in practice if not in the scope of its invitation. Its plenary examples are just the class of ontologically decidable beings.

The three key concepts of this emerging ontology are those of the guiding delta, the situation, and the parameter. Each of these, in turn, is coordinated primarily (though not exclusively) to one of the basic components of the enlarged philosophical toolbox that I advocated in chapter 2.

In order to understand the parameters structuring a given guiding delta, we must have (a) a formulation of the parameter, (b) a description of the development of the delta, and (c) a comparison of the two. The parameter can be formulated in a line-by-line fashion, like a script (as I did with the "fire!" parameter above). The comparison then takes the form of looking at each line of the parameter and matching it against the description of one stage in the delta. This is a straightforward act of subsumption, as has been much discussed in the philosophical tradition, and as such is guided by the norm of truth. This phase of our understanding is keyed primarily to the delta, which must be captured by the parameter as it develops.

We must also look, however, not only at the individual stages of the delta and the parameter, but at their sequence. Here we do not merely match the formulated parameter against the descriptions, but seek to see whether there is more in the one than in the other. If (a) there are developments in the delta that are not matched by lines in the formulation, then we conclude that the parameter in question is not all that is in play, that "something else is going on." If (b) there are lines in the formula that are not instantiated in the delta, we conclude that the parameter is "overdetermined" with respect to the delta. In such cases, we are judging not primarily with reference to truth, though we do make judgments of truth in the course of doing this, but with reference to comprehensiveness and order, with reference to what, in chapter 2, I called Nobility. Our aim is to formulate a parameter, or reformulate it, so that it matches all the (salient) stages of the delta with a stage of its own, and does so in a rationally continuous way. At its extreme, the parameter is thus not only Noble but rational (though not necessarily good or useful or, indeed, anything but rational). On this "narrative" level, then, we are primarily occupied with the parameter.

A "situation," finally, is the convergence of a number of guiding deltas. Such convergence is often incomplete. It is the incompleteness of the convergence among a group of parameters, or what I will call the "gaps" among them, which constitutes what I call the "authentic future" of a situation. I will discuss here three sorts of such gap.

(A) *External gap:* The consequences of a given event, though in some sense coming "close" to those of another, do not actually intersect with it, so that the two deltas develop toward one another, so to speak, but do not completely converge. Such discontinuities are not absent phases within a guiding delta, but occur between one delta and another. Usually the term "close" refers us not to causal convergence in which several "conjoint causes" produce one thing or event, but to an individual life. Effects of my decision to be a philosopher, for example, sometimes intersect with effects of my decision to become a father, but often enough these two stories remain separate, and I must cope with their separation. The fact that I participate in a number of stories (deltas) which do not affect one another but which all affect me, is an important aspect of the freedom with which I shape my life.

The techniques of demarcation highlight such gaps in my situation—the specific ways things do not cohere in it. For a linguistic example, consider the disparity between the different meanings of "cannot" in "the categorical imperative cannot yield concrete ethical recommendations" and "you cannot have the keys to the car tonight." Understanding this discrepancy frees me, who as a philosopher-daddy am able to use "cannot" in both senses, from the specific contexts of those respective uses— and frees me, then, for an unpredictable future.

(B) *Beginning gap:* To say that event *e* begins a new guiding delta is not to say that *e* is uncaused. It is to say that the causes of *e* do not matter, for the moment at least, because we are taking it to trigger a new guiding delta. The parameter under which that delta comes may be an old and familiar one, as when a meaningful glance suddenly turns a friendship into a love affair. Once it has been rendered recognizable (e.g., by being repeated or written down) it may also, however, turn out to be a truly new parameter, one with a structure of its own which has not been formulated before.

Such a new parameter will register its novelty as a series of discrepancies between what is actually being repeated and the sequence of events encoded in already formulated parameters. Registering and interrogating these discrepancies is, once again, an enterprise of demarcation. It enables the new parameter to be formulated in the full breadth of its distinction from all that has been "up to now."

(C) *Ending gap:* When a guiding delta fades away, the fact is not always obvious. At such times, events which seem to be further developments in an ongoing delta are not truly so, or are ambiguous. In that case, discrepancies will once again arise between the way the delta "should" develop and the way it is actually developing. It is easy enough, and often comfortable, to overlook such discrepancies.

Calling attention to such things—as Derrida does on a philosophical level in his obsessive dissections of the fading cultural guidance of the delta he calls "metaphysics" —is an important part of demarcating the future.

Where narrative permits us to connect events by seeing them as successive stages in the development of a parameter, demarcation enables us to see the discrepancies among guiding deltas which become evident on the level of the overall situation.

Subsumption is thus "keyed" to the apprehension of deltas, narrative to the formulation of parameters, and demarcation to the clarification of situations. As I argued in chapter 2, all three philosophical tools should be in use at all times, but each of them is more closely coordinated with one of the dimensions of the emerging ontology than with the others.

Once we understand what ontology is (and why, in fact, ontolog*ies are*), it is easy to see that ontology is both possible and necessary. Actually "doing ontology" in a concrete situation, in such a way as both to clarify and carry forward that situation—to "situate" us in it rationally—is a more difficult matter. For to clarify and carry forward a situation is not only to locate ourselves within it, but to change that situation itself; it is to "construct" our situation. Doing this rationally, and in particular philosophically, requires narrative and demarcation as well as truth-oriented thought.

4 | The Edge of Ethics

"Ethics," as understood in modernity, focuses on the rightness and wrongness of actions. The focus is misleading in that actions never occur outside of wider social and natural contexts to which they respond. Individual, community, and society clearly constitute such contexts, on different levels of the natural and what I will call the "human" world. This world comprises our interpersonal relationships as well as the natural givens, institutions, and arrangements which shape and facilitate them. It is often unhelpful to treat those levels separately from one another, just as it is generally unhelpful to treat the north pole of a magnet without regard to the south.

As I will use the term, then, "ethics" is the set of answers to the ancient question *pôs deî zén,* how is it necessary to live. This Greek formulation expands the scope of ethics beyond the modern conception in two ways. First, it does not specify whether the living "thing" is a person, a community, the whole human species, or indeed the entire biosphere. Ethics so understood is, so to speak, expanded vertically, upwards through the human world so that it incorporates not only ethics in the traditional sense, but social and political philosophy as well. Ethics then comprises the general principles by which life should be navigated, and in particular how individuals and communities should make their way through the human world.

> *Such "vertical expansion" of ethics to embrace relationships and institutions is nothing new. Hegel and Aristotle are only two of the many philosophers who have held that actions cannot be evaluated independently of the historical, cultural, and political contexts in which they occur. For one example of the distortions introduced by a rigid separation of these different levels, consider the "problem" of altruism: Ought I always act in my own self-interest? Can I act any other way?*

> *Such issues are not pressing for thinkers like Hegel and Aristotle because the idea that I can, and maybe occasionally should, place society's interests above my own presupposes that what "society" needs and values is not necessarily what I need and value. What is good for my community, and so my community itself, is seen as something "outside" of me, which I can accept or reject. The levels of individual and community do not, of themselves, affect one another; whether they do so in a given case—whether considerations of the communal good affect my actions—is up to me.*

> *Some divergence between my interests and those of others is normal; the question is whether such divergence is sufficiently great or common to provoke philosophical discussion. Complete separation between self and society obtains, if at all, only on the widest and most paranoid levels of modern society. If, by contrast, I am constituted through my interchanges with others (society, family, perhaps tribe or clan or religion—or other "levels" of the hu-*

*man world), then I will tend, first of all, to learn what I need
and value by watching them. I will value what those around
me value, and they—having also been acculturated in that
society—will do likewise.*

The homogenization of values *is a basic ethical mechanism
obviously necessary to any society; its survival value for the
individual is equally obvious. Together with such homogenizing, in any society successful enough to endure, must go a kind
of* polishing of desire, *which rubs away the sharp corners and
hard edges of individual personality, seeing to it that the things
we all seek will be good for the community as a whole, or at
least not deleterious to it. As Shaftesbury pointed out, such polishing and its result, "politeness," are possible only in society,
and society is possible only through them:*

> All politeness is owing to Liberty. . . . We polish one
> another, and rub off our Corners and rough Sides by a
> sort of amicable Collision. To restrain this, is inevitably to
> bring a Rust upon Men's Understanding 'Tis a destroying
> of Civility, Good breeding, and even Charity itself. . . . [1]

*The often-made case against modern media, especially when
they are employed in the service of advertising, can be phrased
in terms of a disconnect between the homogenizing of desire
and its polishing. Advertising is directed, of course, to making
us all want the same thing (an SUV, a Big Mac, a new house)
without asking whether it is good for society to have large numbers of people wanting that thing. The individual is thus separated from considerations of communal good by the very same
process which homogenizes her with other members of the
community.*

*Both homogenizing and polishing are phenomena of inter-
change between levels of the human world, not a matter of any
one level; they show different levels transforming one another.
Failing to see the many sorts of such interchange leads us to
miss the many complex and highly effective ways in which values and interests are socially coordinated. The presupposition of
a rigid separation between individual and society abets the sepa-*

ration between homogenizing, which is constitutive of individu-
als and their desires, and polishing, which coordinates these
for the common good. Issues like that of whether altruism is
possible or desirable thus owe much of their prominence to mod-
ern media.

The second point about the Greek formulation is that it asks not how it is necessary to act, but how it is necessary to live. It thus pushes toward a "horizontal expansion" of ethics, beyond the sphere of action altogether.

Exchanges among the levels I have identified—individual, community, society, species—are often more ethically significant than what happens on each level separately. But those exchanges happen on the "edge" of ethics as traditionally conceived. The edge of ethics is the place where nature, society, and community guide me, even as I seek to transform them. It is the place where I have to respect things and people instead of act on or with them—i.e., where I must *situate* myself with respect to them. At the edge of ethics, individual actions are channeled by relationships, which can harden into institutions.

My basic claim is that in order to act ethically, we must have defined the situation we are in; we must have satisfied ourselves that we know what sort of thing is happening and what sort of thing needs to happen. Only then can we formulate and decide upon concrete actions and courses of action. What action-oriented views of ethics tend to leave out is that defining our situation is also an ethical undertaking, one which does not impose the clear-cut responsibilities that traditional ethics seeks but is more like a peripheral, "edgewise" envisioning of such responsibilities. Situating us among concrete circumstances, this aspect of ethical "behavior" is best viewed as *responding* to things rather than merely as acting on them; it is the place where my active freedom comes to its edge.

Alasdair MacIntyre, following Aristotle, has eloquently made the argument that ethical evaluation must take culture, society, and politics into account.

> . . . I inherit from the past of my family, my city, my tribe, my nation a variety of debts, inheritances, rightful expectations and obligations. These constitute the givens of my life, my moral starting point.[2]

This view seems to lead to moral relativism,[3] for it apparently construes my ethical "inheritance" (family, city, tribe, nation, religion, etc.) as a monolithic given to whose directives my actions conform, whether I know it or not. If such is the case, any action can only be evaluated in terms of its conformity to its tradition, and so we cannot necessarily condemn slave traders who were only acting in accordance with the accepted social mores of their day.

Such is the case, however, only if we deny—as MacIntyre does not—the phenomenon of exchange among levels. Here we would do so not by separating them too rigidly, but by unifying them so completely as to presume that society speaks with a voice so single as to become silent, something we are not even aware of, much less able to reject.

This view, which Habermas attributes to Heidegger,[4] extols tradition by ignoring history. Such unity may (possibly!) have held for the seamless Athenian polis *extolled by Pericles and (more subtly) by Aristotle. It certainly does not hold for the more complex and conflicted societies of the modern world. A nineteenth-century American slave trader, for example, was hardly following the single silent voice of his society, for he had grown up hearing such Christian teachings as "all men are brothers," and "whatever you do to the least of my brethren, you do to me." Even ancient Athens was not seamless enough to allow its sexism and slavery, however* insouciant, *to pass unchallenged. It strains credulity to think that slaves and women would have been as enthusiastic about their oppression as were the gentlemen who oppressed them, and arguments that women should be given civil status equal to those of men date from Plato's* Republic.

The voices of Christ and Plato, however faint, are not inaudible even today. We can condemn the slave trader or the ancient Athenian, then, for their refusals to hear the quiet voices and thereby to recognize what is actually going on around them— their refusals to allow all the components of their situations to be formulated in such a way that their deliberations and decisions took account of them.

This, for Aristotle, was the job of phronêsis, *practical wisdom. Ethical deliberation incorporates for him a moral scan, which begins from the general goal of all human activity—happiness— and asks what currently available action would most contribute to that. In such moral scanning, I cannot help but evaluate the traditions and institutions around me, so in* phronêsis *interchange among levels becomes rational. I, on the level of the individual, consciously allow my tradition, which is on another, much wider and older level, to affect my actions. But I do so with a view to affecting that tradition as well, i.e., to transforming it if it proves to be defective.*

This kind of rational interchange among levels of the human world reaches to the most general levels of thought, for one case of phronêsis, *noted in the previous chapter, was that of adopting one ontology rather than others on a particular occasion. That MacIntyre could have been accused of moral relativism shows, I suspect, how difficult it is for philosophers to see such interchange.*

Ontology, Agency, and Absolute Causality

No discipline, it would seem, is less "edgy" than ethics. Modern ethics in particular presupposes that we are the conscious origins of our acts, the self-aware centers of our moral lives. Its overall project, in fact, could be characterized as one of increasing our centrality to ourselves by making our decisions, the ways we make them, and the commitments we make by and through them more transparent to, and so controllable by, us—by our own individual ethical center.

And yet when we try and formulate the nature of this center, a problem arises. The problem is one of the exchange between the natural world and the moral agent. It appears, to many, that there cannot be any. On the classical modern (Newtonian) model of nature, beings of nature are wholly unfree; everything about them is caused by previous events. Nature is merely matter in motion, and in the natural order every state of affairs is completely caused by other, previous states. On more recent views of nature, such as those influenced by quantum mechanics, this strict causality is supplemented by various forms of spontaneity, such as proton decay. Since moral agents cannot be conceived either deterministically or in terms of mere spontaneity, they must be exempted from natural causality altogether. Action then becomes mysterious. Our souls, the parts of us considered to be exempt from the natural order, act; our bodies cannot. And yet our souls can only act on the world through our bodies.

We thus arrive at a two-substance problem, which we can reconstruct in more detail as follows. If "ethics" is supposed to inform us about what is good and bad, and if we are to praise what is good and blame what is bad, then ethics teaches us how to apportion praise and blame. "Ethical" praise, as I will use that term here, is special (though not unique) in that it is directed not toward an act or object, but toward whoever produced or performed it. On this first step to defining what is "ethical," to praise something "ethically" is to praise it for being a certain sort of cause.

Ethical praise, unlike other kinds, thus requires at least two good things: a cause and its effect. Praising a sunset for its beauty does not involve ethical categories but aesthetic ones, as praising a horse for its strength involves not ethical but practical categories. It is not until we praise the *cause* of the good sunset or horse or action that we even begin to move toward the ethical dimension. Ethical praise is most closely distinguished not from aesthetic encomium but from blame, which is likewise concerned not with bad things but with their causes.

The fact that ethical praise and blame belong in the realm of the causal places them also in the realm of the contingent, and this gives us the second step toward defining what is "ethical." If I praise something, it is because that thing is better than it could have been; if I criticize it, it is because it is worse than it need have been. To praise someone ethically, or to blame her, thus presupposes that she need not have caused what she caused; she could, as J. L. Austin puts it, have done otherwise.[5] If I have drawn a very bad picture because I am incapable of drawing a good one, your dispraise of my efforts is not "ethical" in this sense, but aesthetic. If I could have drawn a good one but contented myself with a shoddy work, your criticisms may include ethical ones. In sum, a person who could have done otherwise, but did not, is free; ethical praise and blame, and so ethics itself as the art of apportioning them, all presuppose that we are free.

Responsibility and freedom, as I noted, cannot be allocated to nature, so modern ethics comes to reside within a tidy little "supernatural" realm or perspective, that of our freedom; when we cause things in a way we need not have done, we act freely. Among free acts, some are good, and the job of ethics is teaching us how to do good things consistently. Ethical praiseworthiness is the goal and stabilizing principle of this realm, but freedom defines its boundaries. It is therefore worth asking what "freedom" is.

That question takes us to the edge of ethics, the border area where freedom merges into necessity—or, in this case, exchanges with it. Things get murky out there. For in contrast to such categories as "red" or "loud," there exist no indisputable examples of freedom. We know this because there exist no undisput*ed* examples of it. There are always people ready to argue that we are not free at all.

One reason such disputes are always underway is that on the traditional understanding of what an ontology is, all six of the limit and contestatory ontologies I listed in chapter 3 are incompatible with freedom. Substances are purely passive, and so cannot act at all—freely or unfreely. Similarly for nodes. Forces, being irrational, allow at most for what Kant called "spontaneity" (*KRV* B 474f), not for true freedom, and as Spinoza showed most clearly, the pantheistic ontology does not allow for any agent other than God; ethics consists in attaining enough understanding to get out of his way. The negation ontology locates at the core of every being not a freely acting subject, but an ongoing process of change that can be shaped but not stopped, and the diakenic ontology sees us in passive terms, as shaped by various guiding nothings.

The reason for this incompatibility between ontology and ethics is simple: freedom is incompatible not merely with various ontologies, but with the structure of ontology itself. Ontologies, like other theories, seek to explain things. Since nothing is self-explanatory, explaining things requires reducing them to other things. In the (Newtonian) modern world, where explanation normally proceeds according to what medieval philosophers called "efficient" causality, it means reducing the *explanandum* to causes which precede it in time. From an ontological point of view, then, any act is reducible to other things which precede it in time, and to say otherwise is to speak against ontology itself. The causal chain which produced any act of mine thus passes immediately beyond that act itself back to its causal antecedents and at some point beyond me altogether, which means that I can no longer be held responsible for that act. In short, ontology is explanation, and what can be explained is not free.

> *The traditional way around this was to posit freedom as itself an explanatory principle. Thus, for Augustine freedom of the will was a supernatural cause, planted in us directly by God— but a cause nonetheless. Freedom has also been viewed as a sort of "natural" principle, in the sense that its actual exercise on any occasion is determined by pre-existing states and events. Aristotle, as we will see, is a good example, but Leibniz is another. Nothing for him happens without a reason: "We can only will what we think is good, and the more developed the faculty of understanding is, the better are the choices of the will. . . . Choice is always determined by perception."[6] Thus, my choice of x on a given occasion is determined by my previous evaluation or "perception" that x is good, and by my already possessing the power to seek the good.*
>
> *As Kant points out, this destroys moral responsibility. My perception that x is good must come from somewhere, and if such perception is "natural" it must come from pre-existing conditions such as my upbringing or my brain wiring. More generally, for Kant, we know (via the Newtonian structure which the Understanding imposes on experience) that every event, including all our actions, can be explained causally—yet no one would act ethically, i.e., responsibly, unless we had at least the illusion of freedom. Hence what Kant recognized as the great dilemma of modern moral philosophy: the incompatibility of human freedom with Newtonian causality. His moral philosophy consists in trying to show that the belief that we are free, even if false, is more than a mere illusion.*
>
> *This issue has outlived the thought of both Kant and Newton in part, I think, because it expresses the more general issue of interchange among levels of the human and natural worlds, and in part because of the underlying incompatibility of ethics with ontology. Hence, I have put the matter more broadly here by claiming that human freedom is incompatible not only with*

*Newtonian physics, but with any attempt to "explain" an
action, and ultimately with ontology itself.*

Even the ontological coinages developed in chapter 3 do
not allow for freedom. In those terms, to be "responsible"
for something means to stand at the origin of a guiding
delta which includes that thing. But this has an unpleas-
ant consequence: If guiding deltas do not exist independently of our codifying of them, neither does our freedom.
It can come to be only subsequently, when my act is identified as the origin of a guiding delta. My act thus turns
out to have been performed freely only when (and if)
I am called to account for it. By accepting such a call,
and only then, I declare that I am "responsible" for the
act, and hence that I performed it freely. My freedom
dwindles to a retrospected figment of what I and others
think of me.

If ethical freedom is incompatible with any ontological
project, we may wonder why the dilemma I am discussing
arises at all. For what, in the face of our entire experience
of Being—however we experience it—would ever make
us think we were free? In fact, the problem of freedom
arises on the basis of one ontology, and only one: ousia
ontology. For only that ontology views beings not as passive, or as mere components of God, but as discrete beings
having within themselves principles of motion and rest
(cf. Aristotle, *Physics* II.1). These principles—for any given
being, its "nature"—do not precede action the way modern (efficient) causes do. Certain kinds of action are intrinsic to forms, i.e., the form engages in them every
single instant it exists, and the form does not precede
these of its effects in time.

In particular, the form of an ousia actively structures it
according to what I call disposition. It does this in virtue

of its own nature as form. It is simply the nature of form to begin to exercise disposition the moment it begins to exist in some thing, and that overall action (*energeia*) persists as long as the form exists there. To explain something as caused by a form exercising disposition is thus to come to something that requires no antecedent event to explain it. It is to come to an end of explanation, then, and so to freedom of a sort.

Another way to put this is to say that ousia ontology, alone among those I have listed, is incompatible with the claim that all causal relations among different entities may be efficient in nature. Ousia ontology also postulates the kind of formal causality we find in disposition, and that is where freedom can find ontological purchase.

> It is perhaps because ousia ontology alone allows us to conceptualize freedom, even as a problem, that it was retained by modern thought about the human realm even after ousiodic forms had been ejected from nature by modern science. Despite the loudness of their contempt for Aristotle, modern philosophers such as Descartes, Hobbes, Hume, Leibniz, Locke, and Spinoza all take ousia to be the basic structuring principle of human institutions and relationships; for details see Metaphysics and Oppression *109–202.*

Ousia ontology, then, can see moral action as a special case of the kind of activity intrinsic to form. It therefore tends to see freedom as the confluence of the ability to exercise disposition within one's self and the ability to exercise initiative on the external world. Since reason is the human form, freedom becomes the capacity to decide upon and carry out your rational intentions.

Looked at more closely, freedom so viewed presupposes several elements peculiar to ousiodic ontology, including:

(I)   A distinction between "carrying out" and "deciding upon" a course of action. "Deciding upon" an action is internal to the agent, while "carrying it out" is a matter of influencing things in the world outside (boundary).

(II) A second distinction between merely forming or formulating an intention and actually deciding upon it, the former being an intellectual enterprise of articulation and weighing (*logismos*) and the latter being the mobilization of the self around that intention (disposition).

(III) A third distinction between freedom, defined as the ability to carry out one's *rational* intentions and so defined in terms of reason, and power, defined as the ability to get what you want and so defined in terms of desire. In both freedom and power, my intention itself is not changed as it is carried out, but is realized in the world just as it existed in my mind prior to my action (initiative).

The various facets of ousia ontology are thus aligned with important aspects and presuppositions of this concept of freedom. An agent who is free in this sense is responsible both for her intentions and her acts. She is not, as Kant made clear, responsible for the *success* of her acts, i.e., for whether her initiative succeeds in realizing her intentions without change; that depends on many factors beyond her boundaries and so, perhaps, beyond her control. Nor is she responsible, as the Stoics made clear, for the location of her ethical boundaries, for what is and is not "up to her."[7]

This general view of freedom, based on ancient ontology,

carried itself over into the modern world, where it has run into a multitude of problems. Among these are:

(A) The contrast it draws between freedom and power posits the two as generically the same: both consist in the capacity to dominate either the agent's interior circumstances (disposition) or external environment (initiative). This leaves only two ways to conceive of non-oppressive social relations: either in terms of initiative as an equality of power (mutual domination), or in terms of disposition as internal to the agent, i.e., as her right to order her life as she wishes. This latter view restricts non-oppressive social relations to the indifference of a live-and-let-live mentality.

Live-and-let-live, or "negative" freedom, was decisively explored in the modern era by Locke, but its most radical exponent—so radical as to have remained largely unnoticed— was perhaps Descartes. The notable lack of an explicit ethics in Descartes's philosophy is made up for by the fact that his entire philosophy is devoted to establishing the right order of the mind's ideas and faculties, i.e., to establishing freedom as disposition as opposed to freedom as initiative (cf. MO 120–125). Freedom for him is thus entirely immanent to the individual mind; actions have no moral relevance, and Descartes, who never wrote an ethics, *in this sense wrote only on ethics.*

Freedom as mutual domination is explored in Hegel's account of forgiveness and reconciliation in the Phenomenology of Spirit. *There, consciousness is divided against itself because its inner universality is confronted by the many specific words and actions it produces; since universality is here defined as good, these words and deeds are evil, and must be repudiated or denied by consciousness. It is only when another such consciousness forgives it that consciousness is able to integrate its actions and words into its own selfhood "so that they fill out the whole range of the self" (PhS 472/408). When this takes place mutually, we have the birth of "absolute" (i.e., "absolved") Spirit. Put differently, each consciousness is able to help the other attain disposition over its words and acts. In so doing each "dominates" not the other (as in the "master/slave" section), but the other's very dominance over its own acts and words, in the sense that my dominance over my own acts is established with the help of the other. This "second degree" domination is thus mutual and emancipatory.*

(B) Interchange among levels is occluded. The question remains open, but in an oddly closed way, of the level on which such freedom resides; freedom can be either individual or collective, with those alternatives mutually exclusive. This leads to odd intuitions. To the extent that my intentions and acts conform to the mores and dictates of my culture, or to the dictates of a universal reason, their true source would seem to be the collective or "universal" which speaks through them ("I was only following orders"). If they are idiosyncratic, they seem to count as purely individual. They cannot be both. If my act starts with my learning to embody norms and dictates, it does not start with me; if it truly starts with me as an individual and so as unique, it cannot merely be an expression of more general norms.

Hegel locates the view that freedom is to be found either on the communal or the individual level, but not both, in Fichte. He does this in two early writings, The Difference between Fichte's and Schelling's System of Philosophy *(usually called the* Differenzschrift*) and* Faith and Knowledge.[8] *Each rational being, Hegel claims, is present for Fichte both as a free and rational being, on the one hand, and as mere matter to be* *manipulated and formed. This dichotomy, moreover, is absolute; each side of it is what the other side is not (Werke II 81/144).*

Society must for Fichte, continues Hegel, be founded on one principle or the other; the individual must be either a free being of infinite worth, or mere matter. In the latter case we locate rationality not in the individual but above her, in the community— more specifically (of course) in the rational community, the state. As Hegel writes in Faith and Knowledge,

> According to the principle of the system, the lawful, and the erection of the lawful as of the state, is a being-for-self, absolutely opposed to liveliness and individuality. . . . Individuality finds itself under absolute tyranny. The law ought to prevail (*das Recht soll geschehen*) not as inner but as external freedom of individuals, which is just their being subsumed under a completely alien concept. (II 425/183)

The individual thus sinks under a mass of laws and regulations, each rationally enacted for the greater good of the whole. Such a state, the Differenzschrift *tells us, is a "machine" (Werke II 87/148f).*

In the former case, and also countenanced by Fichte's thought (in Hegel's view), the individual as such is accorded infinite worth and full civil rights. The only reason for my doing anything is then my personal insight, in which I pick and choose moral principles to coincide with my own wishes. In such a state, according to Faith and Knowledge, *morality assumes the form of "raising all moral contingencies into the form of the concept and giving immorality (Unsittlichkeit) justification and a good conscience" (Werke II 426f/184).*

As I argued in The Company of Words, *Hegel's presentation of the radical absence of interchange between individual and state was a prescient description of the Cold War (CW 17f).*

(C) Also left open, again in an oddly closed way, is whether the internal ordering which produces an act is itself produced at the moment of the act (*pathos*) or is a fixed disposition of the agent (*hexis*). The former view leads to an ethics of decision and choice; the latter to virtue ethics. Each of these is in turn a threat to the other. The ethics of decision looks for the beginning of the act in the moment, rather as individualistic ethics looks for it in the individual; virtue ethics, like the ethics of the collective, looks for the source of an action in something more general and enduring.

(D) As Aristotle argued (*NE* III.1), I cannot be held responsible for what I do not know (though I can in certain cases be held responsible for my lack of knowledge). Hence, for an act to be truly free, all its conditions must be known to the agent, including both what reason prescribes and what the internal and external circumstances are. If any such condition of action is unknown to the one who performs it, then she cannot be held responsible for the act and did not perform it freely. This requirement is highly counterfactual, which leads—first of all in Aristotle himself—to attempts to discriminate morally relevant conditions of an act, those which make it good or bad, from morally irrelevant ones.

Aristotle (at NE *III.1 1110b 18–1111b 3) distinguishes knowledge of the specific circumstances of an act from knowledge of the moral rules that ought to govern it; the latter is morally relevant knowledge. So is knowledge of the usual way things happen, i.e., in my terms of the parameters currently in play. We are not morally responsible if, unbeknownst to us, unusual circumstances obtain. If I want to practice archery and set my target up*

> next to a road so that when I miss the target my arrow flies into the road and kills someone, I am morally responsible. If I set my target parallel to the road, and my arrow flies into a bush where someone is taking a nap and kills that person, I am not responsible.

> The counterfactuality of the demand for knowledge of all morally relevant conditions is evidenced by Kant's account of ethical action—the "determination of the will"—as having only a single condition, the ethical law; the act itself consists in the submission of the will to that law. This "act" is a profoundly strange one. Not only may it have no effects whatever on the world, we cannot know if we ever commit it or not, because we cannot know if its single condition obtains; we might not be free at all, and we may always have had hidden motives which produced our action but of which we were unaware, in which case our act was not truly free.

The first three of these problems pose a series of unhappy choices (domination/indifference, individual/collective, decision/character), and these are oddly difficult to mediate. Why such closure? Why can these opposed characteristics not simply be, like "hot" and "cold" or "large" and "small" (or, as I argued in chapter 2, "true" and "false") the extremes of continua? Why so many either/ors?

The answer to this question, which also clarifies the presence on my list of the strongly counterfactual (D), lies in the modern deployment of the ousia ontology. Such modern deployments hold that, in order to be held responsible for my actions, I must cause them in the radical sense that on the moral plane I am their *sole* cause—they can have no cause but me, and cannot be explained beyond saying that I chose to perform them. Freedom is thus, in Kant's words, "a power of absolutely beginning a state" (*KRV* B 473). I will call this view of moral agency the "absolute causation" thesis. It is a radical denial of interchange between the moral agent and any other level of nature or society. Even guidance by the mores of one's society is or should be the result of a moral choice, one which I make absolutely alone.

It is unclear why praise and blame should require absolute causation. If my roof leaks, I have no problem assigning responsibility to the hole in it, thus making a sort of "quasi-ethical" judgment on that hole: I view it as the cause of bad things (my judgment is only quasi-ethical because the hole, being just a hole, could not have done otherwise). I can "blame" the hole for the leak, and can undertake to repair it in various ways—all the way to eliminating it altogether, the ultimate sanction. None of this requires me to see the hole as the absolute cause of the leak, in the sense that the leak can only be explained by saying the hole did it, as if nothing could explain the hole itself.

If we apply this view to humans, issues concerning praise and blame can be handled fairly easily. We could justify executing a serial murderer, for example—surely the ultimate in "blaming" someone for her acts—by claiming that whatever wiring is amiss in her brain has rendered her something like a mad dog, from whom society must be protected. So why not protect it? Such a view is in fact very close to Aristotelianism—an eminently respectable position.

> For Aristotle at Nicomachean Ethics III.1, an act is "voluntary" (hêkôn) if its cause is "in" the agent; if the cause is outside, the agent "contributes nothing" and the act is involuntary (NE 1110a 1–b 3). At this point, then, Aristotle seems to agree with the absolute causation thesis: I can only be held responsible for an action if that action originates within me.

> When we look more closely, however, the agreement becomes problematic. According to de Anima III.10, the two things in the mind which contribute to our actions are reason (nous,

dianoia) *and desire* (orexis). *Of these, it is desire which, strictly speaking, produces movement, for "reason is never found without desire"* (de Anima *433a 9–11). Hence, if Aristotle is going to accept absolute causation, desire must be the* only *explanation for a person's action; it cannot itself be caused by anything. But in fact desire is always for something we do not yet have, and hence is caused by something outside itself; it is a "moved mover," while its object is an "unmoved mover"* (de Anima *433b 15–17). Desire is thus "in" the agent, but is caused by something—its object—which can be outside her, such as the glass of water for which she thirsts.*

When the agent is a moral person, however, her ultimate desire is not for an external object but for her own well-being (eudaimonia); *she will drink the water, which contributes to her health, but will pass by the chocolate sundae, which does not. And as Book One of the* Nicomachean Ethics *argues at length, even her most "internal" desire for her own well-being is caused by something—by her human nature, which was received from her father, who therefore can in a very general way be assigned responsibility for her character (see* Generation of Animals *IV.3 767a 36–768b 14). Hence, every action has causes which come from outside the agent; "she desired it" is never the final explanation. Aristotelian ethics thus turns out to deny the absolute causation thesis while salvaging the ethical distinction between good and bad, now seen in terms of the distinction between an ultimate object of desire which is within the self (as its own well-being) or outside it (such as a chocolate sundae).*

This does not mean that Aristotle's account of moral causality is not in some respects kin to absolute causation, or that he escapes all of the problems listed above (particularly A), but discussion of how and when he falls victim to them would take us too far astray here.

The reason for viewing ethical causality as a case of absolute causality is, I take it, the affiliation of this view of ethics with the ousia ontology in its modern deployment. Unlike Aristotle's, that deployment remains, even today, within the Christian horizon of a creator God. As I noted in the preceding "discussion," an Aristotelian human being gets her form from her father. There is no great difficulty, on such principles, in assigning to a father a degree of responsibility for his child's character, and in a general way for her misdeeds (Aristotle even assigns such responsibility to her ethical leaders, the lawgivers who "make the citizens good" [*NE* 1103b 3f]). But for a Christian thinker such as Augustine, a person receives her human form directly from God, and there is enormous difficulty in tracing responsibility for someone's evil deed back beyond the person who actually commits it—for the next candidate in line is God himself, who can do no evil. Hence Augustine's account of free will, all the way through *de libero arbitrio*, is closely associated with his discussion of the problem of evil.

The modern dilemma concerning freedom thus has ontological roots—specifically, in the Christian version of the ousia ontology, which when modulated into the thesis of absolute causation denies all interchange between a moral agent and outside factors. Unless we want to return to the Aristotelian version of that ontology, which has problems of its own, we must find a different ontology for the free agent.

Ethics and Consciousness

In formulating a different ontological basis for conceiving freedom, I will first look at problem (D), the claim that in order for an act to be free, all its morally relevant conditions must be known to the agent. That this claim is untenable is the focus of the postmodern "critique of the subject"—a critique which is in turn given legitimacy by problem (A), which maintains that the only way ousiodic modernity (and the ancient world as well) can conceive of freedom is in terms of domination. Is it possible to formulate a view of freedom which does not require us to be aware of all the conditions of our acts, or even of all the "morally relevant" ones, and which does not conceive freedom as a kind of domination?

> The end game of these aporias is presented most clearly in the work of Michel Foucault. In such "middle" works as Surveiller et punir,[9] Foucault conceives of agency as "power" and also posits power's workings as almost wholly unknown to us. An ethical agent's pathê and hexeis, as well as the agent herself and her community, are all shot through with power, which is the only active force in the Foucaldian universe. Foucault is only drawing more clearly here conclusions which Kant should also have reached, for if we cannot know that we are free, then the free Kantian will is in truth unfathomable. To call it "my" will then has no sense; it is a power beyond comprehension.

I will focus this discussion by referring to empirical research reported by Tor Nørretranders in *The User Illusion*.[10] The upshot of this research is that decisions are actually made about half a second *before* we are aware of making them. All conscious decisions are therefore after the fact—re-enactments of a decision already taken unconsciously.

This possibility is allowed for in my earlier characterization of ethical decision as the mobilization of interior resources around a course of action. For as both Kant and Freud have taught us, our psychic resources, and the ways they organize themselves, are not necessarily conscious. There is then no psychological reason why ethical decisions need to be conscious decisions. This possibility is obviously disturbing to ethics, because it suggests that not only are some morally relevant conditions of an act possibly unknown to the actor, but the very decision to undertake it is unknown as well. Part of what makes this disturbing is that it accords with important testimony about how people undertake ethical actions. Many inhabitants of the French village of Le Chambon-sur-Lignane, for example, did not make a conscious decision to hide Jews from the Nazis during World War II; they simply found themselves doing it.[11] It is not uncommon for spouses to be unable to recall a moment when they decided to get married; at some point they just realized that it was inevitable.

This gives rise to many problems, but also to an insight. One of the problems is that if an action begins before the conscious decision to perform it, as Nørretranders argues, what is the point of our becoming aware of the decision at all? Why consciously re-enact something that has already been enacted unconsciously?

This problem is the problem of the survival value of what I will call ethical consciousness, and insight into it is provided by the same research that raised the problem in the first place. A conscious decision, that research suggests, is merely the re-enactment of a previous unconscious one. But what is really being "re-enacted" here? The French people who hid Jews in Le Chambon-sur-Lignane were re-enacting more than an unconscious decision half a second earlier to do that specific thing. As French Protestants, they were also re-enacting events from their own history of vicious persecution at the hands of Catholics. As former victims of efforts at extermination, they automatically identified with the Jews who came to them for help.

But why did they come to be aware of what they were doing? Why did they not just somehow "fail to notice" the Jews in their midst—as their opposite numbers, the Germans living near concentration camps, "failed to notice" what was going on there? Why did the French not hide Jews out of blind habit?

They could not, I suggest, because in this "re-enactment" they had changed places; they were not victims but providers of refuge. Hence, they could not simply repeat what had happened in the past. Rather, they understood themselves via what, in chapter 2, I called a "communal narrative," here, the story of a community which is no longer personally threatened but which is still able to remember what dire threats are like.

Seen as a stage in a narrative, a conscious decision is not the origin of an act, the way ousiodic ethics takes it to be—the mobilization of interior resources with respect to a future action currently being contemplated. It appears, rather, to have a cybernetic, or feedback, function. This function, in turn, is required by our temporal nature.

If the future were going to be like the past, conscious awareness of our decisions would be unnecessary; we could act strictly from habit or from behavioral principles wired into us by nature, as other animals do and as we in fact do most of the time. In this respect, one can imagine that if the Nazis had gone after the Protestants of Le Chambon-sur-Lignane, they would have run for the hills almost automatically, without thinking about it or remembering it in detail, just as they had in the past. What made it necessary for them to become aware of their situation was the *difference* between their current situation and the past—the fact that they were no longer targets themselves, but providers of refuge. What makes consciousness of our decisions necessary is the possibility that not only will the future not be like the past, but that the present has already begun to diverge from it.

Ousiodic ethics, prearmed with an ontology which posits a single origin of everything significant within the agent (its form), needs to find a single origin for moral acts. It takes for that origin what is in truth merely a conflation of ethical consciousness with ethical decision, thereby mistaking the moment in which I fix *on* the decision to be the moment in which I fix the decision itself.

On the model I am advocating, the dispositive mobilization of internal resources around a course of action (what Nørretranders calls the "readiness potential") occurs naturally, even spontaneously, in light of whatever agglomeration of propensities chemistry and habit have put into the individual who is being mobilized. Then the individual fixes consciously on the decision in order to monitor its effectiveness in circumstances which may have changed. What I will call "ethical consciousness," like ethical decision, is thus an exchange between the individual conscious agent, her chemistry and habits and other features, and natural or cultural givens. For consciousness of this type, three things are therefore necessary: a current situation; a remembered and similar situation of the past; and a cognitive system which compares the two. "Ethical consciousness," as I call it, is this work of comparison.

> This account of ethical consciousness is not advanced as a full account of moral awareness, much less as an account, or even the basis of an account, of consciousness überhaupt. Consciousness is presumably too variegated and complex a field for any single account of it to be possible. The current account does, however, converge intriguingly with two more general accounts of human consciousness.
>
> One is Daniel Dennett's suggestion, following Oscar Neumann, that consciousness arises from the "orienting response" animals take to danger.

> When a specialized alarm is triggered . . . or a general
> alarm is triggered by anything sudden or surprising (or just
> unexpected), the animal's nervous system is mobilized. . . .
> The animal stops what it is doing and does a quick scan or
> update that gives every sense organ an opportunity to con-
> tribute to the pool of available and relevant information. A
> temporary centralized area of control is established through
> heightened activity.[12]

Similarly, moral consciousness as I have described it is a tempo-
rary state triggered by the performance of a particularly conse-
quential action. It poses the question of whether that action was
appropriate for the circumstances, and whether it should be
repeated on future occasions when the circumstances are similar.
It thus requires the kind of generalized, situating scan or update
that Dennett mentions.

The other account with which this one converges is Heideg-
ger's account of the worldhood of the world at Sein und Zeit
§ 16:

> The structure of the Being of what is ready-to-hand as a
> kind of equipment is determined by references [*Verweisun-*
> *gen,* in the broad sense in which a hammer "refers" us in
> turn to the nail, the board, the wall, the house we are
> building, our future life in that house, etc.]. These refer-
> ences are not themselves observed, but are there in that
> we place ourselves among them. But in a disruption of
> reference—in the unusability [of a tool] for [something],
> the reference becomes explicit. . . . The whole context [of
> the tool's use] lights up not as something never seen before
> but as a totality already sighted previously in circumspec-
> tion [*Umsicht*]. With this, the world [the totality of such
> contexts] announces itself. (*SZ* 74)

On all these views, consciousness is not our "normal" state, but
a specific kind of response *to such things as danger, unusually*
consequential action (which is dangerous in its own way), or
blocks and disruptions in our ongoing exchanges with the envi-
ronment. When such response becomes permanent, presumably
via socialization, consciousness comes to be viewed as a realm of
its own—the "inner realm" of our awareness, one version of
Fantasy Island.

Philosophy itself, as situating, would be a function of conscious-
ness as portrayed in these three converging accounts; it is a re-
sponse to dangers or blockages in the environment, to things
not unfolding as they should. For an account of one such
philosophy-inducing check, see chapter 1.

Another intriguing feature of consciousness is directly suggested,
though left unstated, by Dennett's account, and lurks in the
background of the other two: Because it requires the unified
scanning of divergent sensory inputs, consciousness is from the
outset "aesthetic" in character—a point brought out in Heideg-
ger's Der Ursprung des Kunstwerkes, *which shows aesthetic*
consciousness to be an integration of our ways of encountering
things present-at-hand and things ready-to-hand, the two basic
ways of encountering beings which were kept separate in Being
and Time. *Aesthetic consciousness is thus, for the later Heideg-*
ger, full *consciousness.*[13]

Ethical consciousness thus has a past: it re-enacts under-
takings which have already been made. It does this because it also has a future: the monitoring of those under-
takings. The real "future" of conscious decision, that to
which it usually leads, is thus not action, but reflection.
In such reflection, I view my current action as a stage in
a narrative, as carrying forward some development coming from the past (as the French Protestants were carrying
forward their history). Because that development itself is
developing—because it is not going to be a mere repetition of the past—I need to monitor it.

In reflective monitoring, I may evaluate a specific decision with regard to at least three different axes:

(i)   Does it conform to the parameters I have devel-
      oped out of past experiences, both those specifi-
      cally similar to this one and more general ones
      of acculturation?
(ii) Where does the situation which calls forth this

decision—itself a unique intersection of a number of guiding deltas—differ from those previous situations?

(iii) Was this decision successful? What should I do now?

In other words, ethical consciousness enables me to connect reflectively to the past (i and ii) and to open up a future (ii and iii); it is both narrative and demarcative in nature. A free act or decision is not one which originates "within" the actor, and still less one of which she is the only relevant cause. It is one which relates to the past Nobly, and to the future Appropriately; it grows out of a comprehensive and rationally transparent reconstruction of the past which is not allowed to foreclose the future.

So understood, free decision is not an origin but a response. It is not unconditioned, but stands in a dialectical relationship with its conditions—that is, the exercise of freedom changes those conditions, just as they in turn circumscribe the possibilities of such exercise. Freedom, then, is neither universal nor situated. It is situating, and on many levels. I will briefly discuss three of these levels in what follows: the level of the isolated self; of relationships between two people; and finally a single case of institutionalized relations among many people, that of government. The separation of these three levels, to be sure, is artificial.

One

There is no such thing as a truly isolated moral agent, because an individual who was truly alone—without a universe—would have nothing to act on. When we speak of solitary moral agents, we really refer to an individual apart from other humans and from society, but still confronting nature. To get clearer on this, consider yourself confronted by a natural world full of duck-rabbits—those odd little creatures, corralled by Wittgenstein (*Phil Inv* 194), which are equally experienced as ducks and as rabbits. And imagine that, as in Wittgenstein's example, there is no way to decide which sort of creature you are dealing with; your experience remains fundamentally ambiguous.

Wittgenstein is arguing here that we cannot say that "I see the drawing as a picture of a rabbit" (or "as a picture of a duck") because that would imply that the drawing was somehow resolvable; I now see it as a duck, but I will eventually have enough visual information to perceive that it is a duck (or a rabbit). On the contrary, says Wittgenstein; seeing-as is not part of "perception" (Wahrnehmung) *(Phil Inv 197). Wittgenstein is coming from the long debate concerning the possibility of infallible, foundational perception—the kind of experiences whose objects Russell called "sense-data." Heidegger, with a surer grasp of how our perceptual apparatus actually functions, dismissed the possibility of such infallibility, which in turn suggests that there are no such infallible experiences; everything is a bit "duck-rabbity." If that is the case, freedom such as I am about to discuss is an ingredient in all our living, but I do not need that for my argument.*

There are four—and only four—strategies one can adopt in such a case. I have discussed them at length as the four types of what I call "poetic interaction" (cf. *PI*), but a schematic representation may be of help here. Let → be time's arrow; $s_{1...n}$ be a situation constituted by the convergence of guiding deltas 1 through n; $e_{1,2}$ be an event which could be a phase of either of two of these deltas;

and e_p be an event which cannot belong to $\{1 \ldots n\}$. The four strategies can then be schematically (though not elegantly) represented as follows:

1. $s_{1 \ldots n} \rightarrow e_{1,2} \rightarrow s_{(1v2) \ldots n}$
2. $s_{1 \ldots n} \rightarrow e_{1,2} \rightarrow (s_{1,3 \ldots n} \text{ v [and] }_{2 \ldots n})$
3. $s_{1 \ldots n} \rightarrow e_p \rightarrow s_{1 \ldots p}$
4. $s_{1 \ldots n} \rightarrow e_p \rightarrow s_{1 \ldots p \ldots}$

$s_{1 \ldots n}$ is the situation at the beginning of the action, i.e., an intersection of guiding deltas 1 through n. Some of these deltas may be what in chapter 3 I called "intractable"; they are unrolling independently of you, as do those which fall under the heading of "today's weather." You cannot affect their development but have to accommodate yourself to them. Others may be unrolling entirely under your control or even "in your head," like any of a variety of personal narratives you may or may not bring to the situation. Still others may be under your control to some extent, so that you can change their progression in various ways (but not all), order them to one another, and occasionally even stop and start them.

What then does it mean to be a duck-rabbit? It means to have no clear place in the unfolding of a guiding delta, and this can happen in one of two ways: either an event (e) fits within more than one guiding delta currently unrolling, or it does not fit into any of them. It can, we might say, be either a "duck-rabbit" or a "duckrabbit" (or even a "rdaubcbkit"). In any case, dealing with it elicits a response, and I call such an event an "elicitor."

If the elicitor belongs in more than one delta, responding to it throws me onto the usable past, from which comes my knowledge of those deltas—and of the parameters they exemplify. If the elicitor belongs to no delta at all, it is wholly new and my response projects me into the incomprehensibility of the authentic future.

There are, moreover, two ways of situating ourselves: either we define our situation, or we recognize its lack of definition. We thus wind up with four categories of response: defining our relation to the usable past, schematized above as (1); recognizing the lack of definition in our relation to the past (2); defining our relation to the future (3); and recognizing the lack of definition in our relation to the future (4). As I argued at length in *Poetic Interaction,* each of these turns out to be correlated to a specific type of freedom.

Thus, (1) is an obvious example of freedom of choice— but one which has a couple of not-so-obvious features. In the first place, it is not a choice between two courses of action, but rather between two guiding deltas—the more basic horizon within which an action can make sense at all. It thus *precedes* the more familiar action-oriented choice; it is more a matter of getting one's bearings than of deciding what to do. Second, and in keeping with the research cited above, such choice need not be conscious. (Indeed, if duck-rabbits are more prevalent than is generally thought, it can only be because we make many such decisions before becoming aware of them.)

In (2), I respond to the duck-rabbit in ways compatible with its being *either* a duck *or* a rabbit; both the habits of my mind and body associated with ducks and those associated with rabbits play roles in forming my response. The situation is thus left undefined; it could contain delta 1 or delta 2 or both. (2) is aligned with a concept of freedom derived from Aristotle, which holds that to act freely is to act with your whole self: If I can express my whole nature in my acts I am "free," whether I choose to perform those acts or not.

As I noted in the preceding "discussion," an act is "voluntary" for Aristotle when neither of the two things "in us" which can contribute to our actions—reason and desire—is impaired in certain ways. But it is more strictly voluntary when reason and desire cooperate so that what we desire is what reason tells us we should desire. What brings about this harmony of the soul is deliberate choice (proairesis), which is "deliberate desire of things in our power" (NE 1113a13). Reason and desire span the range of action-producing psychic contents for Aristotle, whose account of moral psychology is therefore somewhat impoverished. Freed from this dependence on a specific list of psychic capacities, his view of freedom amounts to the view that to act freely is to act in ways which are produced by, and express, a multitude of psychophysical states.

Modern philosophy, restricting freedom to absolute causality, places this kind of experience into the realm of the "aesthetic." Kant explored this sort of freedom in his Critique of Judgment, from which it moved into the aesthetic and social thought of German Idealism. For Kant, to say that something is "beautiful" is not really to say anything about that object at all. It asserts, rather, something about myself, namely, that my faculties are put into free play by the imaginative presentation of that object. Aesthetic judgment's lack of cognitive status with respect to its object means that the free play, though occasioned by the object, is in a sense independent of it; it depends not on accurate cognition of the object, but on how I receive it. The experience of an object as beautiful is thus "disinterested," first because it requires a harmonious perception of the object, rather than the actual existence of the object as being, in reality, thus harmonious (KU 191, 204ff, 350). Secondly, because I have no concept of the object I experience, I have no guidelines for producing it; unlike moral experience, aesthetic experience does not require us to try and bring about any state of affairs in the actual world. Such disinterested satisfaction, being independent of objective givens (and therefore of nature) is again "free" (KU 210, 350).

Freedom so construed resides not in the self as conceived to be part of a noumenal realm of reason, but in the harmony of the cognitive faculties of an individual who is in nature but not

subject to it. To be "free" here means to have my cognitive facul-
ties put into the free play of their mutual reference, and it also
means to be disinterested, in the two above senses. For Aristotle
action is basic and aesthetic experience, in the Poetics, *is the*
"imitation of an action" (Poetics *1448a)—a reverse imitation,*
which results in the desire to flee rather than pursue, and in
which the desire is not acted upon.[14] *The* Critique of Judgment *grasps aesthetic experience in terms independent of action*
altogether; it grasps it as a situating activity. Such freedom was
first given a political role in Schiller's Letters on the Aesthetic
Education of Humanity.[15]

If (1) was a matter of choice and (2) of expression, (3) is a matter of invention. Suppose an event occurs which is not only not part of any delta currently unrolling, but also not part of any delta I can even understand (i.e., for which I have a parameter). I am then compelled, if I respond at all, to seek a new way of response, and this amounts to inventing a new parameter. This frees me from my dependence on the old repertoire of parameters, one of whose limitations is now evident. That repertoire is now enlarged by the new parameter.

> *An example of this was Einstein's legendary response to the*
> *Lorenz transformations. These transformations explained cer-*
> *tain experimental results, but "made no sense" to many because*
> *they suggested the contraction of length and the dilation of time.*
> *Einstein responded by redefining space and time and their rela-*
> *tionships, via the Special Theory of Relativity—thus beginning*
> *a series of developments whose importance for science, and for*
> *humanity, can hardly be overstated.*

(4) is, like (2), not even a preliminary to action, because it is concerned with recognizing the lack of definition in a situation rather than with "remedying" it. It occurs when something happens which makes no sense and therefore displaces us from our current situation, but does

not lead to any new parameters; we remain in a state of displacement. This, the most ethereal sort of freedom, belongs in the realm of what Kierkegaard called the "religious."

> *Kierkegaard's* Fear and Trembling *is a profound and subtle examination of what it means for humans to encounter absurdity which cannot be cleared up. He focuses on two such humans. One is Abraham. After God has done the impossible by giving Abraham and Sarah a son in their great old age, he speaks to Abraham again and tells him to take the boy up to Mount Moriah and kill him as a sacrifice. No sense whatever is to be made of this command, but, impelled by a faith he also cannot understand, Abraham goes with his son, in silence, to the top of Mount Moriah. At the last minute, he discovers a ram and sacrifices it instead. In thus tolerating a paradox, rather than attempting to resolve it, Abraham prefigures the appropriate response to what for Kierkegaard is the greatest paradox of all: that God, the infinite, became finite and human. True Christianity for Kierkegaard is to dwell within this ultimate paradox without ignoring it or seeking to understand it in any conventional way.*

> *The second human confronting a paradox is the reader, who must try to make sense not out of what God tells Abraham but out of the whole story. In this effort, she is led by Kierkegaard to an understanding of what it is to be Christian. Toward the end of the work, Kierkegaard brings the two humans together in "the paradox":*

>> The distress and anguish in the paradox consisted (as was set forth above) in silence; Abraham cannot speak. So in view of this fact it is a contradiction to require him to speak [i.e., for the reader to make sense of his story], unless one would have him out of the paradox again, in such a sense that at the last moment he suspends it, whereby he ceases to be Abraham and annuls all that went before.[16]

What we find at the edge of ethics, then, is not decision and action but elicitation and response—exchanges between a moral agent and her surroundings. These exchanges are definitions of, or refusals to define, the specific situation within which an action occurs and through which it is guided. Since an "elicitor" is merely something which does not have a unique place within a situation, anything can in principle function as such an elicitor; indeed, if Heidegger is right and everything is duck-rabbity, everything, to some degree, does so function. Nature, seen in this way, is not mere matter in motion—not because it is something more, but because it is something different. Natural beings and events function ethically as elicitors by which I define my situation and my self. They engage me, not as objects, but as partners—from which follow many things which I cannot discuss here.

Two

The edge of ethics is where I encounter beings I cannot act upon, but to which I must respond. I cannot act upon a being if I do not know how it is functioning in the context of my encounter with it, when it can have more or fewer than just one such function. Encounters with beings who, through the ambiguity of their utterances, function ambiguously for me are cases of what I call "poetic interaction." My first encounters with others, and yours as well, were of this type. We watched as our parents and caretakers attempted to decipher the "meanings" of our cries, i.e., tried to figure out what to do about them. And we, in turn, tried to find meanings for their sounds and actions. We wanted to please them.

Some beings are elicitors, but not elicitees. A being which is both can respond to me, i.e., can change its behavior on the basis of mine. Such a being is traditionally called "animate"; the line between animate and inanimate is traditionally, and wisely, difficult to draw. Plants, for example, seem to be a problem for the way I have drawn it (but a plant is, perhaps, what can respond to my cultivation). Some of the beings which present ambiguities to me, moreover, can respond as if I presented an ambiguity to them—by choosing or inventing responses, etc. These beings are other people; the line between "people" and merely "animate beings" is, once again and once again wisely, difficult to draw. When I encounter a human being, then, the elicitation/response cycle is capable of becoming reciprocal. I call the entire set of relationships that obtain among people the "human world," and the possibility of reciprocity is thus definitive for the ingredients of this world.

Philosophical ethics is traditionally concerned with the human world, to such an extent that the idea that we could have ethical relationships with non-human beings is highly controversial. Yet for all its concern with the human world, philosophy has not given great attention to human relationships, at least not since the absolute causation version of ousia, with its internalization of morality, was deployed in the modern era. When philosophy does pay attention to relationships, it looks primarily to what I call ousiodic relationships, which proceed within a defined situation and include those of parent/child, employer/employee, and political leader/politically led—relationships in which one person is the "form" for the other, who is reduced to mere matter to be acted upon. But in order for a situation to be defined, it must previously have been undefined. Ousiodic relationships, which are generally oppressive in character, therefore piggyback on more creative, or as I call them poetic, ones.

For relationships need not be ousiodically structured. A relationship can be a mere node, or site of exchange—what Aristotle called a "friendship of use," as when I buy something from someone in the market. The "network of friendships," again in Aristotle's phrase, that constitutes a society can also be an inert substrate, into which I fall as an individual, and which I depend upon without changing. The "social substance" explored in Hegel's *Phenomenology* is of this type, and it perishes when it is transformed into "subject"—i.e., is viewed in accordance with the negation ontology which Hegel propounds (cf. *PhS* 314/264). So considered, a relationship becomes something which grows and changes in a continuous fashion, dialectically; it can also be something which is defined diakenically, by shattering breaks and failures of understanding. In any case, a relationship is a guiding delta and so is definable, if at all, with respect to parameters.

> *Kant is famous for denying that relationships have any moral value. In his view, the morally right way to treat people—as ends in themselves—is the same at all times, whether I have an ongoing relationship with them or not. Such universality is for him a necessary condition of the moral; if my action toward someone else were to be motivated by their relationship to me, that relationship would have a causal influence on my behavior, of which I would therefore not be the absolute cause.*

> *Ousiodic relationships, i.e., those which obtain among a fixed set of people when some of them order the whole group and interact with the world outside it, have been discussed—often critically— by a variety of modern thinkers. Thus, Locke writes intelligently about patriarchy, and Marx about employment. Neither, however, attempted to provide an overall account of relationships and their types, as Aristotle had done in* Nicomachean Ethics *VIII–IX, perhaps because they did not see that their chosen topics had ontological roots. One of the many ways in which the dominance of ousia ontology has been prolonged is through the locality of the challenges to it.*

> *Hegel, by contrast, can be considered to offer, in the* Phenomenology of Spirit, *a whole inventory of relationships, beginning with the most antagonistic (the "battlers to the death,"*

PhS *143–146/113–115) and ending only on the book's last page, with the* Geisterreich *of freely interacting spirits.*

Ousiodic relationships have attracted disproportionate philosophical attention not only because of philosophy's general obsession with ousia, but because they are (relatively) compatible with the absolute causation thesis. In an ousiodic relationship one person gets to be the form, and so can act without the other person, who is relegated to the passive status of matter. In a more cooperative relationship, each person's actions respond to the other's and so cannot be absolutely caused by either party.

As is well-known, merely inverting an ousiodic relationship, so that what was matter becomes form and vice versa, reinforces the basic pattern of dominance by allowing it to persist through an otherwise basic change. The classification I will propose offers another way out. It is undialectical in that it derives elementary forms of relationship not from each other, but from the "poetic" account of freedom given above. Important in this is that, as I shall argue, such "elementary relationships" are always double; each ousiodic form corresponds to, because it is a deformation of, a non-ousiodic form.

Judith Butler has conceptualized the transition from ousiodic to non-ousiodic relationships, in the case of gender, as a rejection of the fixed roles imposed, on my account, by ousiodic structure:

> The injunction to be a given gender produces necessary failures, a variety of incoherent configurations that . . . exceed and defy the injunction by which they are generated. Further, the very injunction to be a given gender takes place through discursive routes: to be a good mother, to be a heterosexually desirable object, to be a fit worker, in sum, to signify a multiplicity of guarantees in response to a variety of demands all at once. The coexistence or convergence of such discursive injunctions produces the possibility of a complex reconfiguration and redeployment; it is not a transcendental subject who enables action in the midst of such a convergence. There is no self that is prior to its entrance into this conflicted cultural field. There is only a taking up of the tools where they lie, where the "taking up" is enabled by the tool lying there.[17]

In my terms, Butler is saying that gender is a situation *formed by converging and diverging parameters (injunctions to be a* type *of person), and that the recognition of this propels us into a realm where our very selves can be recreated. I do not claim that those recreative practices can be reduced to the practices of poetic interaction which constitute elementary relationships (elementary relationships, I am about to argue, do not remotely have that sort of status). I do suggest, however, that understanding elementary relationships can play an important role in understanding the kinds of "parodic repetition" that Butler advocates.*

Butler's claim about gender can be generalized. All three members of the classic triad of postmodern oppression theory—class, gender, and race—can be seen as imposed on human individuals by ousiodic structure; they are different ways of qualifying people for the role of matter or form in a relationship. The "injunction" which assigns me to a particular race, for example, specifies certain ways in which I can oppress or be oppressed. My racial position does not determine my class or gender, and does not bring with it those forms of oppression and domination (though there are associations: blacks, both male and female, tend to be masculinized; Jews, both male and female, to be feminized). As Sandra Harding has noted (see chapter 2), different stories need to be told about each of these characteristics.

Gender, class, and race thus define the kinds of relationship I can enter into, without themselves being defined by those relationships. They thereby gain a sort of "transcendental" status. They perform on a social level a role somewhat akin to that played by the Kantian faculties in the individual mind: they furnish unchangeable principles which are constitutive of my identity and which delimit my activities.

The common experience that growing friendship renders inoperative stereotypes of class, race, and gender—an experience we have all had—is thus no merely cognitive affair. It testifies to the inherent tendency of ousiodic relationships to revert, under the pressure of interaction, to their more basic non-ousiodic correlates. Once those types have been theorized in what follows, it may not be premature to suggest that reflec-

tion on ousiodic relationships now needs to be balanced by attention to the structures of these "poetic" alternatives.

I will discuss a few of these relationships in the next two sections, but the manifold ways in which we relate to other people are hardly susceptible of even an outline in a book of this scope. My discussion of relations between two people, in this section, and among more than two people, in the next one, will therefore have the status of examples, but of a peculiar type.

They are, first of all, structured in a peculiar way. When another person acts like a duck-rabbit, i.e., becomes an elicitor, my "world" is disrupted; I take up an ethically conscious attitude toward her. At such a point, our relationship becomes structured by the four types of poetic interaction listed schematically above. My examples will, first and foremost, be examples of these types.

This structuring is usually transient; most human relationships include complex mixtures of the four types of poetic interaction, plus many and various other things. Sometimes, however, the kind of interpersonal relation instanced in a given case of poetic encounter among people is generalized enough to persist throughout and structure their whole relationship. The examples I will give are of such relatively pure relationships, each of which owes its structure to just one type of poetic interaction. Though highly simplified (and thus rare), such relationships manifest features which underlie other, more complex sorts of relationship. They can thus furnish, to speak extremely loosely, a set of relational "elements" on which other types of relationship are at least partially built. My examples thus constitute an "exemplary table of elements" for relationships in general.

It is important to note that some degree of reciprocity is

the norm for human relationships, because it results from the random distribution of the roles of elicitor and respondent. A flipped coin will, over time, come up heads (or tails) 50 percent of the time. Similarly, we can expect that between any two people, interacting over time, the roles of elicitor and respondent would be randomly distributed, so that each person would play each about half the time. The random nature of reciprocity, in other words, makes equality "normal." Equality is thus written into the structure of interaction itself; it is only on more complex levels of interaction, where interaction's inherent randomness is disciplined, that equality becomes an ideal that must be fought for.

> *This in turn makes inequality into what the philosophical tradition would call a "privation" (sterêsis) rather than a mere absence. Flight is "absent" from human beings, but then they are not supposed to fly; a blind person, in contrast, is "deprived" of sight, which she ordinarily would have.*

> *Jürgen Habermas has conceptualized this in his account of communicative action. Such basic norms as freedom, equality, and honesty are held to be characteristics of our fundamental way of relating discursively to one another, "communicative action"; their opposites are derived from "strategic" distortions of this more fundamental kind of activity.[18]*

> *Habermas, however, retains the notion of governance throughout. Freedom, equality, honesty, etc., have the status of norms governing all cases of interaction (they govern in the breach, so to speak, if the action is strategic). Habermas never argues effectively for this claim (cf. PF 91–109), and it is more prudent to see his basic norms as arising in and for the sake of one particularly consequential form of interaction rather than as governing all linguistic interaction. The idea that the governing status of norms is the most basic thing about them is itself intrinsically suspect; our capacity to generate norms interactively, while rarely exercised, is more basic to us than our capacity merely*

to follow them. For how can we follow them before we generate them?

Prior to the generation of norms (parameters) for it, an interactive situation is unstructured, and so random, and so reciprocal and free.

When reciprocity does not obtain, interpersonal relations cease to be "poetic" and come to resemble those between an individual and a non-human elicitor (since, as I suggested earlier, a "non-human" is a being which never responds to me as if what I say or do were ambiguous). When reciprocity *never* occurs in the interactions between two (or more) people, their interrelations do not merely resemble relations with non-humans but actually *mimic* them, i.e., are the result of a more or less conscious effort at overcoming the equality inherent in interaction. I call social structures which are constituted through such an effort "oppressive." While oppression is not universal among human relationships, the possibility of it is; interpersonal relations are actually classifiable by the kinds of oppression they produce when their reciprocity is taken away.

(1) Suppose someone says something to me which can mean more than one thing, and I define the situation for both of us by deciding which. From that point on, we are in a situation that has been defined in common. We share in a series of events which can be recounted as a common narrative. Insofar as we do this reciprocally for one another, our relationship is one of *collaboration*. When I capture for myself the role of respondent only, then I alone define the relationship; my collaborator can only function within a narrative I have defined, and becomes my *servant*. In the extreme case, when she is completely defined

by her relationship to me and by no other, she becomes my *slave*.

> American literature is importantly concerned with poetic relationships, and I will elucidate my "elementary table of relationships" with some quick discussions of examples from that literature.
>
> When Huckleberry Finn first meets up with Jim the runaway slave, he is astonished that Jim takes his cheerful "Hello Jim!" to be the call of a ghost. Jim did not, of course, have to do that; he could have assumed the truth, that Huck was somehow still alive though widely presumed dead. Huck's cheery greeting, in and of itself, could have signified either. Jim's response thus defines their common situation, because Huck must then convince Jim that he is very much alive. When Jim then expresses his fear that Huck will tell on him, it is Huck who defines their common situation by declaring that he is never going back to Hannibal, that he is, in effect, dead to the town. Huck's greeting to Jim is ambiguous between that of a living and of a dead man; Jim's comportment to Huck hovers ambiguously between that of a companion and slave. Much of the novel shows how Jim and Huck negotiate their friendship, which always threatens to fall fatally back onto a free man/slave relation.[19]

(2) Suppose my interlocutor's utterance means more than one thing, and my response in turn means more than one thing to her, and we continue in that fashion. A variety of narratives remains open, the aggregate of which engages the sum of our individual selves. We do not collaborate, because there is nothing determinate to work on, but we engage each other in opening a future which, whatever it brings, will include both of us—and all of each. Thus engaging all of each of us, our relationship is no longer *aesthetic,* in the Kantian sense I discussed above, but *erotic,* in a sense which goes well beyond the

strictly sexual to mean the total engagement of two people by each other.

> *When Gatsby gets Nick to invite Daisy for tea so that he can take her on to his house, Gatsby and Daisy conduct a lengthy and complex verbal ballet of polysemic utterances which fall short of defining their situation. Some examples:*
>
> A. *From the next room, Nick hears "a sort of choking murmur and part of a laugh, followed by Daisy's voice on a clear and artificial note: 'I certainly am awfully glad to see you again.'"*
> B. *"'I'm glad, Jay.' Her throat, full of aching, grieving beauty told only of her unexpected joy. 'I want you and Daisy to come over to my house,' [Gatsby] said, 'I'd like to show you around.'"*
> C. *"'They're such beautiful shirts,' she sobbed, her voice muffled in the thick folds. 'It makes me sad because I have never seen such—such beautiful shirts before.'" [There is no response.]*
> D. *"'If it wasn't for the mist we could see your home across the bay,' said Gatsby. 'You always have a green light that burns all night at the end of your dock.' Daisy put her arm through his abruptly."*
> E. *"'I'd just like to get one of those pink clouds and put you in it and push you around. . . . ' [It is not even clear to whom this statement, Daisy's first allusion to an ongoing relationship, is addressed.] 'I know what we'll do,' said Gatsby."[20]*

The total engagement of two people with each other, eros, can thus be viewed as the harmonization of an individual soul through an encounter with another person which engages all components of the self—grief and joy, confusion and clarity, clear speech and choking murmurs—and brings them into unity with each other (the Platonic roots of this conception are discussed at *Poetic Interaction* 185–186). When this harmonization of the soul is not performed reciprocally, it becomes such that one person occasions it in the other, but the other does not occasion it in the one; she unifies my soul, but I do nothing for her. Indeed, in the extreme, she may have no idea at all who I am, or even *that* I am. I am not her lover, but— her *fan*. Until modern times, it was difficult to be around a person without that person's becoming aware of you; fandom was a rare thing, achieved only by those with imaginative capacities as great as, say, Petrarch's. But with modern media, which can put one face before millions, it is becoming increasingly important as an oppressive relationship.

(3) My interlocutor's utterance makes no sense to me. I have to come up with a new way to make sense of it, and the same in turn happens to her. We thus gain intellectual resources through our encounter, but indirectly; we "teach" each other things (in the etymological sense related to *zeigen, indico, deiknumi*). When this happens in a one-sided way, so that she is expanding my mind while I do nothing for hers, she ceases to be my teacher and becomes my *professor*. I do not understand her but she understands herself, and is able to avow it (*profiteor*). Worse, she understands me as well.

> *When Arthur Dimmesdale tells Hester Prynne in* The Scarlet Letter *that he would rather die than leave Boston alone, she whispers to him "Thou shalt not go alone." She thus opens up for him an entire world of possibilities. Understanding their full range, he then says to her, "Do I feel joy again?" This response does the same for Hester. An entirely new, jointly defined future—one which they could not have comprehended moments before—thus surges up before them.*[21] *They show each other the way into a disastrous new world.*

(4) Her utterance makes no sense to me, and my response make no sense to her; we are paradoxes to one an-

other, and yet—when this is generalized into a relationship
—we remain bound to each other through what can only
be called "faith." Displaced from everything but each other,
we are mutual Abrahams, *shamans* to one another. When
this is not reciprocal, one person displaces the other, but
is not herself displaced; she is thus a cult leader, or *prelate*.

> *When, in* The Portrait of a Lady, *the dying Ralph tells
> Isabel, "You'll grow young again. That's how I see you," she
> does not understand him and asks him not to speak. When he
> persists and tells her that she has been not merely loved, but
> adored, she cries out "Oh my brother," which he, too cannot
> fully understand; is it denial of sexual attraction? Or a recogni-
> tion that any such attraction is of no moment now? Both imme-
> diately leave for distant parts—he to death, she to Rome.*[22]

My claim here is that collaborator, lover, teacher, and
shaman are four very basic relational parameters, by which
we situate ourselves and each other. They take on myriad
different forms, which is hardly surprising since they are
in my sense "poetic"; their core is creative. Collaboration, for example, is basic to the many different forms
of teamwork to be found in modern societies; my team-
mate can also be my teacher, shaman, and erotic partner
(whether she can also be my star, professor, or prelate remains open here). Attenuated forms of slavery are ingredients in many employer/employee relationships and, as
Paolo Freire suggests, educational relationships as well.[23]
The present book can do no more than gesture in these
directions.

In addition to the four "elementary relationships," we
also have four ousiodic deformations of them: the relationships of (1) master and slave, (2) star and fan, (3) professor and student, and (4) prelate and lay person. These

are constituted by reducing the reciprocity which "natu-rally" (i.e., randomly) obtains in the corresponding non-ousiodic relationships.

Such reduction can be institutionalized in two basic ways—either materially or juridically. We see many forms of both in the West. The ancient household and the mod-ern factory are material encodings of the master/slave re-lationship, for example, while the standard model of the corporation is a juridical version. Ousiodic structure is cognitively juridified and materially realized in the pro-prietary structures of the modern laboratory, the main engine of Big Science. The star/fan relationship is materi-ally realized in the modern theater and orchestra hall. The layout of a modern classroom, with the professor at its desk or lectern, or of a traditional Christian church, with a prelate at its altar or in its pulpit, clearly shows that someone is going to be allowed to play the role of domi-nant form for all who gather there.

I call a juridico/material realization of ousiodic structure an "engine of oppression." In the ancient world, such engines were nested into one another (the patriarchal household was located within the city and perhaps, in turn, within an empire, etc.). The set of engines of op-pression thus combined into a single system of oppression. The modern world, as I argued in *Metaphysics and Oppres-sion,* rejects such nesting (*MO* 105–193). Modern engines of oppression are thus relatively autonomous and do not unite into an overall system (Marx referred brilliantly to one case of this lack of overarching system as the "chaos and caprice" of the market).[24] The last significant attempt to get dispersed engines of oppression to unite into a single overarching system of oppression was the great to-talitarian misadventure of the twentieth century. With the collapse of that, what confronts us in the postmodern world is a more or less haphazard scattering of engines of oppression across the social landscape, a "state of nature" of what is anything but natural.

> *Disfavored groups can thus, in postmodernity, seize areas where they can dominate; whites are dominated on the basketball court, straights in the West Village, and men in kindergarten. It is anachronistic to suggest that they are allotted these areas by a higher authority, for there is no overarching authority; the disfavored groups seize their terrain of dominance for themselves. Hence the need for Hollywood to provide reassurance that the territories seized are merely marginal and the seizures themselves merely amusing, in popular movies such as* White Men Can't Jump, In and Out, *and* Kindergarten Cop.

As I also argued in *Metaphysics and Oppression,* the reason that modernity does not tolerate nesting lies in its commitment to the existence of an infinite creator-God. Monotheistic theology has it that the modern human individual no longer depends upon an ordered set of ousiai for her subsistence, as Aristotle's ancient citizen depended on his household and polis, but directly on God, and on God alone. Postmodern engines of oppression testify to this divine origin by legitimating themselves in part through mystifying words which, were they allowed to mean anything at all, would convey a sense of divine favor; words such as "charisma," "genius," "leadership ability," "star quality," and "talent" are deployed across the verbal landscape from politics to show business. Those who seem to exhibit these occult qualities benefit enormously, be they American presidents, Hollywood actors, or Nobel laureates, but the legitimacy thus conveyed is a weak and tenuous one. Further critical efforts may demolish it altogether.

Many

To discuss relationships involving more than two people is to come upon a great divide: that between groups of people which, however large, are still small enough for all to meet together face to face, and still larger groups which cannot do that. The former sort of group, for a variety of ancient reasons, has more legitimacy when it comes to making decisions, and so there is generally pressure to reduce the latter sort of group to the former. The general name I will use for strategies which accomplish this is "representation."

At Politics VII.4, Aristotle advances four arguments as to why a well-governed state can have only a limited population. One of the arguments is clearly derived from his metaphysics, in which matter is recalcitrant to form. In states, the individual citizens are analogous to matter, and if there are too many of them, the laws will not be able to order society well. A state with a large population will inevitably be disordered, and there is thus a natural limit to the population of a state—as there is a natural limit in size to plants, animals, and implements. A second argument is empirical: The states which were thought to be well-governed, in Aristotle's Greece, were all relatively small. The other two arguments are pragmatic: In order to choose the right people for the various offices, the citizens of the state must know the character of each, and this is not possible in large states; indeed (and this is misleadingly presented as an independent argument) foreigners and resident aliens can easily pass for citizens in such states. Finally, a speaker cannot even be heard by a large assembly, unless he has the voice of Stentor.

These arguments all presuppose that the business of the state will be conducted by a group of people who are actually in the presence of one another. The basic reason for this is simple: Technology allowing large numbers of people to communicate with each other over appreciable distances did not exist in Aristotle's day, and is still in its infancy today. Since Aristotle's arguments are premised on the size of the governing body (citizens and assembly), not that of the group that is governed (the population as a whole), they also hold for today's much larger societies. Even in such societies, it is thought well to have the common business conducted by a group of people who know each other and who are, when gathered together, a small enough group to be able to communicate easily with each other.

A group which cannot actually meet together and has no mechanism of representation is "present" only in a virtual or imaginary sense. The image of the group thus constituted can fall prey not only to personal whim, but to ontological misfortune. The misfortunes of the social ontology of substance are, as I noted above, exhaustively explored by Hegel in his Phenomenology of Spirit. *The lack of individual initiative is even more characteristic of the force ontology as applied to society by the early Foucault. On the node ontology, as applied to society for example by Robert Nozick, government becomes minimal.*[25]

Let us say that a face-to-face group which represents a wider community and makes decisions by which the members of that wider community must abide is a "government." Called to control a group larger than itself, government has an inherent affinity for ousia ontology; it has a tendency to act in a unitary fashion to bound and dispose the larger group, while reserving to itself relations with entities outside that group. This ousiodic tendency is especially evident when laws and policies are not mere actions of a whimsical ruler but express stable ordering principles. In such cases, they—and even more the groups which make them—are easily viewed as ousiodic forms for the larger community.

There is thus a deep-rooted pull, in the West at least, to see government as bounding and disposing (ordering) the larger community, and as exercising the initiative in dealing with the world outside. This view of government was taken to extravagant theoretical lengths by Hobbes (cf. *MO* 128–144). It was taken to extravagant practical lengths when the twentieth century produced its various forms of totalitarianism. But whatever those excesses, the political deployment of ousia, like other deployments, has also been under attack during the entire modern era; the totalitarian excesses of the last century only enhanced attacks which were already underway.

The task imposed by history—in particular by the modern experiences of governance down through the twentieth century—is, then, how to enable government to carry out its necessary functions without resolving itself into an all-controlling ousiodic form. The problem is thus one of the ontology of government.

This is often missed; the direction of debate has traditionally been toward the question of what the legitimate functions of government are. But this only begs the ontological question. Issues concerning what a government can "properly" do can arise only once we have decided (a) that the government should "do" things (and not act like a substance or a node), and (b) that those things should be "proper" (so that the government does not act randomly, like a force). The deeper problem, then, is one of whether and to what extent government can be conceived in terms of one or more of the non-ousiodic ontologies I listed in chapter 3. Which model, or models, of Being is most successfully applied to government?

The "successful" ontology will not be the one which best captures the nature of government, as if that were some sort of pre-existing thing. It will be the ontology—or ontologies—in conformity with which a group of people can make decisions for a wider community without assuming the unity, stability, or dispositive power of an ousiodic form. This issue, as an ontological one involving a departure from the ousia ontology, comprises three sub-issues. Two of these follow two of the axes of domination inherent in ousiodic ontology: First, how is a government to relate to its own larger community without oppressing that community like an ousiodic form (disposition)? Second, how is it to relate to other communities without that happening (initiative)? The third sub-issue differs from the other two in that it concerns not government's relation to other groups, but its own internal structure: How can it avoid the unity and stability of an ousiodic form?

These two general topics—government's relations with other communities and its own internal structure—tend to be treated in ways which are not only different from, but incompatible with, each other. Certainly that is the case for the country which is most explicitly set up in an antiousiodic way, the United States. Disposition and initiative are contested in ways which presuppose that the government is an ousiodic form, while the government itself is set up so as to be divided and unstable to its very core.

Contestations

Political disposition is the capacity of the government, conceived as an ousiodic form, to order society. In order for this to be possible, the many and various parts of society must primarily relate to the government and not to each other, for if they could *relate* to each other, they could *affect* each other and then even *order* each other. Contesting disposition in the state is then a matter of allowing the parts to do just that. The strategies for doing this are many and often complex; it is important to note that they do not necessarily transgress ousia ontology itself at all, but may attempt to locate ousia exclusively on other levels of the human world. As I noted above, modernity is generally intolerant of what I call "nesting," i.e., of having ousiai exist on different levels. It follows that simply to locate ousia on a different level of the human world weakens it with regard to the society itself. This strategy is deployed in a variety of ways in modern societies, particularly in the United States.

One such way is to locate ousia on the level of the individual, as do for example absolute property rights. If an individual has the initiative to dispose of her property in whatever way she sees fit, the power of the government is considerably weakened. The American slogan for this, often heard during the breakup of the Soviet Union, was "political freedom requires economic freedom."

A second way is to allow for the formation of sub-communities, organizations of citizens which themselves are accorded the status of ousia. In the American system, some of these sub-communities are actually sub-governments—state and local government. The full status of ousia includes initiative, so this strategy allows for the sub-communities and individuals to affect one another. Other examples are street gangs and the Chicago political machine, which have as their disposing forms leaders who make (more or less) rational decisions for their charges.

A sub-community need not, however, have ousiodic structure in order to contest the disposition of the government; anything which brings parts of the society, or individual citizens, in relation to each other rather than to the overarching government will do it. Internet communities, which are often unstructured, open, and temporary, are a case in point. It is no accident that the Internet was invented in the United States.

Other contestations of disposition include applying the node or the force ontology to parts of society. A free market, for example, is a site of transfer which anyone can enter and leave at will. It is a node. Those who use it—producers and consumers—are themselves conceived as forces, in that their activities are not under rational constraints; a person is free to seek or provide whatever she thinks is in her "individual interest."

> *The most important of these tactics has been to view private ownership as itself having ousiodic structure. On this view, there are definite boundaries to my property; within those boundaries, I can operate as I wish, and whatever comes from it is mine to enjoy. The classical case of this is the political philosophy of Locke. See MO 145–162.*

> *Sub-communities have been empowered mainly by according to them the right to own things, producing the ousiodic structure of the modern corporation. But the empowering of other levels, particularly in the American system, goes beyond the accordance of property rights. Freedom of assembly, freedom of religion, and freedom of speech are all ways of impeding the disposition of government over society. It is important to note that in the United States constitution, and particularly in the Bill of Rights, government is limited without making the limitation in favor of anything else, thus encouraging the application of any or all ontologies of contestation.*

Finally, political initiative is the idea that all relations with the outside world should be conducted by the ousiodic form, i.e., by the government. It is contested in that the parts of society, individuals or sub-communities, are enabled to travel freely in and out of the society by porous borders—the kind for which the United States is noted. In the extreme, boundaries are respected but sub-communities are actually allowed to operate in the name of the government by making foreign policy—as United Fruit famously did in Central America, as Union Carbide did more recently in Bhopal, India, and as petroleum interests do today in the Middle East.

Many contemporary protests against "globalization" are actually protests against individual American companies exercising initiative beyond the borders of the United States—as when McDonald's puts restaurants into French cities. The facts that those restaurants are full, or that prior to McDonald's entering France it was very difficult for a working person to afford a hot meal at noon, are not relevant to the indignation, which is metaphysical in origin.

All these strategies of contestation run into serious problems, however. Contesting boundary, for example, weakens not only the government but the society; boundaries must not be so weak that enemies can easily enter the country. A government which must contend with the ousiodic structure of individuals—one whose limits, for example, are established in the name of private property—is relegated to a continual balancing act. The encouraging of sub-communities which are not ousiodically conceived, again, also needs limits on it—otherwise the market (for example) will take over all social functions, remaking government in its own image—as a node.

Contestation of disposition and initiative is not always a good thing. Such contestations need therefore to be adjudicated, and this poses a dilemma. All these contestations presuppose that government itself is a variety of ousiodic form, that it is a stable and unified entity which, for better or worse, exercises bounding, dispositive, and initiatory functions. A government thus stable and unified certainly has the power to adjudicate contestations of its own disposition and initiative, but allowing it to do so merely reimposes it as an ousiodic form on society. As such a form, moreover, government is itself active within the social game, and so is merely one of the contesting parties. Such a government is often unable to provide acceptably impartial guidelines for how the various balancing acts which constitute society are to be conducted. In the absence of such guidelines, the way is open for decisions to be made by force.

The problem, then, is that these arrangements make no provision for a certain level of political discourse. This is what I call the balancing level, on which the various social formations are allocated their appropriate spheres. No place is available for a metadiscourse which would guide the various balancing acts between government and other parts of society. That is left over to the "public sphere" of debate among the citizens. It is their job to improvise, codify, and justify new and old forms of community, situating them with respect to society as a whole and thereby situating government also with respect to that whole.

> Traditional European statecraft does not attempt to adjudicate contestations of its disposition and initiative, because it does not tolerate them—as is attested by the theological warrant given the state in the doctrine of the "divine right of kings." Such legitimation "from above" allows the state to act within society by ordering and/or generating its components, by licensing newspapers and religions, regulating public assemblies, and enforcing a system of compulsory public education. No one (except a conveniently absent God) is allowed to adjudicate its acts, so the dilemma I am sketching does not arise.

The public sphere, however, has become highly problematic. On the one hand, the citizenry expanded, during the twentieth century, to become coextensive with so-

ciety as a whole, as women and minorities got the right
to vote and, more generally, to participate in government.
Absolutely laudable as this is, it has meant that public debate is now carried on by people who have little understanding of, or sympathy for, one another, even when
gathered into face-to-face interaction. The earlier kind of
metadiscourse, conducted among a relatively homogenous
group of gentlemen, was much more effective (that is why
it was so vicious). Furthermore, the gap in understanding
has increasingly been filled by the media, whose function
is to come between ("mediate") the various mutually un-
comprehending groups of a society by providing them
with a relatively clear understanding of that society's current situation. Such understanding does not, usually, go
beyond the lowest common denominator of political understanding. Finally, the centralized (ousiodic) structure
of contemporary media makes it easy for them to be con-
trolled by various well-placed groups, thus skewing the
debate in ways that are very difficult for the citizens to
comprehend.[26] It is hardly a surprise that the first generation to come of age in these altered conditions—the baby
boomers—has abjured the public sphere altogether, re-
treating to the internal debates and issues of the academy.[27]

Limit-Case Ontologies for Government

Allowing government to retain ousiodic form while contesting the disposition and initiative traditionally accorded
to such form cannot, therefore, succeed by itself. The very
structure of government must be reconceived, which
means that a new ontology must be found for it.

The first steps out of the ousia ontology are what I
called, in chapter 3, "limit-case ontologies." Of the four
such ontologies I listed there, two cannot be perspicuously

applied to government. Substance ontology would seek to view government as somehow a passive substrate for the actions and movements of the governed community, which amounts to having no government at all (in Hegel's terms, it would amount to confusing the "social substance" with the state). Pantheist ontology would make government the disposing center of the entire human race—a superstate which is really a dangerous theocratic fantasy.

Force ontology has a bit more plausibility. Much conservative opinion rightly sees government in broad terms of force ontology, as merely random and irrational. Such an approach does not ask where governmental decisions come from or how they are produced, but demands resistance to all equally—an "abstract negation" of government rather than a nuanced appreciation. This approach fails to see that even at its worst, government is not a mere random force but exercises its oppressive functions along three specific axes: boundary, disposition, and initiative. Otherwise it could not do its evil work. Effective resistance to government requires seeing it for what it is: an ousia rather than a force. When we do that, resistance becomes not only effective, but selective.

We are left, of the limit-case ontologies, with node ontology. On such a view, government is legitimated as a site of transfers of various sorts. Because government already has a monopoly on the lawful use of force, no one can transfer power to it, at least not power held lawfully; what gets transferred in this version of the node ontology is not power, but what Habermas calls the other "steering mechanism" in modern society, money.[28] On this model, social actors give money to government in order to get more money in return. A government which is a mere site of transfer for money is unable to provide social order, i.e., unable to act. It is not a government.

Campaign financing and lobbying are two important areas in which node ontology is applied to government. In each case, groups or individuals spend money in order to acquire influence with, or even to help elect, people to the government who will then look favorably on their financial affairs.

It can be seen that the United States has carried these ways of challenging ousia to extremes. An individual American "state" has no control whatsoever over its boundaries. Though some, like California, seek to keep such things as plant materials out of their territory, the free flow of goods and people cannot be impeded by any state government; seeing that they are not impeded is the preserve of the federal government. That government, however, cannot do the job; the boundaries of the United States remain porous, and the resources necessary to enforce them are not allocated. To do so—to set up a "fortress America"—is taken to be an undue interference with individual freedom.

In addition to its false diagnosis of the state as a force, much conservative opinion in America is crippled by its proposed remedy: reducing government from a force to a node. In this it shows its truly "conservative" nature; it is unable to give ousia up altogether and does not go beyond its limit cases. The most acute version of this remains, today, Milton Friedman's view of government as "umpire," adjudicating property disputes. Friedman himself supplements this function of government with those of "setting the rules" for the market and as a "paternalistic" caretaker of incompetents who cannot compete— pre-eminently children and the insane. Among the many problems with his view, however, is that when government is defined solely in terms of its relations to the market, it risks becoming itself subject to market norms—i.e., governmental acts and regulations become commodities which can be bought and sold, reducing government to a mere node or to what Robert Nozick calls an "ultra-minimal state."[29]

Situating Government

Neither contesting ousia nor reconceiving government in terms of limit ontologies is workable or defensible on its own terms. That such efforts are made at all, let alone that they are made with such desperation, is a sign that they are nonetheless serviceable for the great enterprise of America, which is nothing less the political/aesthetic/ religious/economic undoing of ousia ontology.

I have spoken so far of strategies for limiting government and for contesting its metaphysical powers of disposition and initiative. I suggested that such limitation and contestation need to be adjudicated by impartial, and so public, but non-governmental authority: by public opinion, a form of active citizenship which today exists only in residual form.

The prospects for a revival of public opinion are bleak. Though the increasing fragmentation and interactivity of the media offers some hope—cable television is more recalcitrant to central control than traditional television networks, and the Internet is even more so—other conditions remain hopelessly unfulfilled. The ontological roots of public discourse, for example, mean that regaining a public sphere would require the active participation of thinkers who are both ontologically and politically informed— of public philosophers. Only a few such individuals exist, however, and no effort is underway to educate more.

In the absence of hope for a revived sphere of public opinion, the dilemma I sketched above grows more and more acute. Government takes on more and more adjudicative functions and becomes correspondingly less and less effective as an actor in society. The result is what I call "situating government," a government which is set up to define situations as well as to act within them.

We can understand this, if only a bit better, by looking more closely at the kind of discourse the public sphere was supposed to provide. Such a discourse is not merely "balancing" but, in my sense, "situating." In adjudicating contestations it defines the situation of the society, rather than undertaking specific actions within that situation.

To see this, we must construe the various components of a society not as ousiai, nodes, or forces, but as guiding deltas. When I become the operator of a car or a farm, or the owner of a share of stock, a series of events is triggered which falls under one or more of a variety of very general parameters ("driving," "farming," "investing"). When a group of people join together in a sub-community—be it a religion or a gang or anything in between—other deltas are set in motion. Similarly when a foreigner enters my country. Contestations of governmental power are one sort of guiding delta. Adjudicating them is part of the larger enterprise of defining and evaluating the guiding deltas operative in, and on, a society.

Some such deltas may fall unequivocally under established parameters, but others may not. Gangs, for example, may engage in both highly constructive and thoroughly destructive behavior in their communities, and one job of local government is to decide which. Artistic productions often engage a variety of deltas underway in society, and the job of government in such cases may well be to encourage all such productions at once. Other such deltas are radically new, such as the one triggered by Rosa Parks on a bus one day in Montgomery, Alabama.

The "situation" of a society—an immense affair—is the set of guiding deltas converging on it, from within and without, at a given time. The metadiscourse I have in mind is directed toward defining what those deltas are and evaluating them in general terms, rather than to formulating and conducting concrete action within them. It is thus a situating discourse, and one which in the United States is carried out not by the now vestigial public sphere, but by government itself. For like individuals and communities, government too has situating functions, distinct from its more traditionally understood functions of ordering and defending society. It thus performs at least some of the functions which, on an ousiodic model, are assigned to the public sphere.

That governance is, at least in part, a matter of situating, rather than of bounding, disposing, and initiating, suggests that we view it as primarily a matter of specific and provisional responses to ambiguous elicitors, rather than as a clear-cut ordering and defending activity. How must a government be structured in order to carry out this situating function?

Situating here requires, as always, some degree of openness to the future and the past, as well as to the present. When these openings are independent enough to be pursued by different branches of government, we get a tripartite system.

Situation defining with respect to the future requires improvisation in the face of the inscrutable, so as to predict it where possible and hold it open where necessary, thus respecting the difference between the predictable future and the future in itself. It concerns what I call the "invention of parameters," which on the governmental level is legislation.

The aim of legislation so understood is to prevent the origination of certain guiding deltas, and to encourage others. A law is thus a sort of performative prediction. It says that in the future, if x happens then y will happen, and saying that (in the case of legislation) makes it so. Not all these prescriptions and proscriptions are explicit parts of the legislation. If a given law specifies a particular sentence for a particular activity that it defines as criminal, it is today understood that much more than that sentence will actually come to pass in a given case. Those who are merely suspected of a crime may have the police seek them out, read them their rights, and take them away, perhaps in the view of TV cameras, and so on and on.

Legislation is therefore elicited by new phenomena; a situation with no new components does not require new laws. Creating a new law is then what I call "demarcative" in nature. It responds to breaks and ruptures with past patterns, and is predicated on the possibility that new things can happen—that the future is unknowable. The elicitors to which legislation responds, being new, have no current meaning and so require invention. A legislative body which is supposed to do this is best structured, I suggest, as a diakenic interplay itself. The legislative response to the future should therefore be produced jointly by groups which do not understand one another and whose mutual relation therefore mirrors their joint relation to the future. This allows the area of joint agreement—of legal prediction—to be kept small, and society's authentic future to be held open.

The branch of government whose function is to open up the future in this way should, therefore, itself have a structure which institutionalizes discursive gaps within which the future can take shape. It should be composed of a plurality of bodies (the smallest and simplest number is two), neither of which can override the other. These two bodies, moreover, should be different enough from one another that neither is readily comprehensible to the other.

This can be achieved by varying the basis for being elected to them. Terms should vary in length between the two bodies, and the constituencies represented should be of different size and structure—if in one they are small and population-based, in the other they should be large and on some other basis, such as representing some independently existing territory. Since it takes longer for a larger electorate to become acquainted with candidates than for a smaller one, the elections to the large-constituency body should be spaced more widely than those for the small-constituency body; its terms should be longer.

These measures will mean that each body is composed of people whose professional psychology is different from that of those in the other body, and this in turn will give rise to different traditions and procedures in the two bodies. In this way, the two bodies will coexist in what I call a diakenic interplay; each body will cohere with itself, united by a "language" which the other body largely does not understand.

The point of this is not simply that diakenic interplay is a good thing, but rather that when one is trying to cope with something genuinely new, it is best not to have too large a stock of common principles in effect. This could be achieved by abandoning general principles altogether, attempting to treat each case *de novo* and without presuppositions of any kind. That tactic, however, just means the sacrifice of any articulate basis for encountering such a case, and is, in any case, an impossibility. By structuring itself diakenically, the legislative branch allows for (at least) two relatively incommensurable sets of principles, neither of which can be given assured validity, so that the future can be opened up in articulate but flexible ways.

The mutual incomprehension of the two bodies will make the legislative branch tedious and slow to come up with a response, and so will impede the capacity of the government as a whole to act effectively; the hope is that the response will be stronger in the long run. Also possible under this system is the withholding of a response when the bodies cannot come to agreement and so continue their diakenic interplay without producing a law.

Once a response has been formulated and ratified, it can be applied in a defined situation. This function of government is the standard one of action, which here must find a place within government's broader situating functions. The epistemic vehicle of such action is subsumption, which responds to the present facts by deciding what legislation applies to them and how. Since this activity is keyed to the present rather than to the future, it should be carried out by a separate branch of government. The executive branch, which as coming under traditional concepts of action can itself can be ousiodically structured with a single head responsible for the whole, thus receives laws from the legislative and undertakes to enforce them.

A new law is a new parameter for society, and so is a step forward into the future. It may however be what I call an "ignoble" step forward. It may fail to function effectively in the larger context of the society, in the form both of society's deeper, ongoing commitments and traditions and in the narrower sense of its compatibility with previous legislation (including any quasi-legislative written constitution). While such matters of the relation of laws to the past are to some degree taken up by the legislative branch, the very different languages spoken by the separate houses in that branch generally prevent a single answer from being given—one is more likely to get a variety of construals of the relation of the law to the larger social narrative. Laws passed by the legislative branch are thus intrinsically open to challenge, and the challenges single case moves upward from court to court. The challenging of a law, like its application on a given occasion, is the starting point of a new guiding delta. A law which is under challenge is thus part of two narratives at once, the narrative of its enforcement and that of its challenge (this holds even if the law is "stayed" until its constitutionality is decided).

Both narratives are, in different senses, second order; the executive narrative, the overall history of the law's enforcement, is composed of many smaller narratives, while the judicial narrative is a series of reflections on the law itself. The job of the courts is to decide into which of these narratives the law is going to be definitively placed. If the law is upheld, the judicial narrative ceases and the executive narrative goes forward. If it is struck down, the executive narrative ceases and the law, which was never "really" a law, properly has a place only in the judicial narrative, which turns out to have been a narrative of extinction.

In my terms, what Michael Hardt and Antonio Negri describe in Empire *is how ousiodic structure, with the decline of the nation-state, is reconstituting itself on a global level as*

> . . . both system and hierarchy, centralized construction of norms and far-reaching production of legitimacy, spread out over world space. Only an established power . . . relatively autonomous from the sovereign nation-state, is capable of functioning as the center of the new world order, exercising over it an effective regulation and, when necessary, coercion. (*Emp.* 13–15)

There is no doubt that this development is a radical departure from the modern investment of ousia in the nation-state (which I discuss at Metaphysics and Oppression *128–144). The fact that Empire now occupies the entire globe, for example, means that boundaries cannot be given stable definition. On the other hand, they do not disappear entirely. Variously recalcitrant*

*people and groups, though residing geographically within
Empire rather than invading it from without, get defined by
the center as outsiders, or as Giorgio Agamben puts it, are
"included solely through [their] exclusion."*[30] *Thus included
by exclusion, rendered "exceptional," these individuals and
groups lose even the right to speech; they become, as Hardt and
Negri put it, "incommunicable" to each other and to the global
order (*Emp. *54f). The drawing of boundaries in the global
era thus becomes the formation of a "state of exception" which
establishes the power of the sovereign to order what has not been
excluded, a power which is coextensive with sovereignty itself.
The state of exception thus becomes the norm.*[31]

*Certain phrases in the above quote ("centralized construction
of norms," "effective regulation") show that what I call "disposition" holds sway for Hardt and Negri within the unstable
boundaries of the unexceptional, and becomes initiative ("coercion") in "exceptional" cases, where it deals with those excluded
by those boundaries. The dispositive function of ousiodic form,
the establishment and maintenance of internal order, becomes
crucial to Empire in its need to control the movements of (material) multitudes (workers, migrants, refugees) across its* internal
*boundaries (*Emp. *398–400).*

*Agamben's analysis is carried out entirely without reference to
concrete political arrangements, including American ones (he
relates* homo sacer *to Roman law, to the medieval wolf-man,
the Germanic* Friedlos, *and to the bandit, but never mentions
its most important twentieth-century popular icon: the outlaw
of the American West).*[32] *Hardt and Negri's analysis, provocative
though it is, also omits some crucial dimensions which an analysis keyed to ousia brings out. One of the most important of these
concerns the peculiar role of the United States as the one "established power" capable of functioning at "the center of the new
world order."*

*To be sure, the United States cannot in Hardt and Negri's view
"form the center" of an imperialist world order (*Emp. *xiv), but
it does have a privileged position:*

> Just as in the first century of the Christian era the
> Roman senators asked Augustus to assume imperial pow-
> ers of the administration for the public good, so too today

the international organizations (the United Nations, the international monetary organizations, and even the humanitarian organizations) ask the United States to assume the central role in a new world order. (*Emp.* 181)

This is in part because the United States is not merely the strongest possible executor of world Empire, but its archê *or source. Its inventive "open network," is what Empire globalizes (* Emp. *182). What keeps the United States from becoming the kind of center Hardt and Negri say it is not—an ousiodic form exercising disposition and initiative over the entire globe—is that it does not act unless requested to do so by international organizations such as those mentioned above (ibid.).*

The recent predilection of the American government for "unilateralism" raises the question of whether the current situation is anything more than a phase in the passage of the world to a full-blown "American empire" of the classical ousiodic type. Hardt and Negri do not pose this question, which decisively affects both the theoretical and practical tenability of their project; but it is clear that on their analysis there is nothing to prevent its happening.

My terms, by contrast, show why it cannot—but the news is not as comforting as one might expect. To see this, we must note that Hardt and Negri's analysis of America focuses on its relations to what is not America—external relations, a field where the government attempts to speak "with one voice." They completely misunderstand the American principle of "divided sovereignty," which they express as follows:

> Power can be constituted by a whole series of powers that regulate themselves and arrange themselves in networks. (*Emp.* 162)

In fact, the different powers in the American governmental system are not "self-regulating" in a peaceful but expansive network, but are in fundamental, continual, and, as I have noted often, baffled conflict with each other. This means that governing power in the United States is not the kind of unified bounding, disposing, and initiatory agent that the European tradition of political thought would have it be. Its actions, now in the current state of Empire and in a possible future "Ameri-

can empire," will always be conflicting, conflicted, ad hoc, *and temporary. Effective resistance to Empire, and to the sad and frightening role of the United States within it, must exploit this fact. It must operate by setting one branch or level of government against the other—as Americans themselves now do routinely, when they demand federal judicial review of state laws or require the states to enact legislation that the federal government has refused to do, such as bans on smoking in public places. Otherwise our attempt to achieve the unexceptionable goals Hardt and Negri set—such things as the right to global citizenship and a social wage—will remain where Hardt and Negri leave us: with hopeful invocations of the "theurgical teleology" of the multitude (*Emp. 396–411*).*

Conclusion

This sketch of a situating government, rough and brief as it is, is hardly intended as a definitive account of government after the model of, say, Montesquieu. Still less can it pretend to solve the problems with government that I sketched above; that could probably be better done by a revived public sphere.

My discussion here, like the rest of this book, can at best point a way to fuller treatments of the issues it raises. But I hope to have shown that government has situating functions, as well as ordering (dispositive) and defensive (initiatory) ones. I also hope to have revealed a serious problem with such government: that of balancing out its situating function with its ordering and maintaining ones.

If nothing else, I think I have shown the answer to an increasingly important riddle. The American government is notoriously bad at the traditional governmental functions. The United States falls far behind the norm for economically advanced societies on every scale of social order, from crime control to social justice to intelligent use of military power. Yet the American constitution is the oldest of all constitutions in the world today. Why, if it is so bad, has it lasted so long? The answer, I take it, has little to do with free markets, property rights, or "individualism." Markets in America are easily manipulated, property rights are merely a metaphysical residue (see *MO* 145–163), and any European headwaiter can testify that of all national psychologies, that of the Americans is the most sheepishly conformist.

But for all its faults, the American system performs the situating functions of government better than any other system yet devised. It is far more responsive to time itself than any other governmental system the world has known. And this perhaps is why, for better or worse, the passage of time has so far spared it.

| Epilogue

Preposterous!

Preposterous to think that a single issue raised in this book has received any kind of adequate treatment, let alone a definitive one. *Preposterous* to think that the great and ancient domains of logic, ontology, and ethics have been founded anew in a document of approximately two hundred pages. *Preposterous* to think that this book is not far off course on page after page. *Preposterous* to think its arguments do not fail as often as they succeed, even by its own loose standard of "hermeneutical" truth. *Preposterous* to think that the fragmentary "discussions" it proffers could ever add up to the completeness and transparency of a genuine philosophical narrative. *Preposterous* to think that the conclusion to which it has just limped, so small in comparison with the book's themes, is a "defining gap."

Preposterous, in sum, to think that this book has accomplished anything whatsoever.

But *what if* this book did not seek accomplishments or completions or foundations, but merely sought to instigate? *What if* its purpose is merely to elicit a certain sort of debate? *What if* it is intended to contain nothing more than probes and suggestions? *What if* it merely illustrates a way of thinking that, however new it seems, is in reality only one step beyond many things that are going on already in philosophy? *What if* it is a product not so much of its author as of a slow and inevitable reshaping of reason around the achievements and failures of philosophy as we know it? *What if* it seeks only to be one document, among many others, of the emergence of a new philosophy?

What then?

What now?

Notes

PREFACE

1. For an example of what can be done in this regard see Giovanna Borradori, *Philosophy in a Time of Terror: Dialogues with Jürgen Habermas and Jacques Derrida* (Chicago: University of Chicago Press, 2003). That Europe's two most eminent philosophers should collaborate on this project, in spite of their longstanding feud, testifies to the philosophical importance of September 11.

2. This charge is most effectively brought in Jürgen Habermas, "Work and Weltanschauung: The Heidegger Controversy from a German Perspective," trans. John McCumber, *Critical Inquiry* 15 (1989): 431–456.

3. For representative works by these authors, cf. Robert Bernasconi, *The Question of Language in Heidegger's History of Being* (Atlantic Highlands, N.J.: Humanities Press, 1985); Robert Brandom, *Making It Explicit* (Cambridge, Mass.: Harvard University Press, 1994); Daniel Dahlstrom, *Heidegger's Concept of Truth* (Cambridge: Cambridge University Press, 2001); Stephen A. Erickson, *The (Coming) Age of Thresholding* (Dordrecht: Kluwer, 1999); David Kolb, *The Critique of Pure Modernity* (Chicago: University of Chicago Press, 1986); Christine Korsgaard, *Creating the Kingdom of Ends* (Cambridge: Cambridge University Press, 1996); David Krell, *Intimations of Mortality* (University Park: Pennsylvania State University Press, 1986); John McDowell, *Mind and World* (Cambridge, Mass.: Harvard University Press, 1994); Terry Pinkard, *Hegel's Dialectic* (Philadelphia: Temple University Press, 1988); Robert Pippin, *Hegel's Idealism* (Cambridge: Cambridge University Press, 1989); John Sallis, *Echoes after Heidegger* (Bloomington: Indiana University Press, 1990); Reiner Schürmann, *Le principe d'anarchie* (Paris: du Seuil, 1982); Pirmin Stekeler-Weithofer, *Hegels analytische Philosophie* (Paderborn: Schöningh, 1992); Michael Williams, *Unnatural Doubts* (Princeton, N.J.: Princeton University Press, 1995); Robert R. Williams, *Hegel's Ethics of Recognition* (Berkeley and Los Angeles: California University

Press, 1997); Richard Winfield, *Overcoming Foundations* (New York: Columbia University Press, 1989).

4. As Bill Clinton put it in his admirable (but largely unrecognized) distillation of Heidegger, everything "depends on what the meaning of 'is' is."

5. For a general account of this feeling, see my "Just in Time: Towards a New American Philosophy," *Continental Philosophy Review* 1, no. 34 (2003): 61–80.

1. HISTORICO-PHILOSOPHICAL PROLOGUE

1. Immanuel Kant, *Grundlagen zur Metaphysik der Sitten AA* IV 403 (*Groundwork of the Metaphysics of Morals*, in Kant, *Practical Philosophy*, trans. and ed. Mary J. Gregor [Cambridge: Cambridge University Press, 1996], 57–58).

2. For recent examples of such ignoring of Kant's view of the faculties, cf. Karl Ameriks, *Kant's Theory of Mind: An Analysis of the Paralogisms of Pure Reason* (Oxford: Clarendon, 1982); Wayne Waxman, *Kant's Model of the Mind: A New Interpretation of Transcendental Idealism* (Oxford: Oxford University Press, 1991); even the article on Kant by Paul Guyer in *Routledge Encyclopedia of Philosophy*, Edward Craig, General Editor, 8 vols. (London: Routledge, 1998), vol. V, 177–200 never mentions the faculties. For an account which persuasively shows the centrality of the doctrine of the faculties, see Gilles Deleuze, *La philosophie critique de Kant* (Paris: Presses Universitaires de France, 1963). It is noteworthy that one of the most important efforts to appropriate Kant for contemporary philosophy, John McDowell's *Mind and World* (Cambridge, Mass.: Harvard University Press, 1994), makes central use of the doctrine of the faculties.

3. More properly speaking, philosophy performs *part* of the overall task of constructing situations: that of formulating the basic concepts, or as I will call them "parameters," which guide our thinking and acting. The overall task of rationally constructing situations is what I call "situating reason." It is carried out by politics, art, and religion, working through reflective individuals and communities, hopefully in cooperation with philosophy.

4. Embracing things as ontologically disparate as beliefs, propositions, and sentences, assertions may be thought to have a decidedly fuzzy ontological status. That is how it should be.

5. Martin Heidegger, "Das Wort," in Heidegger, *Unterwegs zur Sprache*, 4th ed. (Pfullingen: Neske, 1971), 221ff ("Words," in Heidegger, *On the Way to Language*, trans. Albert Hofstadter [New York: Harper & Row, 1971], 141ff).

6. Ludwig Wittgenstein, *Philosophical Investigations,* trans. G. E. M. Anscombe, 3rd ed. (New York: Macmillan, 1958), § 329.

7. Cited after Hermann Diels and Walther Kranz, eds., *Fragmente der Vorsokratiker,* 6th ed., 3 vols. (Zürich: Weidmann, 1951).

8. This holds more clearly for spoken than for written speech, but can presumably be extended to it via the view that marks on paper are not sentences until someone reads them. And how could it be otherwise? How can we make sense of the idea that if some piece of paper long secreted in a Himalayan cave has on it the marks "All cats are green" and "silently river cancan orphan," the one "is" a sentence (as opposed to having the material shape of a sentence) and the other "is" not?

9. W. V. O. Quine, *Word and Object* (Cambridge, Mass.: MIT Press, 1960), 170.

10. Peter Hylton, *Russell, Idealism and the Emergence of Analytic Philosophy* (Oxford: Clarendon, 1990), vii.

11. As when we investigate the truth of a scientific sentence by inquiring whether the experiment that supposedly establishes it was correctly carried out. But even here, the questions are different; we cannot be sure that creationism will not, someday, turn out to be true. But we can be quite certain that it is not scientific, i.e., cannot be located at the current stage of the growth of scientific knowledge.

12. Friedrich Nietzsche, *Menschliches allzu Menschliches* at *KSA* III 17 (*Human, All Too Human: A Book for Free Spirits,* trans. R. J. Hollingdale [Cambridge: Cambridge University Press, 1986], 13; translation altered).

13. I.e., we take truth, which we know to require a complex time specification ("true after time t − x and before t + y"), to have a simple specification ("true-at-t"). On this sense of "absolute truth," cf. Donald Davidson, "In Defense of Convention T," in Davidson, *Inquiries into Truth and Interpretation* (Oxford: Clarendon Press, 1984), 65–75, 68f.

14. Friedrich Nietzsche, *Zur Genealogie der Moral, KSA* V 399, also cf. 401 (*On the Genealogy of Morality,* trans. Carol Diethe [Cambridge: Cambridge University Press, 1994], 118; also cf. 120).

15. He calls it the "sabbath of sabbaths," the condition of perfect rest which (Augustine thought) will come at the end of time—here scaled down, of course, into the relatively fixed beliefs that come at the end of inquiry. Nietzsche, *Jenseits von Gut und Böse, KSA* V, 120–121 (English translation reprinted at Nietzsche, *On the Genealogy of Morality,* 158).

16. Friedrich Nietzsche, "Über Wahrheit und Lüge im außermoralischen Sinne," *KSA* I, 881–883 (*Philosophy and Truth,* trans. Daniel Breazeale [Atlantic Highlands, N.J.: Humanities Press, 1979], 79–97, 82, 84).

17. W. V. O. Quine, *Methods of Logic*, 2nd ed. (Cambridge, Mass.: Harvard University Press, 1959), xvi.

18. The list is from John Rawls, *A Theory of Justice* (Cambridge, Mass.: Harvard University Press, 1971), 12.

19. Rawls, *A Theory of Justice*, 587.

20. Jürgen Habermas, *Wahrheitstheorien* in *Wirklichkeit und Reflexion: Walter Schulz zum 60e Geburtstag* (Pfullingen: Neske, 1973), 211–265.

21. Jürgen Habermas, *Theorie des kommunikativen Handelns*, 2 vols. (Frankfurt: Suhrkamp, 1981), vol. I, 109 (*The Theory of Communicative Action*, vol. I, trans. Thomas McCarthy [Boston: Beacon Press, 1984], 71).

22. *AA* XXIV: 822 (*Lectures on Logic*, trans. J. Michael Young [Cambridge: Cambridge University Press, 1992], 280); for the date, see xxvi.

23. *AA* XXIV: 50f (*Lectures on Logic* 556f).

24. While external ones are in space, *KRV* B 37, 42, 46.

25. As well as from Kant's wholehearted endorsement of the line as an appropriate analogy to time. We can "deduce from the properties of [a] line *all* the properties of time, except for this one: that the parts of the line are simultaneous, and those of time always follow one another": *KRV* B50, my translation, emphasis added.

26. *KRV* B 257f; cf. Kant's account of the simultaneity of the hot stove and the warm room at *KRV* B 248.

27. *SZ* 327. Thus, beings ready-to-hand for Heidegger are understood in terms of their specific futures; the pen with which I write is grasped in terms of the letter I will send, and of the friend who will read it. Beings merely "present at hand," by contrast, lack any relation to their own future and are, so to speak, inauthentic, *SZ*, 67–71. This opening to futurity has led to attempts to construe Heidegger as a Pragmatist: See, for example, Mark Okrent, *Heidegger's Pragmatism* (Ithaca, N.Y.: Cornell University Press, 1988); Richard Rorty, "Heidegger, Contingency, and Pragmatism," in Rorty, *Essays on Heidegger and Others* (Cambridge: Cambridge University Press, 1991), 27–49. But for Heidegger *the* future is not *my* or even *our* future, and solving the problems of the present may not be solving my, or even our, problems—any more than when Nietzsche talks about life-enhancement as a criterion of truth, as he does recurrently, he is talking about what enhances my life, or even our lives.

28. Daniel Dahlstrom, *Heidegger's Concept of Truth* (Cambridge: Cambridge University Press, 2001), 224, 332, 318.

29. Cf. G. W. F. Hegel, *Werke* VIII, 323 (*Hegel's Logic*, trans. William Wallace [Oxford: Clarendon, 1975], 236); Martin Heidegger, "Vom Wesen der Wahrheit," in Heidegger, *Wegmarken* (Frankfurt: Klostermann, 1967), 74–81 ("On the Essence of Truth," trans. R. F. C. Hull

and Alan Crick, in Heidegger, *Existence and Being* [Chicago: Regnery, 1949], 74–81).

30. G. W. F. Hegel, "Solgers nachgelassene Schriften und Briefwechsel," in Hegel, *Werke,* ed. Eva Moldenhauer and Karl Markus Michel, 20 vols. (Frankfurt: Suhrkamp, 1970–71), vol. XI, 246.

31. Martin Heidegger, "Das Ding," in Heidegger, *Vorträge und Aufsätze,* 4th ed. (Pfullingen: Neske, 1978), 157–179, 162; also cf. *MO* 215–217, 226f, 245–251, and my "Language and Appropriation: The Nature of Heideggerean Dialogue," *The Personalist* 60 (1979): 384–396.

32. Martin Heidegger, *Zur Sache des Denkens* (Tübingen: Niemeyer, 1969), 77 (*On Time and Being,* trans. Joan Stambaugh [New York: Harper & Row, 1972], 70).

33. G. W. F. Hegel, *Enz.* § 24 zus. 2 at Hegel, *Werke* VIII 86/39f.

34. Anyone who tries to assess the contemporary significance of Wilfred Sellars's *Empiricism and the Philosophy of Mind,* for example, is continually put off by the detailed references it contains to sense-datum theory. Hence Robert Brandom's need, in his "study guide" to the book's 1997 reissue, to begin by announcing that "Sense-datum theories, [Sellars's] immediate target, are important only as prominent and influential instances of the appeal to givenness." Robert Brandom, "Study Guide," in Wilfred Sellars, *Empiricism and the Philosophy of Mind* (Cambridge, Mass.: Harvard University Press, 1997), 120.

35. "In philosophy . . . truth is all-important, and determines the structure of the discipline." Roger Scruton, *Modern Philosophy* (London: Sinclair-Stevenson, 1994), 5.

36. Jacques Derrida, *De la grammatologie* (Paris: Minuit, 1967), 68 (*Of Grammatology,* trans. Gayatri Chakravorty Spivak [Baltimore, Md.: Johns Hopkins University Press, 1974], 46).

37. Jacques Derrida, "Le puits et la pyramide: introduction à la Sémiologie de Hegel," in Derrida, *Marges de la philosophie* (Paris: Minuit, 1972), 79–127 ("The Pit and the Pyramid: Introduction to the Semiology of Hegel," in *Margins of Philosophy,* trans. Alan Bass [Chicago: University of Chicago Press, 1982], 69–108).

38. At the end of the lecture "Über Zeit und Sein," in Heidegger, *Zur Sache des Denkens,* 242f (*On Time and Being,* 24).

39. A possibility suggested by the metonymy buried etymologically in the word "tense," derived from Latin *tempus* or time; a "tense" as a time in its own right can be taken for the whole of time, i.e., treated independently of the other two tenses. I prefer here to think of time in terms of "dimensions" which, like those of space, cannot be separated from one another or taken as wholes in their own right.

40. Though parts of it may be known. Similarly for Kant. The "totality of conditions" for a thing is, as totality, unconditioned and un-

knowable, but the individual conditions which are parts of such a totality may indeed be known. *KRV* B, 443–448.

41. Michael S. Gazzaniga, "The Split Brain Revisited," *Scientific American: The Hidden Mind,* ed. John Rennie (special issue of *Scientific American,* 2002), 30.

42. As Heidegger argues. *SZ,* 66–88.

43. Cf. Lee Smolin, *The Life of the Cosmos* (Oxford: Oxford University Press, 1997).

44. Nancy Cartwright, *How the Laws of Physics Lie* (Oxford: Clarendon, 1983).

45. Aristotle, *de Interpretatione* 1 16a11; *Metaph.* IX.9 1051b2f. For problems with the picture theory of truth in Aristotle, see Edwin Hartman, *Substance, Body and Soul* (Princeton, N.J.: Princeton University Press, 1977), 248f. My point here is that Aristotle adopted the theory, in spite of its problems, for metaphysical reasons.

46. See Peter Hylton, *Russell, Idealism and the Emergence of Analytic Philosophy,* 123.

47. Not "discovered"!

48. Saul Kripke, "Naming and Necessity," in Donald Davidson and Gilbert Harmon, eds., *Semantics of Natural Languages* (Dordrecht: Reidel, 1972), 353–355, see especially 314.

49. W. V. O. Quine, *Philosophy of Logic* (Englewood Cliffs, N.J.: Prentice-Hall, 1970), 85.

50. Martin Jay, *Marxism and Totality* (Berkeley: University of California Press, 1984), 509.

51. Cited after Diels and Kranz, *Fragmente der Vorsokratiker.*

52. Martin Jay, "Fin-de-siècle Socialism," in Jay, *Fin-de-Siècle Socialism and Other Essays* (London: Routledge, 1988), 2.

53. Jay, *Marxism and Totality,* 515.

54. For examples of Heidegger on modernity, cf. Habermas, "Work and Weltanschauung: The Heidegger Controversy from a German Perspective," trans. John McCumber, *Critical Inquiry* 15 (1989), 445f and 453; for the history of philosophy, see Heidegger, "Das Ende der Philosophie und die Aufgabe des Denkens," in Heidegger, *Zur Sache des Denkens* (Tübingen: Niemeyer, 1969), 63.

55. For a critical discussion of this "fallacy," see J. L. Austin, *How to Do Things with Words* (New York: Oxford University Press, 1965), 3.

56. The spatial sense of universality approximates to what Kant himself calls "universal" in a loose sense, i.e., what does not (now) admit of exceptions. What I call "temporally universal" approximates to what he calls "necessary," i.e., that which cannot admit of exceptions ever or, in terms of the schematism, is true at all times. *KPV* B3f, 184, 266.

57. *KRV* B 3–10, 89.

58. G. W. F. Hegel, *Lectures on the History of Philosophy*, trans. E. S. Haldane and Frances H. Simson, 3 vols. (London: Routledge and Kegan Paul, 1896), vol. III, 439; the phrase is not in *Werke*, but cf. *Werke* XX, 346.

59. See my "Problems and Renewal in American Philosophy," *Philosophical Studies* 108 (March 2002): 203–211.

60. See the introductions to *CW* and *MO*.

2. ENLARGING THE PHILOSOPHICAL TOOLBOX

1. For this reading of the *Phaedrus*, see my "Discourse and Soul in Plato's Phaedrus," *Apeiron* 16 (1982): 27–39.

2. Jacques Derrida, "La pharmacie de Platon" in Derrida, *La dissémination* (Paris: Éditions du Seuil, 1972), 69–197.

3. See W. V. O. Quine, "Two Dogmas of Empiricism," in Quine, *From a Logical Point of View* (New York: Harper Torchbooks, 1961), 20–46.

4. George Boole, *The Laws of Thought* (1854; reprinted New York: Dover, 1951). Logic as conceived before Boole had remained bound, if only tacitly, to its Aristotelian formulations, which means to Aristotle's metaphysics of ousia and so to specifically Western ways of thinking and acting; see *MO* 48–55 for an overview and *CW* 186–193 for a brief discussion of Aristotelian logic.

5. I call the problems "Berkeleyan" because Berkeley's statement of them, while not the only or even the first, is the most compelling. Cf. George Berkeley, *Three Dialogues between Hylas and Philonous*, in Berkeley, *Principles of Human Knowledge and Three Dialogues*, ed. Howard Robinson (New York: Oxford University Press, 1996), 157.

6. Cf. the fascinating account of toolboxes at Stephen King, *On Writing* (New York: Pocket Books, 2000), 111–115.

7. For which, cf. Patrick Gardiner, "Hume's Theory of the Passions," in D. F. Pears, ed., *David Hume: A Symposium* (New York: St. Martin's Press, 1966), 31–42.

8. Thomas Hobbes, *The Metaphysical System of Hobbes*, ed. Mary Whiton Calkins (La Salle, Ill.: Open Court, 1963), 70.

9. David Hume, *A Treatise of Human Nature*, ed. L. A. Selby-Bigge (Oxford: Clarendon, 1888), 165.

10. Cf. David Hume, *An Enquiry Concerning Human Understanding*, in Hume, *Enquiries*, ed. L. A. Selby-Bigge, 2nd ed. (Oxford: Clarendon, 1902), 60–80.

11. Aristotle, *Poetics* 9 1451b 33–37.

12. Or, as Quine calls it, "minimal mutilation." See W. V. O. Quine, *Philosophy of Logic* (Englewood Cliffs, N.J.: Prentice-Hall, 1970), 86.

13. See also my "Writing Down (Up) the Truth: Hegel and Schiller at the End of the *Phenomenology of Spirit*," in Richard Block and Peter Fenves, eds., *The Spirit of Poesy: Essays on Jewish and German Literature and Thought in Honor of Géza von Molnár* (Evanston, Ill.: Northwestern University Press, 2000), 47–59.

14. Martin Heidegger, "Andenken," in Heidegger, *Erlaüterungen zu Hölderlins Dichtung* (Frankfurt: Klostermann, 1951), 78–80; also cf. *MO* 240–250.

15. Martin Heidegger, *Was Heißt Denken?* (Tübingen: Max Niemeyer, 1971), 106 (*What Is Called Thinking?* trans. Fred D. Wieck and J. Glenn Gray [New York: Harper, 1968], 172).

16. The research is reported in Sylvia Scribner, "Modes of Thinking and Ways of Speaking: Culture and Logic Reconsidered," in P. N. Johnson-Laird and P. C. Wason, *Thinking: Readings in Cognitive Science* (Cambridge: Cambridge University Press, 1977), 483–500.

17. Scribner, "Modes of Thinking and Ways of Speaking: Culture and Logic Reconsidered," 491.

18. J. L. Austin, *How to Do Things with Words* (New York: Oxford University Press, 1965), 132, 144f.

19. Jacques Derrida, "Signature événement contexte," in Derrida, *Marges* (Paris: Minuit, 1972), 367–393.

20. Cf. Austin, *How to Do Things with Words,* 16.

21. J. L. Austin, "A Plea for Excuses," in Austin, *Philosophical Papers* (Oxford: Clarendon, 1961), 149f.

22. See my "Writing Down (Up) the Truth: Hegel and Schiller at the End of the *Phenomenology of Spirit.*"

23. Sandra Harding, *Whose Science? Whose Knowledge?* (Ithaca: Cornell University Press, 1991), 287.

24. Jacques Derrida, *De la grammatologie* (Paris: Minuit, 1967), 68 (*Of Grammatology,* trans. Gayatri Chakravorty Spivak [Baltimore, Md.: Johns Hopkins Press, 1974], 46).

25. For a fuller account, see *MO* passim.

26. Cf. Descartes, *Principles of Philosophy* I 51, AT IXB 25/CSM I 210; *Discourse on Method* V, AT VI 45/CSM II 33.

27. Jacques Derrida, "Le puits et la pyramide: introduction à la Sémiologie de Hegel" in Derrida, *Marges de la philosophie,* 82 ("The Pit and the Pyramid: Introduction to the Semiology of Hegel" in *Margins of Philosophy,* trans. Alan Bass [Chicago: University of Chicago Press, 1982], 72).

3. FROM METAPHYSICS TO ONTOLOGIES

1. David Hume, *A Treatise of Human Nature,* ed. L. A. Selby-Bigge (Oxford: Clarendon, 1888), xvii.

2. Descartes's dismissive note on the prejudices he had imbibed from his education is at the beginning of his *Meditations:* René Descartes, *Oeuvres de Descartes,* ed. Charles Adam and Paul Tannery, 13 vols. (Paris: Cerf, 1896–1913), vol. VII, 17; this pagination given marginally in John Cottingham et al., *The Philosophical Writings of Descartes,* 3 vols. (Cambridge: Cambridge University Press, 1984–1991). Reichenbach's dismissal is throughout his *The Rise of Scientific Philosophy* (Berkeley and Los Angeles: University of California Press, 1951).

3. For Heidegger on Carnap as at the technocratic, and so metaphysical, extreme from his own views, see Heidegger, *Phänomenologie und Theologie* (Frankfurt: Klostermann, 1970), 39–40. On Hegel, see his "Die Onto-theo-Logische Verfassung der Metaphysik," in Heidegger, *Identität und Differenz* (Pfullingen: Neske, 1957), 31–67. For Carnap, see Rudolf Carnap, "The Elimination of Metaphysics through Logical Analysis of Language," in A. J. Ayer, ed., *Logical Positivism* (New York: The Free Press, 1959), 60–81.

4. For a classic statement of emotivism, cf. C. L. Stevenson, *Facts and Values* (New Haven, Conn.: Yale University Press, 1963).

5. Simon Evnine, *Donald Davidson* (Stanford, Calif.: Stanford University Press, 1991), 153f; Jaegwon Kim and Ernest Sosa, "Preface," to Kim and Sosa, eds., *Metaphysics: An Anthology* (Oxford: Blackwell's, 1999), x.

6. Kim and Sosa, *Metaphysics: An Anthology,* ix.

7. Kim and Sosa, *Metaphysics: An Anthology,* x.

8. Richard Gale, ed., *The Blackwell Guide to Metaphysics* (Oxford: Blackwell's, 2002), viii.

9. For a summary of some major thinkers' views on the nature of metaphysics, see "Metaphysics, Definitions and Divisions" in Jaegwon Kim and Ernest Sosa, eds., *A Companion to Metaphysics* (Oxford: Blackwell's, 1995), 310–312.

10. Michael J. Loux, *Metaphysics: A Contemporary Introduction* (London: Routledge, 1998), 2–18.

11. Loux, *Metaphysics: A Contemporary Introduction,* 20.

12. Rudolf Carnap, "The Elimination of Metaphysics through Logical Analysis of Language," 60–61.

13. Jacques Derrida, "Ousia et grammé," in Derrida, *Marges de la philosophie* (Paris: Minuit, 1972), 31–78 ("Ousia and Gramme," in Derrida, *Margins of Philosophy,* trans. Alan Bass [Chicago: University of Chicago Press, 1982], 29–67).

14. Martin Heidegger, "Über Nietzsches Wort: Gott ist Tot," in Heidegger, *Holzwege,* 4th ed. (Frankfurt: Klostermann, 1963), 221. My translation.

15. Jacques Derrida, "Force et signification," in Derrida, *L'écriture et*

la différence (Paris: Éditions du Seuil, 1967), 26 ("Force and Signification," in Derrida, *Writing and Difference,* trans. Alan Bass [Chicago: University of Chicago Press, 1978], 14).

16. Jacques Derrida, "La différance," in Derrida, *Marges de la philosophie* (Paris: Minuit, 1972), 13 ("Differance," in Derrida, *Margins of Philosophy,* trans. Alan Bass [Chicago: University of Chicago Press, 1982], 13).

17. My view, of course, is that as far as we are concerned, there is nothing outside time. The most we can do is talk about things that are in time as if they were not—thus turning members of temporal series into atemporal fantasies such as facts and states of affairs. And my perennial question is: Why do that?

18. A more detailed account of ousia ontology, or metaphysics, is given at *MO* 21–70.

19. Cf. Aristotle, *On the Generation of Animals* IV.3, 767b 8–768a 9.

20. Cf. Aristotle, *Metaphysics* V.7–8, 1017a 8–b 26; also *Physics* II.1 192b 35–40.

21. Heidegger, "Die Onto-theo-logische Verfassung der Metaphysik," 51–67.

22. John Locke, *An Essay Concerning Human Understanding,* ed. Alexander Campbell Fraser, 2 vols. (New York: Dover, 1959), vol. II, § 23.1f; see also the Editor's Note *ad loc.*

23. See, e.g., George Berkeley, *The Principles of Human Knowledge,* in David M. Armstrong, ed., *Berkeley's Philosophical Writings* (New York: Collier, 1965), 74–96. The qualities we actually sense cannot for Berkeley be shown to be caused by external substances, or at least by a plurality of unintelligent ones. They are all caused directly by God, who is thus once again—as he was for Descartes—the only power. See Berkeley, *The Principles of Human Knowledge,* 71f.

24. Daniel Garber, *Descartes' Metaphysical Physics* (Chicago: University of Chicago Press, 1992), 116; also cf. *MO* 109–127.

25. René Descartes to Henry More, April 15, 1649, AT V 340/252.

26. Spinoza, *Ethics,* Part I Prop. 8.

27. Friedrich Nietzsche, *Nachgelassene Fragmente 1887–1889,* in Nietzsche, *Kritische Studienausgabe,* ed. Giorgio Colli and Mazzino Montinari (Berlin: de Gruyter, 2e, durchgesehene Auflage), 15 vols. 1988 XIII 373; reprinted in Nietzsche, *The Will to Power,* trans. Walter Kaufmann (London: Weidenfeld and Nicolson, 1967), 340 (§ 636).

28. Arthur C. Danto, *Nietzsche as Philosopher* (New York: Columbia University Press, 1965), 215.

29. Gilles Deleuze attempts to retain such import by identifying "active" force as "dominant" force and "reactive" force as "inferior" force, but this makes it impossible to understand how reactive forces can gain

the dominance that they have in, for example, Nietzsche's nihilistic Europe. Gilles Deleuze, *Nietzsche and Philosophy,* trans. Hugh Tomlinson (New York: Columbia University Press, 1983), 40.

30. Michel Foucault, *L'archéologie du savoir* (Paris: Gallimard, 1969) (*The Archeology of Knowledge,* trans. A. M. Sheridan Smith [New York: Pantheon, 1972]). On the unexplained unity of Foucauldian discursive formations, see *PF* 110–140; on the absence of moral import, see Nancy Fraser, "Foucault on Power: Empirical Insights and Normative Confusions," in Fraser, *Unruly Practices* (Minneapolis: University of Minnesota Press, 1989), 17–34.

31. See Warren Montag, *Bodies, Masses, Power: Spinoza and His Contemporaries* (London: Verso, 1999).

32. Otto Neurath, *Philosophical Papers 1913–1946,* ed. R. S. Cohen and M. Neurath (Dordrecht: Riedel, 1983), 92.

33. This includes change in place, which I did not discuss because on this reading it does not affect identity.

34. The point is made, without the analogy, at *Werke* VIII 60/39.

35. Martin Heidegger, "Das Ding," in Heidegger, *Vorträge und Aufsätze,* 4th ed. (Pfullingen: Neske, 1954), 157–179, 161 ("The Thing," in Heidegger, *Poetry, Language, Thought,* trans. Albert Hofstadter [New York: Harper & Row, 1971], 169).

36. Heidegger, "Das Ding," at Heidegger, *Vorträge und Aufsätz,* 162/170.

37. Aristotle, *de Anima* II.1 412a 6–21.

38. Aristotle, *On the Generation of Animals* IV.3, 767b 8–768a 9. I have taken the gender inflection out of Aristotle here not in order to save him from his chauvinism but because the problem I am discussing remains even in its absence.

39. On prototype theory, cf. Eleanor Rosch, "Prototype Classification and Logical Classification: The Two Systems," in E. Scholmin, ed., *New Trends in Cognitive Representation: Challenges to Piaget's Theory* (Hillsdale, N.J.: Erlbaum, 1983), 73–86.

40. For overviews, see Norman O. Dahl, *Practical Reason, Aristotle, and Weakness of the Will* (Minneapolis: University of Minnesota Press, 1984), 26–29, and W. F. R. Hardie, *Aristotle's Ethical Theory,* 2nd ed. (Oxford: Clarendon Press, 1980), 240–257.

41. W. V. O. Quine, "Speaking of Objects," in Quine, *Ontological Relativity and Other Essays* (New York: Columbia University Press, 1969), 1–25.

42. Martin Heidegger, "Die Zeit des Weltbildes," in Heidegger, *Holzwege,* 4th ed. (Frankfurt: Klostermann, 1963), 6 ("The Age of the World Picture," in Heidegger, *The Question Concerning Technology and Other Essays,* trans. William Lovitt [New York: Harper & Row, 1977], 115).

43. Jürgen Habermas, "Work and Weltanschauung: the Heidegger Controversy from a German Perspective," trans. John McCumber, *Critical Inquiry* 15 (1989): 431–456.

44. On the contrast between Hume and Mill, cf. Donald Davidson, "Causal Relations," in Davidson, *Essays on Actions and Events* (Oxford: Oxford University Press, 1980), 149f.

45. Jacques Derrida, *De la grammatologie* (Paris: Minuit, 1967), 145–378, 376 (*Of Grammatology*, trans. Gayatri Chakravorty Spivak [Baltimore, Md.: Johns Hopkins University Press, 1974], 266).

46. Donald Davidson, "Actions, Reasons, and Causes," in Davidson, *Essays on Actions and Events* (Oxford: Oxford University Press, 1980), 16. For an attempt to spell out the logical difference between causes and conditions, see J. L. Mackie, "Causes and Conditions," *American Philosophical Quarterly* 2 (1968): 245–264. The complexity of Mackie's analysis is a typical outcome of trying to understand concrete cultural practices as if they were logical truths.

47. Davidson, "Actions, Reasons, and Causes," 17.

48. Robert B. Brandom, *Making It Explicit* (Cambridge, Mass.: Harvard University Press 1994), 134.

49. Ibid.

50. See Roger Shank and Robert Abelson, *Scripts, Plans, Goals, and Understanding* (Hillsdale, N.J.: Erlbaum, 1977), 43f.

51. *Werke* VIII 183/137; Hegel calls this "negativity" at *PhG* 253/209.

52. See, for example, Søren Kierkegaard, *Kierkegaard's Concluding Unscientific Postscript*, trans. David Swenson and Walter Lowrie (Princeton, N.J.: Princeton University Press, 1941), 106–113, 267–282. Also cf. Hermann J. Cloeren, "The Linguistic Turn in Kierkegaard's Attack on Hegel," *International Studies in Philosophy* 17 (1985): 1–13.

4. The Edge of Ethics

1. Quoted in Arthur Herman, *How the Scots Invented the Modern World* (New York: Random House, 2001), 63.

2. Alasdair MacIntyre, *After Virtue*, 2nd ed. (Notre Dame, Ind.: University of Notre Dame Press, 1984), 220.

3. For MacIntyre's response to such charges, see his "Postscript to the Second Edition," *After Virtue*, 264–278.

4. Jürgen Habermas, "Work and Weltanschauung: The Heidegger Controversy from a German Perspective," trans. John McCumber, *Critical Inquiry* 15 (1989): 431–456.

5. J. L. Austin, "A Plea for Excuses," in Austin, *Philosophical Papers* (Oxford: Clarendon, 1961), 123–152.

6. G. W. Leibniz, *Nouveaux essais sur l'entendement par l'auteur du*

système de l'harmonie préétablie, in Leibniz, *Die philosophischen Schriften,* ed. C. J. Erhardt, 7 vols. (Hildesheim: Olms, 1965), vol. V, 166–168 (*New Essays on Human Understanding,* trans. and ed. Peter Remnant and Jonathan Bennett [Cambridge: Cambridge University Press, 1981], 180–182); cf. also Leibniz, *Animadversiones in partem generalem Principiorum Cartesianorum,* in Leibniz, *Die philosophischen Schriften* IV 388f (*Critical Thoughts on the General Part of the Principles of Descartes,* in Leibniz, *Philosophical Papers and Letters,* trans. and ed. Leroy Loemker, 2nd ed. [Dordrecht: Reidel, 1969], 388f).

7. Cf. Charlotte Stough, "Stoic Determinism and Moral Responsibility," in John Rist, ed., *The Stoics* (Berkeley: University of California Press, 1975), 203–231.

8. Both available in volume II of *Werke.* The English translation of *Glauben und Wissen* is *Faith and Knowledge,* trans. Walter Cerf and H. S. Harris (Albany: SUNY Press, 1977); the translation of the *Differenzschrift* is *The Difference between Fichte's and Schelling's System of Philosophy,* trans. Walter Cerf and H. S. Harris (Albany: SUNY Press, 1977).

9. Michel Foucault, *Surveiller et punir* (Paris: Gallimard, 1975) (*Discipline and Punish,* trans. Alan Sheridan [New York: Vintage, 1979]).

10. Tor Nørretranders, *The User Illusion,* trans. Jonathan Sydenham (London: Penguin, 1998), 213–250.

11. For a general account of Le Chambon-sur-Lignane, cf. Phillip R. Haillie, *Lest Innocent Blood Be Shed* (New York: Harper Perennials, 1994). For an American example, cf. Bernard Gordon, *Hollywood Exile: or How I Learned to Love the Blacklist* (Austin: University of Texas Press, 1999), 46–47.

12. Daniel Dennett, *Consciousness Explained* (New York: Little, Brown, 1991), 180.

13. Martin Heidegger, "Der Ursprung des Kunstwerkes," in Heidegger, *Holzwege,* 4th ed. (Frankfurt: Klostermann, 1963), 7–68 ("The Origin of the Work of Art," in Heidegger, *Poetry, Language, Thought,* trans. Albert Hofstadter [New York: Harper & Row, 1971], 15–88).

14. See my "Aristotelian Catharsis and the Purgation of Woman," *diacritics* 18, no. 4 (Winter 1988): 53–67.

15. Friedrich Schiller, *On the Aesthetic Education of Man in a Series of Letters,* trans. and ed. Elizabeth M. Wilkinson and L. A. Willoughby (Oxford: Clarendon, 1967), English text with German facing; see also Philip J. Kain, *Schiller, Hegel, and Marx: State, Society, and the Aesthetic Ideal of Ancient Greece* (Kingston, Ont.: Queen's University Press, 1982).

16. Søren Kiekegaard, *Fear and Trembling and The Sickness Unto Death,* trans. Walter Lowrie (Garden City, N.Y.: Doubleday, 1954), 129.

17. Judith Butler, *Gender Trouble* (New York: Routledge, 1990), 145.

18. Jürgen Habermas, *Theorie des kommunikativen Handelns*, 2 vols. (Frankfurt: Suhrkamp, 1981) (*Theory of Communicative Action* I, trans. Thomas McCarthy [Boston: Beacon Press, 1984–87]).

19. Mark Twain, *The Adventures of Huckleberry Finn* (New York: Heritage Press, 1940), 58–60.

20. F. Scott Fitzgerald, *The Great Gatsby* (New York: Scribner's, 1953), 87–97.

21. Nathaniel Hawthorne, *The Scarlet Letter,* Norton Critical Editions (New York: W. W. Norton, 1988), 135, 137.

22. Henry James, *The Portrait of a Lady,* Norton Critical Editions (New York: W. W. Norton, 1975), 479.

23. Paolo Freire, *Pedagogy of the Oppressed,* trans. Myra Bergman Ramos (New York: Continuum Press, 2000).

24. Karl Marx, *Capital,* trans. Samuel Morse and Edward Aveling (New York: Modern Library, 1906), 390f.

25. Cf. Robert Nozick, *Anarchy, State, and Utopia* (Oxford: Blackwell's, 1974).

26. This is documented in Al Franken, *Lies and the Lying Liars Who Tell Them: A Fair and Balanced Look at the Right* (New York: Dutton, 2003).

27. Cf. Russell Jacoby, *The Last Intellectuals* (New York: Noonday Press, 1989).

28. Cf. Jürgen Habermas, *Theorie des kommunikativen Handelns* (*Theory of Communicative Action* I).

29. Milton Friedman, *Capitalism and Freedom* (Chicago: University of Chicago Press, reissued 2002), 7–36; Nozick, *Anarchy, State, and Utopia,* 26–28.

30. Giorgio Agamben, *Homo Sacer: Sovereign Power and Bare Life,* trans. Daniel Heller-Roazen (Stanford, Calif.: Stanford University Press, 1998), 18.

31. *Emp.* 16f; Agamben, *Homo Sacer,* 20.

32. Agamben, *Homo Sacer,* 104, 183.

Bibliography

Agamben, Giorgio. *Homo Sacer: Sovereign Power and Bare Life*. Translated by Daniel Heller-Roazen. Stanford, Calif.: Stanford University Press, 1998.

Ameriks, Karl. *Kant's Theory of Mind: An Analysis of the Paralogisms of Pure Reason*. Oxford: Clarendon, 1982.

Aristotle. *Works* (Bekker pagination; English translation). In *The Basic Works of Aristotle*, edited by Richard McKeon. New York: Random House, 1941 (contains marginal pagination to Greek edition).

Austin, J. L. *How to Do Things with Words*. New York: Oxford University Press, 1965.

————. "A Plea for Excuses." In *Philosophical Papers*, 123–152. Oxford: Clarendon, 1961.

Berkeley, George. *The Principles of Human Knowledge*. In David M. Armstrong, ed., *Berkeley's Philosophical Writings*. New York: Collier, 1965.

————. *Principles of Human Knowledge and Three Dialogues*. Edited by Howard Robinson. New York: Oxford University Press, 1996.

Bernasconi, Robert. *The Question of Language in Heidegger's History of Being*. Atlantic Highlands, N.J.: Humanities Press, 1985.

Boole, George. *The Laws of Thought*. 1854. Reprint, New York: Dover, 1951.

Borradori, Giovanna. *Philosophy in a Time of Terror: Dialogues with Jürgen Habermas and Jacques Derrida*. Chicago: University of Chicago Press, 2003.

Brandom, Robert. *Making It Explicit*. Cambridge, Mass.: Harvard University Press, 1994.

Butler, Judith. *Gender Trouble*. New York: Routledge, 1990.

Carnap, Rudolf. "The Elimination of Metaphysics through Logical Analysis of Language." In *Logical Positivism*, edited by A. J. Ayer, 60–81. New York: The Free Press, 1959.

Cartwright, Nancy. *How the Laws of Physics Lie*. Oxford: Clarendon, 1983.

Cloeren, Hermann J. "The Linguistic Turn in Kierkegaard's Attack on Hegel." *International Studies in Philosophy* 17 (1985): 1–13.

Dahl, Norman O. *Practical Reason, Aristotle, and Weakness of the Will.* Minneapolis: University of Minnesota Press, 1984.

Dahlstrom, Daniel. *Heidegger's Concept of Truth.* Cambridge: Cambridge University Press, 2001.

Danto, Arthur C. *Nietzsche as Philosopher.* New York: Columbia University Press, 1965.

Davidson, Donald. "Actions, Reasons, and Causes." In *Essays on Actions and Events,* 3–19. Oxford: Oxford University Press, 1980.

———. *Inquiries into Truth and Interpretation.* Oxford: Clarendon Press, 1984.

Deleuze, Gilles. *Nietzsche and Philosophy.* Translated by Hugh Tomlinson. New York: Columbia University Press, 1983.

———. *La philosophie critique de Kant.* Paris: Presses Universitaires de France, 1963.

Dennett, Daniel. *Consciousness Explained.* New York: Little, Brown, 1991.

Derrida, Jacques. "Force et signification." In *L'écriture et la différence,* 26. Paris: Éditions du Seuil, 1967. Translated by Alan Bass under the title "Force and Signification" in *Writing and Difference* (Chicago: University of Chicago Press, 1978).

———. *De la grammatologie.* Paris: Minuit, 1967. Translated by Gayatri Chakravorty Spivak under the title *Of Grammatology* (Baltimore, Md.: Johns Hopkins University Press, 1974).

———. "Ousia et grammé." In *Marges de la philosophie,* 31–78. Paris: Minuit, 1972. Translated by Alan Bass under the title "Ousia and Gramme," in *Margins of Philosophy* (Chicago: University of Chicago Press, 1982).

———. "La pharmacie de Platon." In *La dissémination,* 69–197. Paris: Éditions du Seuil, 1972.

———. "Le puits et la pyramide: introduction à la Sémiologie de Hegel." In *Marges de la philosophie.* Paris: Minuit, 1972, 79–127. Translated by Alan Bass under the title "The Pit and the Pyramid: Introduction to the Semiology of Hegel," in *Margins of Philosophy.*

———. "Signature événement contexte." In *Marges.* Paris: Minuit, 1972.

Descartes, René. *Oeuvres de Descartes.* 13 vols. Edited by Charles Adam and Paul Tannery. Paris: Cerf, 1896–1913: VII. 17. This pagination is given marginally in John Cottingham et al., *The Philosophical Writings of Descartes,* 3 vols. (Cambridge: Cambridge University Press, 1984–1991).

Diels, Hermann, and Walther Kranz, eds. *Fragmente der Vorsokratiker.* 6th ed. 3 vols. Zürich: Weidmann, 1951.

Erickson, Stephen A. *The (Coming) Age of Thresholding.* Dordrecht: Kluwer, 1999.

Evnine, Simon. *Donald Davidson.* Stanford, Calif.: Stanford University Press, 1991.

Fitzgerald, F. Scott. *The Great Gatsby.* New York: Scribner's, 1953.

Foucault, Michel. *L'archéologie du savoir.* Paris: Gallimard, 1969. Translated by A. M. Sheridan Smith under the title *The Archeology of Knowledge* (New York: Pantheon, 1972).

———. *Surveiller et punir.* Paris: Gallimard, 1975. Translated by Alan Sheridan under the title *Discipline and Punish* (New York: Vintage, 1979).

Franken, Al. *Lies and the Lying Liars Who Tell Them: A Fair and Balanced Look at the Right.* New York: Dutton, 2003.

Fraser, Nancy. "Foucault on Power: Empirical Insights and Normative Confusions." In *Unruly Practices.* Minneapolis: University of Minnesota Press, 1989.

Freire, Paolo. *Pedagogy of the Oppressed.* Translated by Myra Bergman Ramos. New York: Continuum Press, 2000.

Friedman, Milton. *Capitalism and Freedom.* Chicago: University of Chicago Press, reissued 2002.

Gale, Richard, ed. *The Blackwell Guide to Metaphysics.* Oxford: Blackwell's, 2002.

Garber, Daniel. *Descartes' Metaphysical Physics.* Chicago: University of Chicago Press, 1992.

Gardiner, Patrick. "Hume's Theory of the Passions." In *David Hume: A Symposium,* edited by D. F. Pears, 31–42. New York: St. Martin's Press, 1966.

Gazzaniga, Michael S. "The Split Brain Revisited." *Scientific American: The Hidden Mind,* edited by John Rennie. Special issue of *Scientific American,* 2002: 30.

Gordon, Bernard. *Hollywood Exile: or How I Learned to Love the Blacklist.* Austin: University of Texas Press, 1999.

Guyer, Paul. "Kant." In *Routledge Encyclopedia of Philosophy,* Edward Craig, general editor, 8 vols., vol. V, 177–200. London: Routledge, 1998.

Habermas, Jürgen. *Theorie des kommunikativen Handelns.* 2 vols. Frankfurt: Suhrkamp, 1981. Vol. I, 109. Translated by Thomas McCarthy under the title *Theory of Communicative Action* (Boston: Beacon Press, 1984–87).

———. *Wahrheitstheorien.* In *Wirklichkeit und Reflexion: Walter Schulz zum 60e Geburtstag,* 211–265. Pfullingen: Neske, 1973.

———. "Work and Weltanschauung: The Heidegger Controversy from a German Perspective." Translated by John McCumber. *Critical Inquiry* 15 (1989): 431–456.

Haillie, Phillip R. *Lest Innocent Blood Be Shed.* New York: Harper Perennials, 1994.

Hardie, W. F. R. *Aristotle's Ethical Theory.* 2nd ed. Oxford: Clarendon Press, 1980.

Harding, Sandra. *Whose Science? Whose Knowledge?* Ithaca, N.Y.: Cornell University Press, 1991.

Hardt, Michael, and Antonio Negri. *Empire.* Cambridge, Mass.: Harvard University Press, 2000.

Hartman, Edwin. *Substance, Body and Soul.* Princeton, N.J.: Princeton University Press, 1977.

Hawthorne, Nathaniel. *The Scarlet Letter.* Norton Critical Editions. New York: W. W. Norton, 1988.

Hegel, G. W. F. *Werke.* Edited by Eva Moldenhauer and Karl Markus Michel. Frankfurt/Main: Suhrkamp, 20 vols., 1970–71; *Vorlesungen über die Ästhetik* translated by T. M. Knox under the title *Aesthetics.* Oxford: Oxford University Press, 2 vols. with consecutive pagination, 1975; *Enzyklopädie der philosophischen Wissenchaften, erster Teil* translated by William Wallace under the title *Hegel's Logic.* Oxford: Clarendon, 1975; *Phänomenologie des Geistes* translated by A. V. Miller under the title *Hegel's Phenomenology of Spirit.* Oxford: Clarendon Press, 1977.

———. *Wissenschaft der Logik.* Edited by Georg Lasson. 2 vols. Hamburg: Meiner, 1932. Vol. II, 259–264. Translated by A. V. Miller under the title *Science of Logic* (New York: Humanities Press, 1969).

Heidegger, Martin. "Andenken." In *Erläuterungen zu Hölderlins Dichtung,* 1st ed., 75–143. Frankfurt: Klostermann, 1951.

———. "Das Ding." In *Vorträge und Aufsätze,* 3 vols., vol. II, 37–59. Pfullingen: Neske, 1954. Translated by Albert Hofstadter under the title "The Thing," in *Poetry, Language, Thought,* 163–186 (New York: Harper & Row, 1971).

———. "Die Onto-theologische Verfassung der Metaphysik." In *Identität und Differenz,* 51–67. Pfullingen: Neske, 1957.

———. *Phänomenologie and Theologie.* Frankfurt: Klostermann, 1970.

———. *Zur Sache des Denkens* (Tübingen: Niemeyer, 1969), 77. Translated by Joan Stambaugh under the title *On Time and Being* (New York: Harper & Row).

———. *Sein und Zeit.* 11th ed. Tübingen: Niemeyer, 1967. Translated by John MacQuarrie and Edward Robinson under the title *Being and Time* (New York: Harper and Row, 1962).

———. "Über Nietzsches Wort: Gott ist Tod." In *Holzwege,* 4th ed., 193–247. Frankfurt: Klostermann, 1963.

———. "Der Ursprung des Kunstwerkes." In *Holzwege*, 4th ed., 7–68. Frankfurt: Klostermann, 1963. Translated by Albert Hofstadter under the title "The Origin of the Work of Art," in *Poetry, Language, Thought*, 15–88 (New York: Harper & Row, 1971).

———. *Was Heißt Denken?* Tübingen: Max Niemeyer, 1971. Translated by Fred D. Wieck and J. Glenn Gray under the title *What Is Called Thinking?* (New York: Harper, 1968).

———. "Vom Wesen der Wahrheit," in Heidegger, *Wegmarken*. Frankfurt: Klostermann 1967. Translated by R. F. C. Hull and Alan Crick under the title "On the Essence of Truth," in Heidegger, *Existence and Being* (Chicago: Regnery, 1949).

———. "Das Wort." In *Unterwegs zur Sprache*, 4th ed., 217–238. Pfullingen: Neske, 1971. Translated by Albert Hofstadter under the title "Words," in *On the Way to Language*, 139–158 (New York: Harper & Row, 1971).

———. "Die Zeit des Weltbildes." In *Holzwege*, 4th ed., 6. Frankfurt: Klostermann, 1963. Translated by William Lovitt under the title "The Age of the World Picture," in *The Question Concerning Technology and Other Essays*, 115–154 (New York: Harper and Row, 1977).

Herman, Arthur. *How the Scots Invented the Modern World*. New York: Random House, 2001.

Hobbes, Thomas. *The Metaphysical System of Hobbes*. Edited by Mary Whiton Calkins. La Salle, Ill.: Open Court, 1963.

Hume, David. *An Enquiry Concerning Human Understanding*. In *Enquiries*, 2nd ed., edited by L. A. Selby-Bigge. Oxford: Clarendon, 1902.

———. *A Treatise of Human Nature*. Edited by L. A. Selby-Bigge. Oxford: Clarendon, 1888.

Hylton, Peter. *Russell, Idealism and the Emergence of Analytic Philosophy*. Oxford: Clarendon, 1990.

Jacoby, Russell. *The Last Intellectuals*. New York: Noonday Press, 1989.

James, Henry. *The Portrait of a Lady*. Norton Critical Editions. New York: W. W. Norton, 1975.

Jay, Martin. "Fin-de-siècle Socialism." In *Fin-de-Siècle Socialism and Other Essays*, 1–13. London: Routledge, 1988.

———. *Marxism and Totality*. Berkeley: University of California Press, 1984.

Kain, Philip J. *Schiller, Hegel, and Marx: State, Society, and the Aesthetic Ideal of Ancient Greece*. Kingston, Ont.: Queen's University Press, 1982.

Kant, Immanuel. *Critique of Pure Reason*. Translated by Werner S. Pluhar. Indianapolis: Hackett, 1996.

———. *Kants gesammelte Schriften*. 29 vols. Berlin: Akademie-Ausgabe, 1902–.

Kierkegaard, Søren. *Fear and Trembling and The Sickness unto Death.* Translated by Walter Lowrie. Garden City, N.Y.: Doubleday, 1954.

———. *Kierkegaard's Concluding Unscientific Postscript.* Translated by David Swenson and Walter Lowrie. Princeton, N.J.: Princeton University Press, 1941.

Kim, Jaegwon, and Ernest Sosa. Preface to *Metaphysics: An Anthology.* Oxford: Blackwell's, 1999.

King, Stephen. *On Writing.* New York: Pocket Books, 2000.

Kolb, David. *The Critique of Pure Modernity.* Chicago: University of Chicago Press, 1986.

Korsgaard, Christine. *Creating the Kingdom of Ends.* Cambridge: Cambridge University Press, 1996.

Krell, David. *Intimations of Mortality.* University Park: Pennsylvania State University Press, 1986.

Kripke, Saul. "Naming and Necessity." In *Semantics of Natural Languages,* edited by Donald Davidson and Gilbert Harmon, 353–355. Dordrecht: Reidel 1972.

Leibniz, G. W. *Animadversiones in partem generalem Principiorum Cartesianorum.* In *Die philosophischen Schriften,* vol. IV. Translated and edited by Leroy Loemker under the title *Critical Thoughts on the General Part of the Principles of Descartes,* in *Philosophical Papers and Letters,* 2nd ed. (Dordrecht: Reidel, 1969).

———. *Nouveaux essais sur l'entendement par l'auteur du système de l'harmonie preétablie.* In *Die philosophischen Schriften,* edited by C. J. Erhardt, 7 vols. Hildesheim: Olms, 1965. Translated and edited by Peter Remnant and Jonathan Bennett under the title *New Essays on Human Understanding* (Cambridge: Cambridge University Press, 1981).

Locke, John. *An Essay Concerning Human Understanding.* Edited by Alexander Campbell Fraser, 2 vols. New York: Dover, 1959.

Loux, Michael J. *Metaphysics: A Contemporary Introduction.* London: Routledge, 1998.

MacIntyre, Alasdair. *After Virtue.* 2nd ed. Notre Dame, Ind.: University of Notre Dame Press, 1984.

Mackie J. L. "Causes and Conditions." *American Philosophical Quarterly* 2 (1968): 245–264.

Marx, Karl. *Capital.* Translated by Samuel Morse and Edward Aveling. New York: Modern Library, 1906.

McCumber, John. "Aristotelian Catharsis and the Purgation of Woman." *diacritics* 18, no. 4 (Winter 1988): 53–67.

———. *The Company of Words.* Evanston, Ill.: Northwestern University Press, 1993.

———. "Discourse and Soul in Plato's Phaedrus." *Apeiron* 16 (1982): 27–39.

———. "Just in Time: Towards a New American Philosophy." *Continental Philosophy Review* 1, no. 34 (2003): 61–80.

———. "Language and Appropriation: The Nature of Heideggerean Dialogue." *The Personalist* 60 (1979): 384–396.

———. *Metaphysics and Oppression.* Bloomington: Indiana University Press, 1999.

———. *Philosophy and Freedom.* Bloomington: Indiana University Press, 2000.

———. *Poetic Interaction.* Chicago: University of Chicago Press, 1989.

———. "Problems and Renewal in American Philosophy." *Philosophical Studies* 108 (March 2002): 203–211.

———. *Time in the Ditch.* Evanston, Ill.: Northwestern University Press, 2001.

———. "Writing Down (Up) the Truth: Hegel and Schiller at the End of the *Phenomenology of Spirit.*" In *The Spirit of Poesy: Essays on Jewish and German Literature and Thought in Honor of Géza von Molnár,* edited by Richard Block and Peter Fenves, 47–59. Evanston, Ill.: Northwestern University Press, 2000.

McDowell, John. *Mind and World.* Cambridge, Mass.: Harvard University Press, 1994.

"Metaphysics, Definitions and Divisions." In Jaegwon Kim and Ernest Sosa, eds., *A Companion to Metaphysics.* Oxford: Blackwell's, 1995.

Montag, Warren. *Bodies, Masses, Power: Spinoza and His Contemporaries.* London: Verso, 1999.

Neurath, Otto. *Philosophical Papers 1913–1946.* Edited by R. S. Cohen and M. Neurath. Dordrecht: Riedel, 1983.

Nietzsche, Friedrich. *Sämtliche Werke: Kritische Studienausgabe in 15 Bänden.* 15 vols. 2nd ed. Edited by Giorgio Colli and Mazzino Moninari. Berlin: de Gruyter, rev. 1988.

———. *The Will to Power.* Translated by Walter Kaufmann. London: Weidenfeld and Nicolson, 1967.

Nørretranders, Tor. *The User Illusion.* Translated by Jonathan Sydenham. London: Penguin, 1998.

Nozick, Robert. *Anarchy, State, and Utopia.* Oxford: Blackwell's, 1974.

Okrent, Mark. *Heidegger's Pragmatism.* Ithaca, N.Y.: Cornell University Press, 1988.

Pinkard, Terry. *Hegel's Dialectic.* Philadelphia: Temple University Press, 1988.

Pippin, Robert. *Hegel's Idealism.* Cambridge: Cambridge University Press, 1989.

Plato. *Platonis Opera.* Edited by John Burnet. 5 vols. Oxford: Clarendon, 1907. Translated and edited by Edith Hamilton and Hamilton Cairns under the title *The Collected Dialogues* (Princeton, N.J.: Princeton University Press [Bollingen], 1961). Both editions give Stephanus pagination marginally.

Quine, W. V. O. *Methods of Logic.* 2nd ed. Cambridge, Mass.: Harvard University Press, 1959.

———. *Philosophy of Logic.* Englewood Cliffs, N.J.: Prentice-Hall, 1972.

———. "Speaking of Objects." In Quine, *Ontological Relativity and Other Essays.* New York: Columbia University Press, 1969.

———. "Two Dogmas of Empiricism." In *From a Logical Point of View.* New York: Harper Torchbooks, 1961.

———. *Word and Object.* Cambridge, Mass.: MIT Press, 1960.

Rawls, John. *A Theory of Justice.* Cambridge, Mass.: Harvard University Press, 1971.

Reichenbach, Hans. *The Rise of Scientific Philosophy.* Berkeley and Los Angeles: University of California Press, 1951.

Rorty, Richard. "Heidegger, Contingency, and Pragmatism." In *Essays on Heidegger and Others.* Cambridge: Cambridge University Press, 1991.

Rosch, Eleanor. "Prototype Classification and Logical Classification: The Two Systems." In *New Trends in Cognitive Representation: Challenges to Piaget's Theory,* edited by E. Scholmin, 73–86. Hillsdale, N.J.: Erlbaum, 1983.

Sallis, John. *Echoes after Heidegger.* Bloomington: Indiana University Press, 1990.

Schiller, Friedrich. *On the Aesthetic Education of Man in a Series of Letters.* Translated and edited by Elizabeth M. Wilkinson and L. A. Willoughby. Oxford: Clarendon, 1967.

Schürmann, Reiner. *Le principe d'anarchie.* Paris: du Seuil, 1982.

Scribner, Sylvia. "Modes of Thinking and Ways of Speaking: Culture and Logic Reconsidered." In P. N. Johnson-Laird and P. C. Wason, *Thinking: Readings in Cognitive Science.* Cambridge: Cambridge University Press, 1977.

Scruton, Roger. *Modern Philosophy.* London: Sinclair-Stevenson, 1994.

Sellars, Wilfred. *Empiricism and the Philosophy of Mind.* Cambridge, Mass.: Harvard University Press, 1997.

Shank, Roger, and Robert Abelson. *Scripts, Plans, Goals, and Understanding.* Hillsdale, N.J.: Erlbaum, 1977.

Smolin, Lee. *The Life of the Cosmos.* Oxford: Oxford University Press, 1997.

Stekeler-Weithofer, Pirmin. *Hegels analytische Philosophie.* Paderborn: Schöningh, 1992.

Stevenson, C. L. *Facts and Values*. New Haven, Conn.: Yale University Press, 1963.

Stough, Charlotte. "Stoic Determinism and Moral Responsibility." In *The Stoics*, edited by John Rist, 203–231. Berkeley: University of California Press, 1975.

Twain, Mark. *The Adventures of Huckleberry Finn*. New York: Heritage Press, 1940.

Waxman, Wayne. *Kant's Model of the Mind: A New Interpretation of Transcendental Idealism*. Oxford: Oxford University Press, 1991.

Williams, Michael. *Unnatural Doubts*. Princeton, N.J.: Princeton University Press, 1995.

Williams, Robert R. *Hegel's Ethics of Recognition*. Berkeley and Los Angeles: California University Press, 1997.

Winfield, Richard. *Overcoming Foundations*. New York: Columbia University Press, 1989.

Wittgenstein, Ludwig. *Philosophical Investigations*. 3rd ed. Translated by G. E. M. Anscombe. New York: Macmillan, 1958.

Index

JOHN MCCUMBER is Professor of Germanic Languages at UCLA and has taught at Northwestern University, The Graduate Faculty of the New School for Social Research, and the University of Michigan–Dearborn. He is most recently the author of *Metaphysics and Oppression* (Indiana University Press, 1999), *Philosophy and Freedom* (Indiana University Press, 2000), and *Time in the Ditch: American Philosophy and the McCarthy Era* (2001).